KT-428-833

perfect plants
for every season

perfect plants
for every season

An illustrated directory of the best shrubs, roses, climbers, conifers and small trees and how to choose, plant and care for them to provide a year-round structure to the flower garden

Andrew Mikolajski
Consultant: John Swithinbank

southwater

This edition is published by Southwater

Southwater is an imprint of Anness Publishing Ltd
Hermes House, 88–89 Blackfriars Road, London SE1 8HA
tel. 020 7401 2077; fax 020 7633 9499; www.southwaterbooks.com; info@anness.com

© Anness Publishing Ltd 2006

UK agent: The Manning Partnership Ltd, 6 The Old Dairy, Melcombe Road, Bath BA2 3LR
tel. 01225 478444; fax 01225 478440; sales@manning-partnership.co.uk

UK distributor: Grantham Book Services Ltd, Isaac Newton Way, Alma Park Industrial Estate,
Grantham, Lincs NG31 9SD; tel. 01476 541080; fax 01476 541061; orders@gbs.tbs-ltd.co.uk

North American agent/distributor: National Book Network, 4501 Forbes Boulevard,
Suite 200, Lanham, MD 20706; tel. 301 459 3366; fax 301 429 5746; www.nbnbooks.com

Australian agent/distributor: Pan Macmillan Australia, Level 18, St Martins Tower, 31 Market St,
Sydney, NSW 2000; tel. 1300 135 113; fax 1300 135 103; customer.service@macmillan.com.au

New Zealand agent/distributor: David Bateman Ltd, 30 Tarndale Grove, Off Bush Road, Albany,
Auckland; tel. (09) 415 7664; fax (09) 415 8892

All rights reserved. No part of this publication may be reproduced, stored in a retrieval system,
or transmitted in any way or by any means, electronic, mechanical, photocopying, recording or
otherwise, without the prior written permission of the copyright holder.

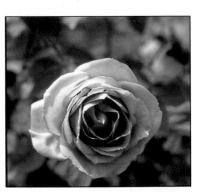

A CIP catalogue record for this book is available from the British Library.

Publisher: Joanna Lorenz
Editorial Director: Judith Simons
Executive Editor: Caroline Davison
Project Editors: Claire Folkard and Mariano Kälfors
Assistant Editor: Lindsay Kaubi
Copy Editor: Lydia Darbyshire
Editorial Readers: Rosanna Fairhead, Penelope Goodare and Richard McGinlay
Designer: Michael Morey
Photographers: Peter Anderson, Jonathan Buckley, Derek Cranch, Helen Fickling,
Paul Forrester, John Freeman, Michelle Garrett, Janine Hosegood, Andrea Jones,
Simon McBride and Marie O'Hara
Illustrators: Neil Bulpitt, Liz Pepperell, Michael Shoebridge
Cover Design: Balley Design Associates
Production Controller: Steve Lang
Picture Research: Gary Murphy, Joanna Skordis and Nansong Lue

Material in this book has previously been published in *The Encyclopedia of Garden Techniques*,
The Encyclopedia of Garden Plants and *The Illustrated Practical Encyclopedia of Pruning, Training and Topiary*

10 9 8 7 6 5 4 3 2 1

NOTES
Bracketed terms are intended for American readers.

Contents

INTRODUCTION

This directory aims to help you choose the permanent plants that will form the structure of your garden, all year round. Flowers are easy to add, and easy to change from year to year, once you have established a basic framework; but for a successul garden that will always look good, whatever the season, it is essential to make the right choices of structural plants, particularly trees. Shrubs and climbers complete the picture, and you should make sure you include some that are evergreen, or have an attractive shape when not in flower.

Th plants in this book include all those you need to create a beautifully designed garden that will never look dull, and they are conveniently grouped into five sections: trees, conifers, shrubs, roses and climbers. There follows a useful chapter covering the techniques needed to look after your plants and ensure they flourish. Having taken care of the basic structure of your garden, you will find adding flowers is so much easier and more rewarding.

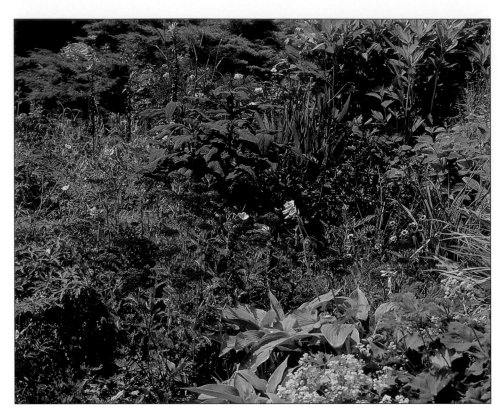

This border has been designed in a "hot" colour scheme with a combination of red-flowered and purple-leaved plants, both hardy and tender.

The summer-flowering *Itea ilicifolia*, though hardy, benefits from the shelter of a warm wall.

Hardiness

All the plants in this book have been assessed for their hardiness, and for the US, the range of zones where they can be grown outdoors is given (see page 155). Most can be grown outdoors in most temperate areas, and are able to withstand lows of -15°C (5°F). Plants described as "borderline hardy" will need some form of protection from the coldest weather, either by being grown in a warm, sheltered spot (for instance in the lee of a sunny wall) or by being covered in winter with a dry mulch of straw or other similar material. However, severe lows in themselves are less detrimental to plants than cold, drying winds.

Hardiness in any case is relative, and the ability of many plants at least to survive cold is largely dependent on how hot the weather is the previous summer. Deciduous trees and shrubs have an in-built mechanism for surviving unfavourable weather. During hot, dry periods, plant growth stops altogether. As the soil dries out, roots delve deeper in search of moisture, while bark thickens in the heat. The result is a tough, sturdy plant with an extensive root system that is better able to withstand severe cold than one that has grown sappy through excess moisture during the growing season. These plants are able to survive colder winters than usual, simply because the preceding summer was a hot one. Winter temperatures in certain regions with a Mediterranean climate can drop as low as they do in temperate areas, but plants such as olives are able to survive simply because of the long hot summers that ripen the wood. Hence the necessity of growing plants of borderline hardiness in a microclimate where they can ripen sufficiently.

How to use the directory

The directory section of this book is divided into five plant categories: Trees; Conifers; Shrubs; Roses; and Climbers. Within each directory plants are arranged alphabetically, by genus. Each main entry features an introduction to that genus and concise information on cultivation. These are followed by a selection of individual plant entries from that genus, also organized alphabetically according to their most common and internationally accepted names. A plant entry might be a species, hybrid or group of hybrids, a variant or a cultivar. As well as a useful description of the plant, information is given on height and spread; best time of interest for flowers, foliage and fruits/berries/hips; and plant hardiness zones.

Lavandula angustifolia 'Hidcote'

LAVANDULA
Lavender

Lavenders are well-known herb garden plants, but they have a number of other uses, principally as flowering hedging. When they are in flower, these evergreen shrubs and subshrubs will be alive with bees. They make a classic combination with old roses and can also be trained as standards.

Cultivation Lavenders will grow in all soil types but must have good drainage and a position in full sun. Clip hedging lightly in spring.

L. angustifolia
(syn. *L. officinalis*)
Old English lavender
The species has grey-green leaves and scented blue-grey flowers all summer. H and S 60cm (2ft). Hardy/Z 6–9. There are many selections, including '**Hidcote**' (syn. *L.* 'Hidcote Blue'), which has rich deep lavender-blue flowers; '**Munstead**', which has soft, lilac-blue flowers; and the strong-growing '**Rosea**', with pink flowers. H and S 60cm (2ft).

Caption
A full botanical name is given with each photograph.

Genus name
This gives the botanical name for a group of related species.

Genus introduction
This is a general description of the genus and may give the number of species or state that the genus is monotypic (there is only one species in the whole genus). There is also some information on preferred conditions and natural habitat, country or countries of origin, and occasional advice on how the plants can be used in the garden.

Cultivation
This section gives the level of sun or shade that the plants described in the selection either require or tolerate as well as advice on the type of soil in which they should be grown.

Varieties and cultivars
The descriptions of cultivars, forms, subspecies and varieties appear within the main plant entry. Heights and spreads are only included if they differ from those of the main plant entry.

Height and spread
This gives the average expected height and spread, though growth rates may vary, depending on location and conditions. If the height and spread are the same, then only one measurement is given. Metric measurements always precede standard measurements.

Photograph
Each entry features a full-colour photograph to make identification easy.

Common name or names
These apply to the whole genus, if given.

Main plant entry
This starts with the current botanical name of the plant in bold and can refer to a species, hybrid or hybrids, a variant or a cultivar.

Synonym or synonyms
If given, this provides the synonym or synonyms for the main plant entry. A synonym is an alternative name for the same plant.

Common name or names
If given, this provides the common name or names for the main plant entry.

Hardiness rating/Zones
This gives the plant's temperature tolerance as either tender, down to 5°C (41°F); half-hardy, down to 0°C (32°F); or hardy, down to -15°C. Plants described as "Borderline hardy" will need some form of protection from the coldest weather. A slightly different system is used in the US and Canada. Zones are based on the average annual minimum temperature for each zone. The lower number indicates the northernmost zone a plant can survive in and the higher number the southernmost zone the plant will tolerate. In some cases only one zone is given for a plant entry. See page 155 for details of zones and a zone map.

How plants are named

All living things are classified according to the binomial system, devised by the Swedish taxonomist Carl Linnaeus (1707–78) in his *Species Plantarum* (1753). Under the rules of this system, plants have Latin names consisting of the genus name (e.g. *Viburnum*) followed by the species epithet (e.g. *davidii*). Some genera comprise only one species, while others are vast. *Euphorbia*, for instance, is made up of some 2,000 plants, annuals, perennials, shrubs and trees as well as some cactus-like plants, and is widely distributed. (Such genera are sometimes rather grandly described as "cosmopolitan".)

All members of a genus are assumed to have some relationship to each other (though this may not necessarily be immediately apparent to the naked eye) and different species can often be crossed with each other. At the higher level, some genera seem to be related to each other (roses, pyracanthas and rowans, for instance, which all have cup-shaped flowers in their wild state), suggesting some common ancestry, though much remains conjectural or relies on the evidence of fossilized remains.

Naming plants

Nomenclature is not an exact science, and although there are certain internationally agreed rules, how they are put into use is often a matter of individual prejudice. Botanists and taxonomists frequently disagree over which name certain plants should bear, and in many cases there can be no "right" answer, since much depends on individual opinion. Hence the advisability of retaining synonyms, which can be as valid as the name officially sanctioned. The well-known mile-a-minute plant (here *Fallopia baldschuanica*) has

 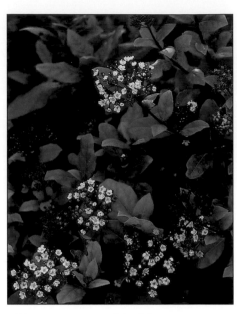

Plant names can be a complex and confusing matter. Here are two examples of the genus *Viburnum*: species *plicatum*, cultivar 'Marliesii (left) and species *tinus*, cultivar 'Eve Price' (right).

migrated several times between *Polygonum* and *Fallopia*, with ports of call at *Bilderdykia*. Another popular plant (also known as angel's trumpets because of its dramatic trumpet-shaped flowes), has been officially *Brugmansia* for many years, but many gardeners have been reluctant to adopt the new name. To avoid confusion, the old one, *Datura*, is universally retained as a synonym.

It occasionally happens that two plants thought to be distinct, with two separate names, are discovered to be, in fact, one and the same, and here a decision has to be taken as to which name has precedence.

Cultivars

Many plant species have the genetic potential to assume different characteristics to adapt to changes in the environment. In the wild, the habitat will favour seedlings best suited to the prevailing conditions, while the rest will not survive. Hence any population of a particular species in the wild will look more or less the same.

In the more controlled conditions

of a garden, the genetic potential becomes manifest, since gardeners are able to germinate and grow on a larger proportion of the seed. All manner of variations can arise: double flowers, albino forms, plants with variegated leaves etc. Such forms, if they have garden potential and are sufficiently distinct from the species, are given names and known as cultivars (a contraction of "cultivated varieties") or selections of the species, and the name is put in single quotes as, for instance, *Viburnum tinus* 'Eve Price'.

Hybrids

Certain species can be crossed with each other to produce hybrids. This can occur in nature, but is more usually deliberately practised by plant breeders. Hybridization generally results in robust plants with bigger flowers. For instance, at Bodnant in Wales, *Viburnum farreri* was crossed with *V. grandiflorum* to produce *V. × bodnantense* (the cross indicating that the plant is a hybrid). Outstanding seedlings were given names, including 'Dawn' and 'Deben'.

Hybrids can be back-crossed with one of the parents, to consolidate a particular feature, or can be crossed with other species or hybrids. Some garden forms have such complex parentage that it becomes meaningless to try to ascribe them to one or other species or hybrid group. Indeed, if precise records were not kept, the ancestry of a plant can only be guess-work. Such plants are styled with the genus name followed by the cultivar name, e.g. *Ceanothus* 'Dark Star'. Many roses and rhododendrons come into this category.

In general, garden forms can only be propagated vegetatively (cloning). Seedlings will revert back to the parent species (or one of them). Over time, the quality tends to deteriorate: repeated vegetative propagation is like photocopying a photocopy of a photocopy. Hence only the most vigorous of the older cultivars will stand the test of time, and there is good reason for replacing them with newly created hybrids. Many gardeners regret this, but while there is every reason to

wish to preserve species that may be under threat in the wild to maintain the biodiversity of the planet, the disappearance of certain garden forms from cultivation does not represent a comparable loss.

Garden forms usually do not survive in the wild, but some species have been known to "escape", as with *Rhododendron ponticum*, from the Mediterranean, which has colonized areas of the UK and Ireland to the extent that it has become a weed.

Name changes

As previously mentioned, nomenclature is never precise and can lead to disputes amongst botanists. For instance, the genera *Berberis* and *Mahonia* were formerly united in a single genus, and members of the two will in fact hybridize, suggesting that there is some close relationship between them. Many botanists would like to see them reunited. Recent research into cacti and bamboos has resulted in reclassification; some species formerly considered to belong to separate genera are now thought

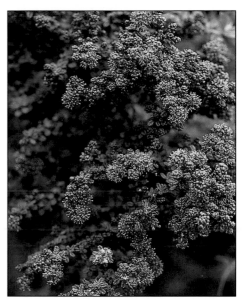

Ceanothus 'Dark Star' is a popular hybrid that flowers in spring.

to be related, and some species have been switched from one genus to another.

Name changes result in synonyms. A new name is not necessarily more valid than the old, and merely represents the opinion of whoever has come up with the new name. Although many gardeners despair at what seem like constant changes, there is usually a good reason for a change (even though agreement may not be universal).

Names of cultivars that have been bred abroad and given foreign names are often given translated names (or even new names) once imported. There are arguments for and against this: on the plus side, it results in names that are easier to remember and spell; on the down side, it leads to potential confusion. Modern rules require translated names to be set in a different font and without quotes.

The same name is sometimes ascribed to two different plants, as is the case with the clematis 'Princess of Wales', a name that applies to two cultivars, one honouring Alexandra, wife of Edward VII, the other Princess Diana.

Rhododrendron 'Dopey' (left) and Rhododrendron 'Curlew' (right) are examples of rhododrendron hybrids, with the genus name followed by the cultivar name.

Choosing plants for your garden

When deciding which plants to include in your garden, obviously your first consideration must be the style you want to create. An informal, cottage-type garden may focus on traditional favourites such as shrub roses, honeysuckle and jasmine, whereas if you want a contemporary look, you are more likely to choose conifers with striking shapes to form the backbone of your design.

Having thought about your ideal choice of plants to suit your style, there are further points to consider before you make your final planting decisions. Most gardeners know only too well the disappointment that comes from trying to grow a plant in the wrong place – it will either rapidly die, or linger on but become more and more miserable. The solution – as gardeners tend to learn the hard way – is to find out before you start what kind of soil and microclimate you have, and choose plants that will do well in those conditions. This book gives the growing requirements of all the plants listed, to help you make the right choices.

The plants that were chosen for this scheme, including the aromatic shrub *Artemisia*, are perfectly adapted to hot, dry conditions.

Designing with plants

Even if you have a very tiny garden, it is surprising what effects you can achieve with careful design; and in a large garden, it is even more important to think about overall structure. Hard landscaping, such as paths and patios, comes first, along with the shape of the lawn and any water features or statues. The structure of the garden will then depend mainly on plants.

The most permanant elements of your planting, and the most important when it comes to design, are of course trees. Even the smallest gardens can usually accommodate a tree or two, but don't forget to check how large they will eventually become. Some gardeners are ruthless enough to plant trees knowing that they will have to be removed when they outgrow their space, but it is usually more sensible to grow ones that can be left to reach their natural size. Beware of trees sold as "dwarf" varieties: many are not as small as they claim, and conifers in particular are often slow-growing, rather than dwarf, and may eventually become larger than you expected.

Shrubs form the other major group of structural plants in your garden, and they can be effective either in groups or as specimens, perhaps to create a focus in a lawn. For year-round interest, include some that are evergreen, preferably with a good shape, as well as winter-flowerers, or varieties such as *Cornus* that can be cut down to the ground each year to make them produce attractive coloured stems in winter.

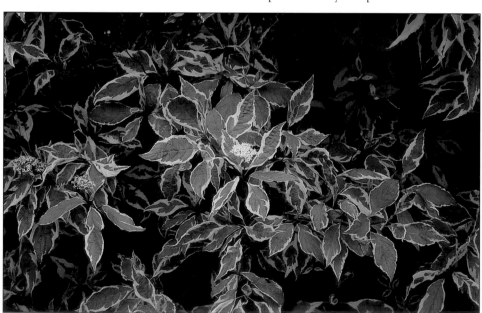

Cornus alba 'Sibirica Variegata' is a good all-year-round choice, with its variegated leaves, excellent autumn leaf colour and attractive red winter stems.

Climbers can be added wherever there is a suitable wall or fence, as well as on free-standing trellises, pergolas and poles – and even up trees, if you have any large and sturdy enough. Once you have laid out the framework of the garden to your satisfaction, you can enjoy adding the flowers that will complete the picture. They are sure to be more effective if they are set against an interesting backdrop of permanent plants, and it is easy to change the choice of flowers from year to year until you find the ones you like best.

The aspect

Light is essential to all plants as it provides the energy that is needed to manufacture food during daylight hours, so providing the right levels of light is crucial if the plants are to thrive. For this reason, one of the first considerations is the aspect of your garden. You will need to study your garden to work out which areas are sunny, shady or in partial shade at different times of the day. In their natural environment, some plants will grow in dense shade on the forest floor while others are exposed to intense bright sunlight for long periods of time. This wide diversity of natural habitat explains why so many of the different ornamental plants we grow require different conditions. The ability to adapt to unfamiliar conditions is a major reason for the popularity of many common plants.

The soil

It is worth finding out whether your soil is acid or alkaline, since not all plants will do equally well in both (though the majority are indifferent). The most reliable method is with a chemical soil testing kit, or you can make an educated guess by looking to see what is growing successfully in the surrounding countryside, or in other people's gardens if you live in a built-up area. Geological maps also indicate the presence of limestone or silt, for instance.

Equally important, perhaps more so, is the soil profile. The ideal – a loam that binds easily into crumbs, allowing for both moisture-retention and free drainage of excess water – suits nearly all plants. Stiff clays, cold and heavy to work, are usually nutrient high, suiting bog plants and others adapted to reliably wet conditions. Dry, sandy soils, easy to work and quick to warm up in spring, are nutrient poor but are the ideal medium for many of the Mediterranean plants and herbs. All soils can be improved by digging in organic matter, in the form of garden compost or well-rotted farmyard manure, greatly increasing the range of plants you can grow.

If a plant is doing well in your garden, either plant more of the same kind, or some of its near relatives or others that enjoy the same conditions. The reverse is also true. If you have trouble establishing a particular plant, you are also unlikely to succeed with others of the same type.

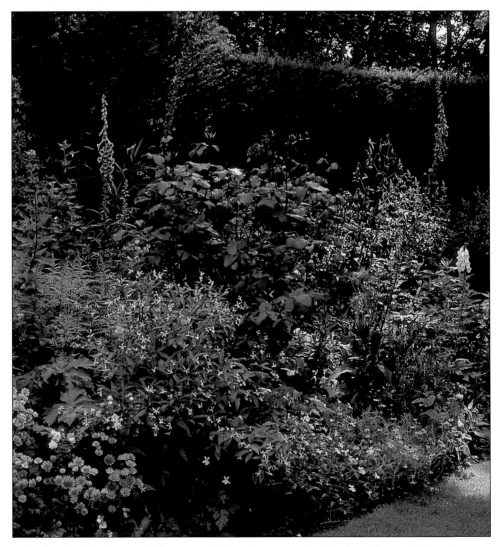

A classic mixed border, combining roses, lilies and a range of easily pleased perennials against a backdrop of clipped yew.

Trees

A tree completes a garden. Whether it is grown for its flowers, fruits, foliage or overall appearance, a tree adds dignity and style to any garden. From mighty oaks to the more manageable Japanese maples, there is a tree for every type of garden, whether you have rolling acres or a suburban plot. Even if you have only a courtyard, balcony or roof garden, there are trees suitable for containers. Careful selection is necessary, however. Remember: a tree often outlives the gardener.

A flowering tree makes a splendid eye-catcher at the peak of its glory, dominating the garden.

What is a tree?

Trees comprise a large and diverse group of plants that defies precise botanical classification. What distinguishes a tree from other forms of plant life is in fact no more than its overall appearance. Most people understand a tree as having a single woody trunk and a branching crown, while shrubs produce a number of stems from ground level. However, many trees can develop as multi-trunked plants, while certain shrubs become tree-like on maturity. Climatic factors also play a part: certain plants are unequivocally trees when growing at the foot of a mountain, for instance, but behave as shrubs at the mountain top, where strong winds will have a dwarfing effect, resulting in a thick trunk and gnarled branches. In isolation on open ground, trees will branch from ground level (or very near it) and be clothed in leaves; in forests, where the planting is denser and they are competing for light, they tend to develop tall, slim trunks, branching only near the top to form the characteristic leaf canopy. Generally, trees are assumed to have a height greater than 3m (10ft) and shrubs to be below that. But some weeping trees have a much shorter trunk than that and can in no way be mistaken for shrubs.

Trees occur in a range of plant families and have adapted to most environments except deserts and tundra. Most belong to the largest group, the angiosperms (all flowering plants). Gymnosperms include conifers and cycads, while even the most primitive plant group, the ferns and mosses (pteridophytes), includes the tree ferns (but treated as a fern in this book). Most trees are deciduous, shedding their leaves in autumn and experiencing a period of dormancy

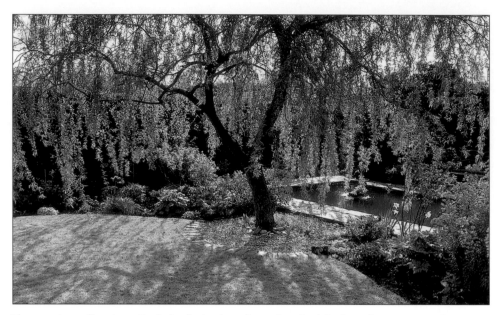

The weeping willow is particularly alluring in spring, when its delicate, pale green emerging leaves cast dappled shade.

over winter, though some are evergreens that in favourable climates will be more or less permanently in growth. Evergreen trees tend to be less hardy than deciduous trees.

Essential to the planet's ecology, trees store carbon dioxide and produce oxygen, and the material they shed – leaves and twigs – breaks down in the soil to release nitrogen, carbon and oxygen to feed the next generation of plants. Their roots help prevent soil erosion, which is why they are often planted in railway cuttings and to retain the banks at the sides of motorways, and the vast amount of water stored in a mature tree helps prevent local flooding. Trees also provide food and shelter for a wide range of mammals, birds and invertebrates.

Most trees grown in gardens today are either species or very closely related to naturally occurring forms. A few have been extensively hybridized, however, most notably the Japanese maples (forms of *Acer palmatum* and *A. japonicum*) and flowering cherries (*Prunus*), resulting in a vast number of highly desirable garden plants.

Trees in the garden

Even the smallest of gardens should include at least one tree. Trees give an air of maturity and permanence to any plot, quite apart from whatever ornamental qualities they may possess, and have the additional benefit – inestimable to environmentalists – of attracting wildlife into the garden. Birds will perch and sometimes nest in the branches, as well as feed off any autumn fruits or berries. Trees also attract pollinating insects when in flower, and harbour a wide range of invertebrates in their bark. Before making a choice, however, you need to consider the impact the tree will make on the rest of the planting. Deciduous trees that cast dappled shade in summer but are bare in winter can be underplanted with dwarf spring bulbs for early interest, followed by shade-loving perennials later on, but the shade cast by evergreens will be too dense to allow much other plant life to thrive. In a very small garden, a narrow, columnar tree, such as *Prunus* 'Amanogawa', is often the best choice.

Trees have a range of ornamental qualities, but whether you are planning an avenue of mighty oaks or have room for only a small tree, think long and hard over which species to plant. Most trees will outlive you. If it is flowers that you want, you could scarcely do better than look to the magnolias, with sumptuous, waxy, chalice-like flowers in spring; for more delicacy, a flowering cherry (*Prunus*) could fit the bill. In favoured areas, a catalpa or paulownia would provide spring flowers, while *Acacia dealbata* (perhaps trained against a warm wall) will flower in late winter. Rather less exotic, but equally attractive in their way, as well as being tough and hardy, are the rowans (*Sorbus*) and hawthorns (*Crataegus*).

Many trees have a second period of interest in autumn when the fruits ripen. Crab apples (*Malus*) are among the best, and their red, yellow or orange fruits, as well as looking good and attracting birds, can be cooked or made into a preserve. Rowans also have spectacular trusses of berries, which often change colour or turn translucent as the temperature drops in winter.

That elusive moment when the leaves of deciduous trees change colour in autumn just before they are shed is one of the most keenly anticipated events in the gardening calendar. The display will vary from year to year, depending on the conditions of the season. One reliable performer is the katsura tree (*Cercidiphyllum japonicum* var. *magnificum*), whose leaves turn brilliant orange and then give off the scent of burnt toffee as they fall to the ground. Many of the acers produce glorious autumn colour, particularly the Japanese maples, as do amelanchiers, rowans and beeches (*Fagus*).

Trees that have attractive bark are interesting in every season of the year. The birches are especially noted for this feature.

Many trees are surprisingly effective in winter, and not only the evergreens such as hollies (*Ilex*) or *Quercus ilex*. *Prunus serrula*, for instance, has shiny mahogany red bark, while that of *Betula utilis* var. *jacquemontii* (to name only one birch from a genus outstanding for this very feature) is a gleaming white. Site them where they will be dramatically lit up by the winter sun.

If space is restricted, a surprising number of trees will do well in containers. Not the large forest trees, obviously, but any of the evergreens that take kindly to pruning, such as bay (*Laurus*) or holly, as well as more modest trees, such as Japanese maples (stylish in glazed Eastern-style pots). Citrus and acacias make a good choice for a conservatory or porch.

Fruit trees have two-fold attractions: breathtaking when in flower in spring, they earn their keep by providing edible crops in autumn.

The trees described below are deciduous unless otherwise indicated.

ACACIA
Wattle

The main drawback of this delightful genus is that few wattles are hardy enough to grow as freestanding specimens in any but favoured climates. In the right spot, however, they make airy, elegant trees, laden with scented flowers. They are sometimes used as pavement trees, to spectacular effect. In cold areas they can be grown in conservatories (porches), but need cutting back to restrict their size. The genus also includes some shrubs.
Cultivation Moderately fertile, lime-free soil in full sun, with shelter from strong winds.

A. dealbata
Mimosa, silver wattle
This evergreen Australian and Tasmanian species has silver-grey, fern-like leaves and masses of fragrant, fluffy yellow flowers in late winter to early spring. It is suitable for training against a warm wall. H 15m (50ft), S 10m (33ft). Borderline hardy/Z 9–10.

ACER
Maple

This is a huge and important genus, and there is a maple for every garden, large or small. *A. pseudoplatanus* (sycamore) is almost a weed in some gardens, but that should not blind you to the

Acacia dealbata

Acer × conspicuum 'Phoenix'

beauties of the other species. Maples suit a woodland planting or lightly shaded area.
Cultivation Acers tolerate most soil types, although *A. rubrum* does best in lime-free soil. Japanese maples like a leafy, fertile but well-drained soil. Smaller species are best in light shade. *A. palmatum* cultivars are particularly susceptible to frost, which can damage the young growth, and they do best in a sheltered spot.

A. capillipes
The young stems of this erect, deciduous Japanese species are reddish. The leaves open red, mature to mid-green and turn crimson and orange in autumn. The grey-green bark is striped white. H and S 10m (33ft). Hardy/Z 6–9.

A. × conspicuum 'Phoenix'
This is grown mainly for the beauty of its green bark, which turns vivid pink with silver stripes in winter. The autumn display is also good, with the leaves turning a bright golden-yellow. H 5m (16ft), S 3m (10ft). Hardy/Z 6–9.

A. davidii
Snake-bark maple, Père David's maple
Native to China, the species has (usually) spreading branches. The leaves are tinged bronze as they emerge and turn red and purple in autumn. The grey bark is striped white. It does best in semi-shade. H 6m (20ft), S 3m (10ft). Hardy/Z 6–8.

'George Forrest' has larger, red-stalked, dark green leaves, but the autumn colour is not as good. H 4m (13ft), S 2m (6ft).

A. griseum
Paperbark maple
Also native to China, this slow-growing species is one of the most outstanding members of a fine genus. The leaves turn a brilliant red before they fall in autumn, but the principal interest is the cinnamon-red bark, which peels to reveal a richer colour beneath. H and S 10m (33ft). Hardy/Z 6–8.

A. japonicum
Japanese maple, full-moon maple
The Japanese maples, which also include selections of *A. palmatum* (see below), are among the most attractive of all small trees, staying fairly compact and ending up as broad or broader than they are tall. They all have spectacular autumn leaf colour. The species is a spreading, rather shrubby tree. H and S 10m (33ft). Hardy/Z 6–8. **'Aconitifolium'** (syn. 'Filicifolium') is a slow-growing tree or large shrub, generally broader than it is tall. The soft green, deeply cut leaves turn vivid orange-red in autumn. H 5m (16ft), S 6m (20ft).

A. palmatum
Japanese maple
The species, which is native to Korea and China as well as to Japan, is a rounded tree or shrub

Acer griseum

Acer japonicum 'Aconitifolium'

displaying glorious autumn colour. H 8m (25ft), S 10m (33ft). Hardy/Z 5–8.
A. palmatum f. *atropurpureum* (syn. 'Atropurpureum') is notable for the vibrant purple of its leaves, in spring and autumn. H 8m (25ft), S 10m (33ft).
A. palmatum var. *dissectum* makes a dome-shaped tree with elegant ferny foliage, which turns red or yellow in autumn. It has a number of cultivars with coloured or variegated leaves. H and S to 4m (13ft) but usually less. Acers in the **Dissectum Atropurpureum Group** have similar colouring to *A. palmatum* f. *atropurpurem* but with very finely dissected leaves, giving the plant a more filigree appearance. Slow-growing, they eventually make attractive, dome-shaped, spreading trees. H and S 4m (13ft). **'Dissectum Nigrum'** (syn. 'Ever Red') has finely dissected, blackish-purple leaves and forms a low, rounded bush. H 3m (10ft), S 4m (13ft). **'Fireglow'** (syn. 'Effegi') carries rich burgundy-red leaves, which turn orange-red in autumn. This requires some sun to enhance the leaf colour. H and S to 3m (10ft). **'Kagiri-Nishiki'** (syn. 'Roseomarginatum') has pale green leaves margined with pink, later turning cream. H and S 3m (10ft). **'Katsura'** has the typical palm-shaped leaves of the species. Pale orange-yellow when young, they mature to a rich bronze, then redden in autumn. H 1.2m (4ft), S 2.5m (8ft). **'Ôsakazuki'** carries mid-green leaves, which turn brilliant orange, crimson and scarlet in autumn. H 5m (16ft), S 2.5m (8ft). The red-tinted leaves of **'Rubrum'** turn bright red in autumn. H 5m (16ft), S 2.5m (8ft). **'Sekimori'** has very finely divided, filigree foliage,

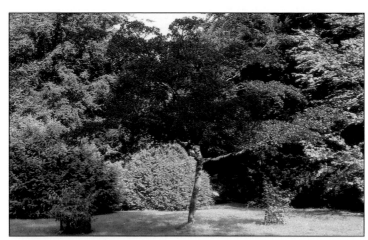

Acer palmatum f. *atropurpureum*

which is bright green, turning red or yellow in autumn. H and S to 3m (10ft).

A. platanoides
Norway maple
This fast-growing acer offers startling autumn colour, which is usually yellow but sometimes red. H 25m (80ft), S 15m (50ft). Hardy/Z 4–7. **'Crimson King'** has rich red-purple foliage. H 15m (50ft), S 5m (16ft). **'Drummondii'** is less vigorous with mid-green leaves that are variegated with creamy-white. H 12m (40ft), S 5m (16ft).

A. rubrum
Red maple, scarlet maple, swamp maple
This species has leaves that turn rich red-orange in early autumn. H 20m (65ft), S 10m (33ft). Hardy/Z 4–9. **'Scanlon'** is a slow-growing, densely upright form with good autumn colour. H 15m (50ft), S 5m (15ft).

A. shirasawanum 'Aureum'
Moonglow maple
A round-headed, slow-growing tree, with distinctive butter-yellow

Acer palmatum 'Rubrum'

leaves, which turn red in autumn. It needs some sun to colour the foliage but can scorch in full sun. H and S to 6m (20ft). Hardy/Z 6–8.

AESCULUS
Horse chestnut, buckeye
A spectacular show of late-spring flowers is just one of the attributes of these majestic trees. Most are for big gardens only, although *A. pavia* is well worth considering for a smaller plot.
Cultivation Grow in moist, fertile, well-drained soil in full sun.

A. hippocastanum
Common horse chestnut
This giant of a tree, which is native to south-eastern Europe, has mid-green leaves. The white, candle-like flowers are spectacular in late spring. H 25m (80ft), S 20m (65ft). Hardy/Z 4–7.

A. × neglecta 'Erythroblastos'
Sunrise horse chestnut
This slender, slow-growing, conical hybrid has red leaf stalks and leaves that emerge cream and pink, then turn yellow before maturing green by midsummer. H 10m (33ft), S 8m (25ft). Hardy/Z 7–8.

A. pavia
(syn. *A. splendens*)
Red buckeye
A shrubby, North American species, this has mid-green leaves and upright panicles of bright red flowers in late spring to early summer. H 3m (10ft), S 2.5m (8ft). Hardy/Zone 6–9.

ALNUS
Alder
One of the few genera adapted to boggy conditions, alders are often planted near to water.
Cultivation Alders will grow in any fertile soil in full sun.

A. glutinosa
Common alder
This species has purplish catkins (pussy willows) in late winter. Dark green leaves emerge from sticky buds in spring. H 25m (80ft), S 10m (33ft). Hardy/Z 4–7.

AMELANCHIER
June berry, snowy mespilus, serviceberry
These are charming trees for the spring garden, the dainty flowers appearing around the same time as tulips. They also provide good autumn colour and fruits that will attract birds. They make good specimen trees but are small enough for a mixed planting.
Cultivation Grow in a lime-free soil in sun or light shade.

A. × grandiflora 'Ballerina'
A profusion of starry white flowers appears on this spreading, shrubby hybrid in spring. The leaves turn red and purple in autumn. H 6m (20ft), S 8m (25ft). Hardy/Z 4.

A. lamarckii
This beautiful small tree bears copper-red young leaves, which turn orange and red in autumn.

Aesculus hippocastanum

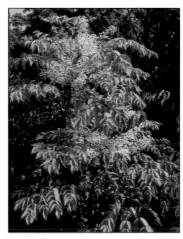

Aralia elata

The white spring flowers are followed by black berries. H 10m (33ft), S 8m (25ft). Hardy/Z 4–8.

ARALIA
Angelica tree
The genus includes some of the most elegant and architectural trees for the small garden. The species described makes a good specimen, but it can also be used in mixed plantings when young.
Cultivation Fertile soil in partial shade, but they will tolerate full sun if the soil is reliably damp.

A. elata
(syn. *A. chinensis* of gardens)
Japanese angelica tree
This has spiny stems and coarsely toothed leaves, which turn yellow, orange or purple in autumn. White flowers appear in late summer to autumn. H and S 10m (33ft). Hardy/Z 4–9.

Betula albosinensis var. septentrionalis

ARBUTUS
Strawberry tree, madroña, manzanita

A genus with many attractions, not the least of which are the charming, strawberry-like fruits that give the trees their common name. (The fruits are edible, if on the insipid side.) The lily-of-the-valley-like flowers, which appear at the same time as the ripening fruits, are also beautiful. Add peeling bark to the list of attractions, and the surprise is that they are not more widely planted. There are two main reasons for this: not all are reliably hardy, and some will grow well only in acid soil.
Cultivation Most strawberry trees need lime-free soil in a sheltered position; *A. unedo* tolerates lime.

A. × andrachnoides
This evergreen hybrid has peeling, reddish-brown bark and clusters of small ivory-white flowers, which are borne between autumn and spring. Fruits appear only occasionally. H and S 8m (25ft). Hardy/Z 8–9.

Arbutus unedo 'Rubra'

A. unedo
This evergreen species has a spreading, sometimes rather shrubby habit. It is native to south-eastern Europe and the Middle East. The white flowers appear in autumn, at the same time as the strawberry-like fruits from the previous year ripen. The red-brown bark, which peels in shreds, is also an attractive feature. H and S 6m (20ft). Borderline hardy/Z 8–9. The form **'Rubra'** reaches the same size as the species, but has deep pink flowers.

BETULA
Birch

The genus includes some of the best garden trees. They are hardy and easy to grow in addition to being graceful and quick growing. Most have attractive, usually white, bark and good autumn leaf colour. They are among the most reliable trees for alkaline soils.
Cultivation Birches will grow in any fertile soil in sun or light shade; they also tolerate poor soil.

B. albosinensis var. septentrionalis
In a genus renowned for the beauty of its bark, this form of *B. albosinensis* (Chinese red birch) is outstanding for that feature. Creamy white when young, on mature specimens (those 15 or more years old) it develops a pinkish bloom and peels to reveal a mahogany red underlayer. The oval leaves are deep green, turning yellow in autumn and persisting on the tree until early winter. In favourable conditions trees can exceed the dimensions indicated, but only after 20 years or so. H 10m (33ft), S 6m (20ft). Hardy/Z 6–8.

B. ermannii
Erman's birch, gold birch, Russian rock birch
The species is native to Russia (the Kamchatka peninsula), Japan and Korea, and is valued by gardeners because of its beautiful peeling white bark, which is sometimes tinged pink or cream. This feature is particularly apparent on multi-stemmed trees. H 7m (23ft) or more, S 4m (13ft) or more. Hardy/Z 5–8.

Betula utilis var. jacquemontii

The vigorous **'Grayswood Hill'**, which has an attractive conical habit of growth, has pure white bark. H 7m (23ft) or more, S 4m (12ft) or more.

B. pendula
(syn. B. alba, B. verrucosa)
Silver birch
This familiar tree, which is native to Europe and northern Asia, has slightly drooping branches and greyish-white bark, which cracks attractively on mature specimens. It may not always be long-lived in gardens. H 25m (80ft), S 10m (33ft). Hardy/Z 3–8. Notable selections include **'Youngii'** (Young's weeping birch), which is less vigorous and has more pendulous branches. H 8m (25ft), S 5m (15ft). Hardy/Z 3–8.

B. utilis var. jacquemontii
(syn. B. jacquemontii)
This naturally occurring variety of the Himalayan birch has white bark, which makes it an outstanding plant for the winter garden. The oval leaves turn yellow in autumn. Many of the plants sold in the trade under this name are raised from seed collected in the Himalayas, so habits and growth rates can vary, but most will not exceed the dimensions indicated in 20 years. H 12m (40ft), S 5m (16ft). Hardy/Z 6–8. Selected seedlings include **'Grayswood Ghost'**, which has glossy leaves, the fast-growing **'Jermyns'**, which has rounded leaves and large catkins (pussy willows), and **'Silver Shadow'**, which has large, drooping, dark green leaves; all three forms have particularly brilliant bark. H 12m (40ft), S 5m (16ft).

CATALPA
Indian bean tree
Catalpas are among the most impressive flowering trees, bearing orchid-like flowers in mid- to late summer. The large, soft leaves are also appealing, particularly in the coloured-leaf forms. Suitable trees for sheltered, sunny gardens, they are hardier than is commonly supposed, although flowers are not always freely borne in cold areas. They can also be grown as foliage plants in mixed borders and cut back hard annually in spring, which produces luxuriant foliage, albeit at the expense of the flowers. The common name refers to the seedcases, which dangle from the branches from late summer onwards.
Cultivation Grow in any fertile soil in sun. Provide protection from strong winds.

C. bignonioides
Southern catalpa, smoking bean
Native to the south-eastern United States, this has long seed pods hanging from the branches in autumn. Its most striking feature, however, are the panicles of orchid-like flowers, which are white marked with yellow and purple-brown. A mature catalpa in full flower is an impressive sight in midsummer. The large, soft green leaves are also handsome, making this a highly valued shade tree in hot climates. Flowering is

Catalpa bignonioides 'Aurea'

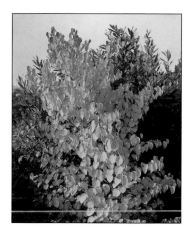

Cercidiphyllum japonicum var.
magnificum

reliable only during hot summers.
H and S 15m (50ft). Hardy/Z
5–9. **'Aurea'** is less vigorous. The
soft yellow-green leaves, tinged
bronze as they unfurl in spring,
benefit from some shade from
direct sun. Given that this tree is
more reluctant to flower than its
parent, plus the fact that it is
slightly tender, in cool climates it
is best treated as a pollard or
coppice and enjoyed for its leaves
alone. H and S 10m (33ft)
unpollarded.

CERCIDIPHYLLUM

The genus contains a single
species, which is native to western
China and Japan. It is a choice
tree for the garden grown for its
spectacular autumn foliage.
Cultivation These trees do best in
woodland conditions – in fertile
soil in light dappled shade – and
although they are tolerant of lime,
the best autumn colour occurs on
acid soil.

× *Citrofortunella microcarpa*

C. japonicum var. *magnificum*
(syn. *C. magnificum*)
Katsura tree
This rare Japanese upright species
has rounded leaves that turn
yellow, orange and red in autumn
and smell of toffee when they fall
to the ground. H 10m (33ft),
S 8m (25ft). Hardy/Z 5–9.

CERCIS

All six species in the genus are
small trees, with rounded leaves
and pea-like flowers in spring.
Cultivation The trees need fertile
soil in a sunny, sheltered spot
where the late-spring flowers will
not be damaged by frosts.

C. siliquastrum
Judas tree
The connotations of the common
name (this is supposedly the tree
from which Judas hanged himself)
do not militate against its garden-
worthiness. The species, which is
native to south-eastern Europe
and south-western Asia, is quick-
growing and produces dark pink
flowers on the bare wood in
spring. The kidney-shaped, blue-
green leaves turn yellow in
autumn. The tree can be trained
against a wall. H and S 10m
(33ft). Hardy/Z 8–9. The
shrubby form *C. siliquastrum* f.
albida has white flowers and pale
green leaves.

× CITROFORTUNELLA

The trees in this hybrid genus
(a cross between *Citrus* and
Fortunella) are easy to grow, being
hardier than most *Citrus*.
Cultivation Grow in neutral to
acid soil in full sun. Container-
grown plants can be clipped to
keep them within bounds.

× *C. microcarpa*
(syn. × *C. mitis*)
Calamondin
This evergreen tree bears fragrant
white flowers at the same time as
the fruits from the previous
season are ripening. H 3m (10ft),
S 2m (6ft). Half-hardy/Z 9.

CORNUS
Dogwood
The dogwoods are among the best
trees for a small garden. Some are
grown for their overall appearance

Cornus alternifolia 'Argentea'

and hence make good specimens,
while others have striking spring
flowers and good autumn leaf
colour. The genus also includes
many shrubs and a few perennials.
Cultivation They need fertile soil,
preferably lime-free, in sun or
light shade. The species described
need neutral to acid soil.

C. alternifolia
(syn. *Swida alternifolia*)
Pagoda dogwood, green osier
This species from eastern North
America is usually grown in the
variegated form **'Argentea'** (syn.
'Variegata'), one of the most
beautiful of small trees. It has a
distinctive tiered habit, but it is
slow-growing and takes several
years to develop its characteristic

'wedding-cake' appearance.
Careful staking is necessary
initially to establish an upright
leader. H 3m (10ft), S 2m (6ft).
Hardy/Z 4–8.

C. 'Eddie's White Wonder'
This conical tree or large shrub
has white flowers in late spring
and leaves that reliably turn
orange, red and purple in autumn.
H 6m (20ft), S 5m (16ft).
Hardy/Z 6–9.

C. kousa
White flowers in summer are
followed by red fruits on this
elegant species, native to Japan
and Korea. The wavy-edged leaves
redden in autumn. H 7m (23ft),
S 5m (16ft). Hardy/Z 5–8.

Cercis siliquastrum

Crataegus laevigata 'Crimson Cloud'

CRATAEGUS
Hawthorn

Despite their ubiquity as roadside plants, hawthorns make excellent garden trees, particularly in exposed situations and on poor, limy soils. They are tough and hardy and make excellent hedges, particularly in country gardens.
Cultivation Grow hawthorns in any fertile soil, preferably in full sun. They can be grown in exposed positions.

C. laevigata
(syn. C. oxyacantha)
Common hawthorn, may
Widely seen as a hedgerow plant in northern Europe, this bears white flowers in spring. These are followed in autumn by red haws, a valuable food source for birds. H and S to 8m (25ft). Hardy/Z 5–8. **'Crimson Cloud'** is a distinctive selection, producing brilliant red flowers with white centres, which are a strong contrast to the glossy,

Crataegus laevigata 'Paul's Scarlet'

dark green leaves. H and S 5m (16ft). **'Paul's Scarlet'** is one of the most popular of the hawthorns, but its double, deep pink flowers, produced in vast quantities, are usually sterile and haws are seldom produced. H and S 5m (16ft). Hardy/Z 5–8.

C. × lavallei 'Carrierei'
This spreading, densely branched hawthorn has glossy green leaves that turn red in late autumn and winter. Clusters of white spring flowers are followed by orange-red fruits. H 7m (23ft), S 10m (33ft). Hardy/Z 5–7.

C. persimilis 'Prunifolia'
(syn. C. prunifolia)
A compact, spreading hawthorn of garden origin, this bears clusters of white flowers in spring, which are followed by bright red fruit. The glossy, deep green leaves are tinted orange and scarlet in autumn. H 8m (25ft), S 10m (33ft). Hardy/Z 6–7.

EUCALYPTUS
Gum tree, ironbark

A familiar sight in many urban areas, eucalyptus are widely planted as pollution-tolerant street trees. Although potentially very large, they respond well to pruning. The foliage of most species changes shape as the tree matures, the juvenile leaves being generally considered the more attractive. Cutting back stems regularly ensures that trees retain their youthful appearance.
Cultivation Grow in any well-drained soil in full sun. (Some sources specify acid soil, but many species tolerate chalk.)

E. gunnii
Cider gum
This evergreen from Tasmania is one of the most versatile of garden trees. Not only can it be allowed to develop freely as a single- or multi-stemmed tree, but it can also be kept within bounds by hard pruning so that it can be grown as a shrub in a mixed border. Pruning also encourages the ready production of juvenile foliage, which is coin-shaped and a gleaming pewter grey. Unless cut back, mature trees can become unstable. H 20m (65ft), S 6m (20ft). Borderline hardy/Z 8–10.

E. pauciflora subsp. niphophila
(syn. E. niphophila)
Snow gum, alpine snow gum
This slow-growing evergreen tree is grown for its brilliant, peeling, cream and grey bark, which is shown to best advantage when the plant is grown as a multi-stemmed tree. The bluish-grey juvenile leaves are oval; adult leaves are sickle shaped. To retain the juvenile foliage, treat as a pollard. H and S to 6m (20ft). Hardy/Z 9–10.

E. perriniana
Spinning gum
An evergreen species from Australia, this has flaking, white,

Eucalyptus gunnii

Eucryphia glutinosa

green or grey bark and bluish-green, rounded juvenile leaves, while adult leaves are lance-shaped. It is best treated as a pollard. H 5.5m (18ft), S 2m (6ft). Borderline hardy/Z 9–10.

EUCRYPHIA

These trees deserve to be better known. Not only are the myrtle-like flowers beautiful, but they also appear late in the season, when few other woody plants are flowering. A mature eucryphia in full flower is an impressive sight. Choose among the species carefully because some are particular as to soil type.
Cultivation Plant in neutral to acid soil in sun or light shade in a sheltered spot. E. × nymansensis 'Nymansay' tolerates chalk.

E. glutinosa
Nirrhe
This slow-growing small tree or shrub from Chile is an excellent flowering tree for an acid site. The large white flowers cover the plant in mid- to late summer. In mild areas the tree is evergreen; in cold areas the leaves turn rich orange-red before falling in autumn. H 10m (33ft), S 6m (20ft). Hardy/Z 8–10.

E. × nymansensis 'Nymansay'
This columnar, evergreen hybrid is better known than E. glutinosa, probably because it tolerates alkaline conditions and has fragrant flowers. H 5m (16ft), S 2m (6ft), ultimately probably larger. Borderline hardy/Z 8–9.

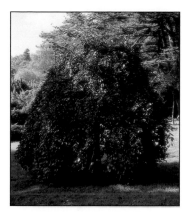

Fagus sylvatica 'Purpurea Pendula'

FAGUS
Beech

The 10 species in this genus have a number of uses. While most – magnificent though they are – grow too large for the average garden, some are more modest and make fine specimens. Beech also makes a splendid hedge. While not evergreen, the faded leaves hang on the branches over winter in a most appealing way. The autumn colour of all beeches can be spectacular.
Cultivation Grow in any soil except wet, sticky clays. Forms with coloured leaves do best in full sun, but other forms prefer light shade.

F. sylvatica
Common beech
This large European species is widely planted in parks and large public gardens. It can be unstable as a large specimen and its branches are brittle, especially in strong winds. It is, however, the parent of a number of handsome

Fortunella japonica

selections. Those listed are both hardy/zone 4–7. The excellent **'Dawyck Gold'** is a narrow, conical, slow-growing tree with leaves that are bright yellow as they unfurl in spring, becoming paler by summer. The dead leaves are held on the tree over winter. For the best leaf colour, plant in a sunny position. H 6m (20ft), S 2m (6ft). **'Purpurea Pendula'**, the weeping copper beech, is popular as a specimen in gardens both for its elegant habit and its rich purple leaves, which turn red in autumn. H up to 5m (16ft) (but often less), S to 2.2m (7ft).

FORTUNELLA
Kumquat
The four or five species in the genus are popular for their orange-yellow fruits, which, unlike other types of *Citrus* (to which *Fortunella* is related), can be eaten whole. Kumquats are native to southern China, and they make good conservatory (porch) plants.
Cultivation In frost-free climates they will grow in any well-drained soil in full sun or light shade, but elsewhere they need protection from frost.

F. japonica
(syn. *Citrus japonica*, *C. macrophylla*)
Marumi kumquat, round kumquat
This small evergreen tree or shrub carries fragrant white flowers from spring to summer. These are followed by edible, oval, golden-yellow fruits, each up to 4cm (1½in) long. When grown in a container under glass the dimensions will be smaller than indicated here. H 3m (10ft), S 1.5m (5ft). Tender/Z 9.

GLEDITSIA
Few trees have the charm of gleditsias, which look graceful all year round. In areas where there are hot summers the stems turn almost black, creating a sensational contrast with the lime green leaves. They are excellent as specimens or underplanted with prostrate ceanothus.
Cultivation Grow in any well-drained soil in sun or light shade. They are tolerant of pollution.

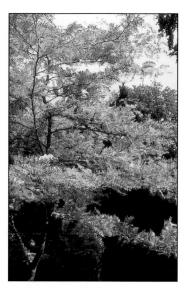

Gleditsia triacanthos 'Sunburst'

G. triacanthos
Honey locust
This popular species, from North America, is usually represented in gardens by **'Sunburst'**. The leaves of this cultivar are bright yellow on emergence, changing to pale green by the end of summer. This does best in a sunny position, where it can be sheltered from strong winds, and it is definitely a better choice for a small garden than the more vigorous *Robinia pseudoacacia* 'Frisia', which it superficially resembles. H 12m (40ft), S 10m (33ft). Hardy/Z 5–9.

HIPPOPHÄE
Buckthorn
These attractive small trees and shrubs make good windbreaks or barrier plantings, but they also combine well with other plants in mixed borders, providing a good

Hippophäe rhamnoides

foil to flowering shrubs and herbaceous perennials.
Cultivation Buckthorns will grow in any well-drained soil, including sandy soil, in sun or partial shade. They are well adapted to coastal conditions and will withstand strong, salt-laden winds.

H. rhamnoides
Sea buckthorn
The spiny shoots of this native of Europe and temperate Asia are clothed in long, silver-green leaves. Small yellow flowers in spring (almost lost among the branches) are followed by showier orange berries in autumn. Male and female flowers are borne on separate plants, so for reliable berrying, plant members of both sexes. H and S 6m (20ft). Hardy/Z 3–8. **'Freisendorf Orange'**, **'Hergo'** and **'Leikora'** are female; **'Pollmix'** is male.

IDESIA
The genus, from China and Japan, contains only one species, an elegant, understated plant, which is probably at its best as a specimen in a minimalist-style garden or in light woodland.
Cultivation Idesias need neutral to acid soil in sun or light shade.

I. polycarpa
This is an unusual, spreading tree, with heart-shaped leaves, usually tinged bronze as they open in spring. Male and female flowers are carried on separate plants, so for the bright red berries that are a feature on female plants in autumn, trees of both sexes must be grown. H and S up to 12m (40ft). Hardy/ Z 7–9.

Idesia polycarpa

Ilex aquifolium 'J.C. van Tol'

ILEX
Holly

Indispensable plants in any garden for their healthy, glossy leaves, the hollies are either trees or shrubs depending on age and how they have been pruned (if at all). If you inherit a garden with a large holly, think twice before ousting it – it will undoubtedly be of venerable age. Holly also makes an excellent hedge. Berries will be produced only on females, which will need a pollinating male nearby, so choose carefully among the cultivars. (*I. aquifolium* 'J.C. van Tol' is self-pollinating.) Those listed here are evergreen.
Cultivation Grow in any fertile soil, in sun or light shade. Variegated forms produce their best leaf colour in full sun. They are tolerant of atmospheric pollution and wind.

I. aquifolium
Common holly, English holly
Seedlings of the species, which is native to northern Africa and western Asia as well as to Europe, often appear in gardens, but the many cultivars generally make more attractive plants. The following selections are all hardy/Z 7–9. **'Aurea Marginata Pendula'** is a slow-growing, rounded, weeping tree with purple stems and spiny, glossy, bright green leaves that are margined with creamy yellow. It is a female form, producing red berries in autumn. It is an outstanding plant for year-round interest. H and S up to 3m (10ft). The male **'Ferox Argentea'** carries very prickly dark green leaves margined with cream. H 6m (20ft), S 4m (13ft). **'J.C. van Tol'** is self-fertile, with bright red berries among the plain leaves. H 6m (20ft), S 4m ((13ft). **'Silver Milkmaid'**, a female cultivar, has an open habit and leaves with white margins. The berries are scarlet. H 6m (20ft), S 4m (13ft). **'Silver Queen'** (syn. 'Silver King'), which is a slow-growing male form, also has white-edged leaves. It has a dense, upright habit of growth. H 10m (33ft), S 4m (13ft).

KALOPANAX

The genus, which is native to China, Korea, Japan and parts of Russia, contains a single species, which, while not exactly beautiful, nevertheless makes a striking

statement in the growing season with its maple-like leaves and, in winter, its barbed branches.
Cultivation Grow in any fertile, well-drained soil either in sun or light shade.

K. septemlobus
(syn. *Eleutherococcus pictus*,
E. septemlobus, *Kalopanax pictus*,
K. ricinifolius)
Castor aralia, tree aralia
This spreading tree has lobed, dark green leaves and large heads of small white flowers, which appear in autumn and are followed by small black berries. H and S 10m (33ft). Hardy/Z 5–9. The leaves of **K. septemlobus var. maximowiczii** are more deeply lobed. H and S 10m (33ft).

× LABURNOCYTISUS

This curiosity would be a talking point in any garden, although it is not an entirely beautiful tree. It is a hybrid of *Chamaecytisus purpureus* and *Laburnum anagyroides*, grafted on to laburnum seedlings. It retains some of the characteristics of both its parents.
Cultivation Grow in any well-drained, moderately fertile soil in full sun.

× *L.* 'Adamii'

This tree is grown for its laburnum-like flowers in late spring or early summer. Some are yellow (like laburnum), others purple (like *Chamaecytisus*), while a third group are purplish-pink, flushed yellow, all colours appearing simultaneously. H 8m (25ft), S 6m (20ft). Hardy/Z 6–8.

LABURNUM
Golden rain

These decorative trees with their long pendulous flowers have one drawback, which is a serious one for many gardeners: all parts of the plant are poisonous. Effective as they are as specimens, laburnums are at their most attractive when planted in avenues and trained as a tunnel. In a small garden, they can be very effective when planted as a pair and trained to make an archway.
Cultivation Plant in any well-drained soil in sun or light shade.

Kalopanax septemlobus var. *maximowiczii*

L. × *watereri* 'Vossii'
This laburnum, a naturally occurring hybrid of *L. alpinum* and *L. anagyroides*, is one of the best-loved trees, with its racemes of golden-yellow flowers, which are followed by pea-like seed pods. Initially upright, it becomes more rounded on maturity. H and S 8m (25ft). Hardy/Z 6–8.

LAURUS
Bay laurel, sweet bay

The small genus, which contains two species, is a typical plant of the Mediterranean littoral. In colder areas bays are usually grown as shrubs, principally for their leaves, which, while not edible in themselves, can be used to flavour a variety of dishes. Bay looks effective in containers and incomparably stylish when arranged in pairs to frame a doorway. It is also a good choice for a seaside planting.
Cultivation Plant in any well-drained soil in sun or light shade.

Ilex aquifolium 'Aurea Marginata Pendula'

Laburnum × *watereri* 'Vossii'

Laurus nobilis

Choose a sheltered spot in all but the warmest gardens because cold, drying winds can kill it.

L. nobilis
Bay laurel
This handsome evergreen foliage plant has glossy mid- to dark green leaves. The flowers, produced in spring, are inconspicuous. Although it can be grown as a standard, it is often pruned to a shape, such as a cone or ball. H 12m (40ft), S 10m (33ft). Borderline hardy/Z 8–10.

LIGUSTRUM
Privet
Most of the privets are shrubs, planted mainly as hedging, although they are widely considered inferior to many other evergreen hedging plants. The genus includes a number of fine trees, which are tough, tolerant plants.
Cultivation Grow in any garden soil in sun or shade.

L. lucidum
Chinese privet
The evergreen species, which originates in China, Korea and Japan, has oval, glossy, dark green leaves and white flowers in late summer. It can be kept smaller than the dimensions shown by regular clipping. H and S 10m (33ft). Hardy/Z 7–10.

MAGNOLIA
Sumptuous and stately, magnolias are among the most handsome of garden trees, as well as being among the hardiest. Drawbacks of some of the species are their enormous size, slowness of growth and reluctance to flower until some 20 or more years after planting. Fortunately, most of the modern selections are free from these vices. All magnolias make incomparable specimens and are best appreciated when grown in isolation. A few are shrubs.
Cultivation Grow in well-drained, humus-rich soil in sun or light shade. Not all magnolias will tolerate chalky (alkaline) soil.

M. campbellii
The species is found in a range from the Himalayas to China. The large, cup-and-saucer-shaped flowers, to 30cm (12in) across and either white or pink, emerge in late winter to early spring before the glossy green leaves. H to 15m (50ft), S to 10m (33ft). Hardy/Z 7–9. The vigorous **'Charles Raffill'** is a well-known selection, with claret-stained, white flowers, opening from rose pink buds. H 10m (33ft), S 5.5m/18ft.

M. 'Elizabeth'
A conical tree, this bears fragrant, goblet-shaped, pale yellow flowers, to 15cm (6in) across, in mid- to late spring. The leaves are attractively tinged with bronze when they emerge. This needs acid soil. H 10m (33ft), S 6m (20ft). Hardy/Z 5.

M. grandiflora
Bull bay, laurel magnolia
One of the few evergreen magnolias, the species is native to the south-eastern United States. Sadly, it is less hardy than some other species. In an open situation, it makes a magnificent, broadly conical tree, with long, glossy, dark green leaves and citrus-scented, waxy-textured, creamy white, cup-shaped flowers, which are borne in late summer. It is tolerant of lime, and it may be grown against a wall in cold areas. H 18m (60ft), S 15m (50ft), less when wall-trained. Borderline hardy/Z 7–9. The selection **'Victoria'** is hardier than the species but has smaller flowers. The leaves are brownish-red beneath. Hardy/Z 6.

Magnolia campbellii

M. 'Heaven Scent'
This lovely spreading tree hybrid bears a profusion of fragrant, goblet-shaped, white flowers, heavily flushed with deep pink outside, from mid-spring to early summer. The leaves are glossy dark green, lighter green beneath. This needs to be planted in acid soil. H 10m (33ft), S 6m (20ft). Hardy/Z 5.

M. 'Pickard's Schmetterling' (syn. *M. 'Schmetterling'*)
A spreading tree, this bears goblet-shaped, rich pinkish-purple flowers in mid-spring. The flowers open as the leaves emerge. H 10m (33ft), S 6m (20ft). Hardy/Z 5.

M. × soulangeana
The hybrid of *M. denudata* and *M. liliiflora* has given rise to a large range of garden-worthy plants, all with goblet-shaped

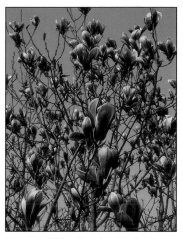

Magnolia 'Pickard's Schmetterling'

flowers from mid-spring and a candelabra-like habit as they mature. The plants are moderately tolerant of lime. The following are all hardy/Z 5–9. The slow-growing **'Amabilis'** has pure white flowers. H and S to 6m (20ft). The flowers of the conical **'Brozzonii'** are heavily flushed with purple on the outside and white within. They are produced over a long period from mid-spring to early summer. H and S to 8m (25ft). The large flowers of **'Rustica Rubra'** (syn. 'Rubra') are a dramatic deep purple. H and S to 6m (20ft).

M. sprengeri
This slow-growing species, which is native to China, carries large, cup-shaped, white or pink-tinged flowers in early spring before the leaves appear. It has a compact habit. H 20m (65ft), S 10m (33ft). Hardy/Z 7–9.

Magnolia × soulangeana 'Amabilis'

Magnolia sprengeri

Malus 'Evereste'

Mespilus germanica 'Nottingham'

Morus alba 'Pendula'

MALUS
Crab apple

As well as a plethora of fruit-bearing trees (forms of *Malus domestica*), this genus includes a number of trees of purely ornamental value, although even with these it is worth bearing in mind that the fruits, small and hard though they are, can be cooked or made into jellies. These ornamental trees are smaller than the flowering cherries, to which they are, therefore, a useful alternative, and, having a more 'rustic' appearance, they suit cottage-style gardens.
Cultivation Grow in any ordinary, fertile garden soil which is not too wet, in sun or light shade.

M. coronaria
Wild sweet crab apple

The species, native to North America, is usually represented in gardens by the form **'Charlottae'**, an attractive small tree. Fragrant, semi-double, pink flowers are borne in late spring, and these are followed by yellowish-green fruits. The leaves take on good autumn colour. H and S 9m (30ft). Hardy/Z 5–8.

M. 'Evereste'

In spring this conical small hybrid bears a profusion of large white flowers, opening from reddish-pink buds. The fruits, which develop in autumn as the leaves turn yellow, are bright orange to red. H 7m (23ft), S 6m (20ft). Hardy/Z 4.

M. floribunda
Japanese crab apple

A spreading species from Japan, this bears pale pink flowers in late spring and small yellow fruits in autumn. H and S 10m (33ft). Hardy/Z 5–8.

M. 'John Downie'

This is one of the finest crab apples, and the best for making jelly. The cup-shaped, white flowers, borne in late spring, are followed by quantities of egg-shaped, orange and red fruits. H and S 6m (20ft). Hardy/Z 5–8.

M. × robusta 'Red Sentinel'

This hybrid produces a wonderful display of deep glossy fruits, which stay on the tree for most of the winter. H and S up to 7m (23ft). Hardy/Z 4–8.

M. tschonoskii

A notable introduction from Japan, this strong-growing, erect species bears pink-flushed, white flowers in spring. Fruits ripen to glossy yellow (with a red flush) in autumn as the leaves turn orange, red and purple. H 12m (40ft), S 7m (23ft). Hardy/Z 5–8.

M. × zumi 'Golden Hornet' (syn. M. 'Golden Hornet')

A small, rounded tree with deep pink buds that open to white flowers in late spring. They are followed by a good crop of bright yellow fruits. H 10m (33ft), S 8m (25ft). Hardy/Z 5–8.

MESPILUS
Medlar

Although medlars have been known since the Middle Ages, they are not grown commercially, so most people are unaware of the unique delights of the fruits, which are edible only once they have been frosted (or 'bletted') on the plant. The flowers, in late spring, are also attractive. The one species in the genus makes a charming specimen.
Cultivation Grow in well-drained soil in sun or light shade.

M. germanica

This medlar is found growing wild in forests and woodlands in south-eastern Europe and south-western Asia. The white flowers, borne in late summer, are followed by rounded brown fruits. As an added bonus, the leaves turn yellow-brown in autumn. H 6m (20ft), S 8m (25ft). Hardy/Z 6–9. The most widely grown selected form is **'Nottingham'**, which is less thorny than the species and has larger leaves.

MORUS
Mulberry

These handsome trees are sometimes found in old cottage gardens: they can live for several hundred years. Although the raspberry-like fruits are edible, mulberries are grown more for their stately overall appearance.
Cultivation Mulberries need fertile, humus-rich soil in full sun. For the best fruiting, provide some shelter from strong winds.

M. alba
White mulberry

The shiny, heart-shaped leaves of this mulberry turn yellow in autumn as the fruits ripen from white through red to black. The species is native to China. H and S 10m (33ft). Hardy/Z 5–9. **'Pendula'** is a weeping form, ideal for a smaller garden. Unfortunately, it does not fruit freely. H 3m (10ft), S 5m (16ft). Hardy/Z 5–9.

PAULOWNIA

Only one species of this fairly small genus of deciduous trees is at all common, and the climate of your garden will determine how you grow it. Where summers are long and hot, it can make an excellent specimen, but in colder areas, where it is less likely to flower, it is best treated as a pollard, when the huge leaves make it an exotic-looking foliage plant for a mixed border.
Cultivation This needs well-drained fertile soil in full sun with shelter from wind.

P. tomentosa
Foxglove tree, empress tree, princess tree

The most usual common name of the species, which is native to central and western China, derives from the upright spires of foxglove-like, mauve flowers. Unfortunately, the overwintering flower buds are generally killed by frosts in cold climates. In areas with hard winters, therefore, it is usually best enjoyed for the hairy young shoots and leaves and cut

Paulownia tomentosa

Populus alba

back hard annually in early spring. The leaves on coppiced plants will be up to 60cm (2ft) across. H to 12m (40ft), S 10m (33ft) (uncoppiced). Hardy/Z 6–9.

POPULUS
Poplar, aspen, cottonwood
Lombardy poplars are a familiar roadside tree in Europe, but the genus contains many other handsome species, although the majority are suitable only for larger gardens. Poplars are fast growing and are useful for providing a barrier in a relatively short time. All have invasive roots, however, so take care not to plant them near buildings whose foundations they could damage.
Cultivation Most poplars will grow in any garden soil, including wet, sticky clay (as long as it is not waterlogged), in an open position.

P. alba
White poplar, abele
The species, from central and southern Europe, central Asia and northern Africa, is recognizable from the white, woolly undersides of the leaves (turning yellow in summer), which create a charming effect as they flutter in the breeze. H to 40m (130ft), S 15m (50ft). Hardy/Z 4–9. **'Richardii'** is a more compact form, with leaves that are golden-yellow above and white beneath. H 15m (50ft), S 12m (40ft).

P. × candicans 'Aurora'
This decorative, slow-growing hybrid forms a pillar-like tree with oval leaves that are splashed with white, cream and pink. Some shelter is desirable if the leaves are not to scorch. Pollarded, it makes a pretty specimen in a small garden. H 15m (50ft), S 6m (20ft). Hardy/Z 5–9.

P. nigra
Black poplar
Although handsome, the species is eclipsed in popularity by the selected form **'Italica'** (Lombardy poplar), an elegant, narrowly columnar tree. It tends to be short-lived in cultivation and seldom reaches the dimensions indicated. H 30m (100ft), S 5m (16ft). Hardy/Z 3–9.

Prunus 'Pandora'

PRUNUS
Ornamental cherry
This large genus contains evergreens and deciduous plants, shrubs as well as trees. Apart from the fruiting varieties (cherries, plums, apricots, peaches and almonds), there are a huge number of ornamental ones, many being hybrids of Japanese origin. A cherry orchard is a spectacular sight when in flower in spring, and an ornamental cherry should be among the first choices for a flowering specimen.
Cultivation Grow ornamental cherries in any well-drained, moderately fertile soil in full sun. A little lime seems to suit them.

P. 'Amanogawa'
(syn. *P. serrulata* 'Erecta')
This is an upright ornamental cherry with, usually, semi-double, shell-pink flowers in late spring. The leaves, which are tinged with bronze when young, redden in autumn. It is an ideal specimen for a small garden, but is also effective when planted in pairs or

Prunus 'Hillieri'

Prunus 'Shirofugen'

avenues. H 8m (25ft), S 4m (13ft). Hardy/Z 6–8.

P. 'Hillieri'
A spreading tree, this hybrid bears clusters of soft pink flowers in mid-spring. H and S to 10m (33ft). Hardy/Z 6.

P. 'Okame'
This cherry is laden with clusters of carmine-pink flowers in spring. The leaves turn orange and red in autumn. H 10m (33ft), S 8m (25ft). Hardy/Z 5–8.

P. 'Pandora'
This makes a spreading tree, with deep pink buds in early spring opening to paler pink flowers. Good autumn leaf colour adds to its attractions. H 10m (33ft), S 8m (25ft). Hardy/Z 6–8.

P. sargentii
Sargent cherry
A spreading species from Japan, Korea and Russia whose pale lilac-pink flowers are followed by cherry-like fruits that ripen to a glossy crimson. The leaves are a magnificent crimson and orange in autumn. It may grow too large for most gardens. H 25m (80ft), S 20m (66ft). Hardy/Z 5–9.

P. serrula
(syn. *P. tibetica*)
Tibetan cherry
This species from western China is usually planted for its gleaming mahogany red bark which peels off in strips to produce an eye-catching feature in winter. Site where the tree will be well lit by winter sun. H and S 10m (33ft). Hardy/Z 6–8.

P. 'Shirofugen'
One of the best of the cherries, this makes a spreading tree. The abundant double white flowers, which open from pink buds and age to pink, are fragrant. They may not appear until early summer. H 8m (25ft), S 10m (33ft). Hardy/Z 6–8.

P. 'Spire'
(syn. *P.* 'Hillieri Spire')
This upright, vase-shaped tree is a good choice for a small garden, and a possible alternative to the roughly similar 'Amanogawa'. It has pale pink flowers, which appear with the leaves in mid-spring, and good autumn colour. H 10m (33ft), S 7m (23ft). Hardy/Z 6–8.

P. × subhirtella 'Autumnalis'
Autumn cherry
This cultivar, which was developed in Japan, is probably the finest winter-flowering tree, producing flushes of pink-tinged white flowers throughout winter, during mild spells. The peak display usually occurs right at the end of winter, shortly before the equinox. The leaves turn yellow in autumn. H and S to 8m (25ft). Hardy/Z 6–8.

Prunus × *subhirtella* 'Autumnalis'

PTEROCARYA
Wingnut

This Asiatic genus consists of towering trees that make handsome specimens where there is lots of space. The common name relates to the winged seeds, which dangle in strings from the branches in autumn.

Cultivation Wingnuts need fertile, well-drained soil in sun, in a position where they will not be exposed to late frosts, which can damage young foliage.

P. stenoptera
Chinese wingnut

A fast-growing tree, this is particularly happy near water. Once mature, it produces greenish-yellow catkins (pussy willows) in early summer. The glossy green leaves turn yellow in autumn at the same time as the winged nuts develop. H 30m (100ft), S 15m (50ft). Hardy/Z 7–9.

PYRUS
Pear

"Pears for your heirs" is a familiar saying among the gardening fraternity – in other words, fruiting varieties will not produce any worthwhile crops until some years after you have planted them. Apart from the fact that this is not strictly true, the genus does include a number of attractive ornamental trees, which reward the gardener from the word go.

Cultivation Grow in fertile, well-drained soil in sun or light shade.

Pyrus elaeagnifolia

P. calleryana
Chinese pear, callery pear

This Chinese species is usually represented in cultivation by the selection 'Chanticleer', a conical ornamental tree with white flowers in spring followed by inedible brown fruits. The leaves redden attractively in autumn. H 15m (50ft), S 6m (20ft). Hardy/Z 5–8.

P. elaeagnifolia

A dainty specimen when young, this is an unusual species from Asia Minor that deserves to be better known. Its thorny branches are covered with attractive, grey-felted leaves. White flowers in spring are followed by green fruits. H 12m (40ft), S 8m (25ft). Hardy/Z 5–9.

P. salicifolia 'Pendula'
Weeping willow-leaved pear

This is the form of the species that is, deservedly, most commonly encountered, and it makes a delightful and elegant specimen in a small garden. The narrow, silver-grey leaves are borne on pendulous branches, and creamy white flowers appear in spring. H 5m (16ft), S 4m (13ft). Hardy/Z 5–9.

QUERCUS
Oak

All the oaks are magnificent trees, and you shouldn't be put off by their final size. They stay small for quite a long time and can be pollarded to keep them within bounds, even if this prevents them from achieving their full

Quercus ilex

splendour. Oak trees are also important for wildlife, providing shelter for an enormous range of insects, birds and small mammals.

Cultivation Oaks should be grown in ordinary, well-drained soil, preferably in a sunny, open site. They tolerate light shade, but need space to expand.

Q. ilex
Holm oak

This majestic evergreen does particularly well in coastal situations. The variable leaves, often lance-shaped are silver-grey when young, darkening to a glossy green as they age. H 25m (80ft), S 20m (65ft). Borderline hardy/Z 7–9.

Q. robur
(syn. Q. pedunculata)
Common oak, English oak

The large species has the characteristically lobed leaves and

clusters of acorns in autumn. H 35m (120ft), S 25m (80ft). Hardy/Z 5–8. More manageable in smaller gardens are some of the selections, including the shrubby 'Compacta', which is very slow growing. H 5m (16ft), S 4m (13ft). Also slow growing is 'Concordia' (golden oak), a small, rounded form carrying bright yellow-green leaves in spring. H and S 10m (33ft). The neatly upright 'Hungaria' resembles *Populus nigra* 'Italica' (Lombardy poplar) in outline. H 9m (30ft), S 1.5m (5ft).

ROBINIA

These handsome trees are often, rather ill-advisedly, recommended for small gardens. Most make quite large plants and grow rapidly. A safer bet if space is at a premium is the shrubby *R. hispida* (rose acacia) at 2.5m (8ft) in height.

Cultivation These trees need well-drained soil in a sunny, sheltered spot. Avoid excessively windy sites: the branches are brittle and snap easily.

R. pseudoacacia
False acacia, black locust

The species from the United States is less widely grown than the selected form 'Frisia', a golden-leaved variety, which has become one of the most popular of all garden trees, although it

Pyrus calleryana 'Chanticleer'

Quercus robur

can eventually grow quite large. Unlike other yellow-leaved trees and shrubs, it holds its colour well through the summer, making a splendid foil for purple-leaved shrubs. The shoots are very thorny and brittle. H 15m (50ft), S 8m (25ft). Hardy/Z 4–9. At the other end of the scale, **'Lace Lady'** is a compact, even bonsai-like form, which is good for a container. H and S 45cm (18in).

SALIX
Willow

The genus contains creeping shrubs as well as some quite large trees. Willows offer a variety of attractions for the garden. Many are grown for their catkins (pussy willows) or brightly coloured young shoots – regular annual or biennial hard pruning ensures a good supply of these – and weeping varieties look attractive growing at the water's edge. Some willows are also prized for their handsome summer foliage.
Cultivation Willows need reliably moist soil, ideally in full sun.

S. alba
White willow

The fast-growing species, from Europe and western Asia, is a spreading tree with a large number of garden forms, some with coloured stems, which are best coppiced or pollarded. H 25m (80ft), S 10m (33ft), but considerably less if cut back hard annually. Hardy/Z 2–8. **'Hutchinson's Yellow'** has clear golden-yellow stems. *S. alba* subsp. *vitellina* **'Britzensis'** (scarlet willow, coral-bank willow) has brilliant orange-scarlet shoots. *S. alba* var. *sericea* (syn. *S. alba* 'Splendens'; silver willow) is also best if cut back hard, but in this case to create a vase-like clump of silvery foliage.

S. babylonica var. pekinensis 'Tortuosa'
(syn. *S. matsudana* 'Tortuosa')

This bizarre tree is grown exclusively for the interest of its twisted stems, at their most striking in winter. H 15m (50ft), S 8m (25ft). Hardy/Z 5–8.

S. caprea 'Kilmarnock'
(syn. *S. caprea* var. *pendula*)
Kilmarnock willow

This is a weeping miniature, with cascades of silver-white catkins in late winter. The tree is created artificially by grafting a prostrate plant on to rootstocks of varying height. H 1.5–2m (4–6ft), S 2m (6ft). Hardy/Z 5–8.

S. daphnoides
Violet willow

The species, an upright, fast-growing tree, is found from

Robinia pseudoacacia 'Frisia'

Europe to central Asia. The young shoots are purple. H 8m (25ft), S 6m (20ft). Hardy/Z 5–9. The superior selection **'Aglaia'** has bright red shoots and silvery catkins before the dark green leaves appear. H 8m (26ft), S 6m (20ft).

S. 'Erythroflexuosa'
(syn. *S.* 'Golden Curls', *S. matsudana* 'Tortuosa Aureopendula')

This spreading tree has twisting stems and leaves, which are useful in flower arrangements. Pale yellow catkins appear in spring. It can be kept smaller by regular cutting. H and S 5m (16ft). Hardy/Z 5–9.

S. integra 'Hakuro-nishiki'
(syn. *S.* 'Albomaculata')

This willow is actually a shrub that is usually sold grafted on to a clear stem to create a round-headed miniature tree. The leaves, which follow the slender catkins, are strikingly variegated with pink and cream. They keep a good colour well into summer. This graceful tree is a good choice for a container. The height varies according to the rootstock. H to 1.5m (5ft), S to 1m (3ft). Hardy/Z 5–8.

S. × sepulcralis var. chrysocoma
(syn. *S.* 'Chrysocoma')
Golden weeping willow

The fast-growing weeping willow is possibly the most familiar of all willows, and it is an evocative sight when the tips of its arching branches trail in water. It is equally attractive when bare in winter as when it is clothed in its bright green, lance-shaped leaves in summer. H and S 15m (50ft). Hardy/Z 6–8.

Salix integra 'Hakuro-nishiki'

Sophora microphylla

Sorbus mougeotii

Sorbus scalaris

SOPHORA

An interesting genus, *Sophora* contains both deciduous and evergreen trees and shrubs and some perennials. In many ways they are plants for the connoisseur, and they do look rather exotic with their wisteria-like flowers. They are good as specimens or, in cold areas, trained against a warm wall.
Cultivation Grow sophoras in fertile, well-drained soil in a sunny, sheltered spot.

S. japonica
Japanese pagoda tree, Chinese scholar tree
The tree, which is native to China and Korea, is grown for its late summer flowers, which are white and scented, although these appear only after a hot summer and on mature trees. The leaves turn yellow in autumn. H 30m (100ft), S 20m (65ft). Hardy/Z 5–9.

S. microphylla
(syn. *Edwardsia chilensis*)
Kowhai
A spreading species from New Zealand and Chile, this evergreen tree bears rich yellow, pea-like flowers in mid- to late spring, followed by dangling seed pods. Train against a warm wall in frost-prone areas. H and S 8m (25ft). Borderline hardy/Z 8–10.

SORBUS
Rowan
The rowans are splendid plants for cold gardens. They are hardy and provide a valuable food source of berries for birds in winter. Attractive flowers and outstanding autumn colour add to their appeal.
Cultivation Grow in any well-drained soil in sun or light shade. Most rowans tolerate winds and urban pollution.

S. aria
Whitebeam
A large number of cultivars have been developed from this European species. **'Lutescens'** has a more conical habit than the species and is thus better suited to small gardens. The leaves are covered in creamy-white hairs and are particularly brilliant as they emerge in spring. The heads of white flowers that appear in late spring are followed by dark red berries. H 10m (33ft), S 8m (25ft). Hardy/Z 6–8.

Sorbus aria 'Lutescens'

S. aucuparia
Mountain ash, rowan
The species, which is a conical to rounded tree with good autumn colour, is found in Europe and Asia. **'Sheerwater Seedling'** is a narrowly upright selection with white flowers in spring followed by orange berries. The leaves turn red or yellow in autumn. H 10m (33ft), S 5m (16ft). Hardy/Z 4–7.

S. cashmiriana
Kashmir rowan
Native to the western Himalayas, this is a light, airy tree with finely toothed greyish-green leaves. The pink-flushed flowers are followed by round white berries, which remain on the tree after the leaves have fallen. H 4m (13ft), S 3m (10ft). Hardy/Z 5–7.

S. commixta
This compact tree, from Korea and Japan, is generally grown in the form **'Embley'**, which fruits

Sorbus cashmiriana

rather more freely. The white spring flowers are followed by an abundance of brilliant orange-red berries at the same time as the leaves turn red. H 10m (33ft), S 7m (23ft). Hardy/Z 6–8.

S. 'Joseph Rock'
This upright hybrid has white flowers in spring followed by bright yellow fruits in autumn as the leaves colour brilliant red. This is the best yellow-fruited variety, but is susceptible to fireblight. H 10m (33ft), S 7m (23ft). Hardy/Z 7–8.

S. mougeotii
This unusual small tree or shrub is native to mountainous regions of northern Europe. The broad leaves have greyish hairs on their undersides. The fruits, sometimes lightly speckled, turn red in autumn. H 4m (13ft), S 3m (10ft). Hardy/Z 6–7.

S. 'Pearly King'
The glossy dark green foliage of this spreading hybrid colours yellow or red in autumn. White flowers in spring are followed by pinkish berries. H and S 6m (20ft). Hardy/Z 6–8.

S. sargentiana
Sargent's rowan
Native to south-western China, this rowan is one of the most outstanding members of the genus. The large, crimson, sticky leaf buds make a strong statement in late winter, emerging as matt green, feathery leaves that turn brilliant orange-red in autumn. Masses of red berries develop from the clusters of white spring flowers. H and S 10m (33ft). Hardy/Z 7–8.

Sorbus thibetica 'John Mitchell'

S. scalaris
(syn. *S. aucuparia* var. *pluripinnata*)
Ladder-leaf rowan
This Chinese species makes a
spreading tree or large shrub, with
glossy green leaflets that turn red
and purple before they fall in
autumn. The white flowers, which
appear in late spring to early
summer, are followed by red
berries. H and S to 10m (33ft).
Hardy/Z 6–8.

S. thibetica 'John Mitchell'
(syn. *S. aria* 'Mitchellii')
A notable selection of a Chinese
species, this has leaves that are
covered with white hairs on their
undersides in spring, making a
brilliant effect in the wind. They
turn yellow in autumn, when the
green berries ripen to red.
H 20m (65ft), S 3m (10ft).
Hardy/Z 5–7.

S. vilmorinii
Vilmorin's rowan
An outstanding specimen for a
small garden, this tree is native
to south-western China. Arching
branches carry glossy green, fern-
like leaves, which turn red and
purple in autumn. The white
flowers, produced in late spring
to early summer, are succeeded by
berries that are initially red but
turn to white flushed with pink
as winter advances. H and S 5m
(16ft). Hardy/Z 6–8.

STYRAX
These graceful trees are
delightful, but the cultivation
requirements restrict their use to
woodland gardens.
Cultivation These trees need
fertile, well-drained, humus-rich,
lime-free soil in light shade with
shelter from wind and late frosts.

Sorbus vilmorinii

S. japonicus
Japanese snowbell
An elegant species from China,
Korea and Japan, this bears
fragrant, bell-shaped white flowers
in summer. The leaves turn yellow
or red in autumn. H 10m (33ft),
S 8m (25ft). Hardy/Z 6–8.
'Pink Chimes', with pink flowers
with yellow stamens, is rare and
worth looking out for. H 9m
(30ft), S 7m (23ft).

S. obassia
Fragrant snowbell
The species, from China, Korea
and Japan, has bell-shaped white
flowers in summer amid dark
green leaves that turn yellow in
autumn. H 12m (40ft), S 7m
(23ft). Hardy/Z 6–9.

TILIA
Lime, linden
Avenues of these long-lived trees
are often a feature of stately
homes and they were also
commonly planted in town
squares. Although the scent of
the inconspicuous flowers is
incomparable, their suckering
habit made them unpopular for a
while. The following selections

are improvements that make
excellent garden plants. Pollard
or pleach them to restrict their
size, albeit at the expense of
the flowers.
Cultivation Grow lime trees in any
moderately fertile, well-drained
soil (preferably alkaline), in sun
or light shade.

T. cordata
Small-leaved lime
The upright European species
flowers in midsummer, and the
heart-shaped leaves turn yellow
in autumn. H 25m (80ft),
S 15m (50ft). Hardy/Z 4–8.
'Winter Orange' is a desirable
selection with golden-orange
young stems that are a feature in
winter. Cut back hard for the best
winter display. H 25m (80ft),
S 15m (50ft) (unpollarded).

T. × europea
(syn. *T. intermedia*, *T. × vulgaris*)
Common lime
This long-lived and vigorous tree
is a hybrid of *T. cordata* (small-
leaved lime) and *T. platyphyllos*
(large-leaved lime) and is too
large for most gardens. It has dark
green leaves and, in midsummer,
clusters of pale yellow flowers.
H 35m (120ft), S 15m (50ft).
Hardy/Z 4–7. 'Wratislaviensis' is
a more modest size, but its
distinction is obvious only at

maturity, when the bright yellow
young leaves contrast vividly with
the older green ones, creating a
spectacular golden halo effect.
H 20m (65ft), S 12m (40ft).
Hardy/Z 5.

TRACHYCARPUS
Chusan palm, windmill palm
The hardiest of all palm trees,
this remarkably tough evergreen
makes an exotic-looking specimen.
Cultivation These palms will
grow in any well-drained soil in
sun or light dappled shade. It
is important to provide shelter
from strong winds.

T. fortunei
(syn. *Chamaerops excelsa*
of gardens)
This evergreen is the only palm
hardy enough to be grown outside
in northern Europe. Its exact
origins are unknown, but it is
widely naturalized in China and
Japan. It is grown for its stiff,
pleated, fan-like leaves and, on
mature specimens, its fibrous
bark. It needs a position sheltered
from cold winds, and young
plants should be protected from
the worst winter weather with
horticultural fleece. In favourable
situations it can grow larger than
the dimensions indicated. H 4m
(13ft), S 2.5m (8ft). Borderline
hardy/Z 8–10.

Trachycarpus fortunei

Conifers

The backbone of the garden, conifers are a diverse group of plants ranging from mighty giants such as the redwoods to dwarfs suitable for rock and scree gardens, troughs and windowboxes. Mainly evergreen, tough and hardy, they give year-round pleasure, providing backdrops to the transient flowers of summer and coming into their own in autumn and winter as their firm outlines begin to dominate the scene. Conifers embrace a wide range of colours, from blue-grey through many shades of green to vivid golden yellow.

This collection of conifers indicates something of the variety of textures and forms to be found in this fascinating plant group.

What is a conifer?

Conifers are a fascinating group of plants. Within the plant kingdom, they belong to a division called gymnosperms – plants that produce naked seed. The word conifer itself means "cone-bearing". Other gymnosperms include palms and cycads. Conifers are assumed to be "lower" or more primitive plants than the angiosperms (all flowering plants), which produce covered seed.

Conifers do not flower in the conventional sense. In spring, male and female cones, not necessarily conspicuous at this stage, appear together with new shoots and leaves. Male and female cones can be borne on separate plants (such species are described botanically as dioecious) or on the same plant (monoecious). The cones are either held erect on the branches or hang down; in many cases, the female cones are a conspicuous and decorative feature. The males ripen and shed their pollen grains then wither and drop. The pollen adheres to the sticky surface of the female cone's ovule (the structure on which fertilization takes place). The female cone deve-lops as a woody structure, whose scales part to release the ripe seed, between a few months to two and a half years after pollination, depending on the species. Conifer seed usually has a papery "wing" attached to it and is wind-borne.

A few conifer genera, however, generally assumed to be younger in evolutionary terms for this reason, have fleshy berries instead of cones, notably yew (*Taxus*), juniper (*Juniperus*) and the nutmeg yew (*Torreya*). Seed dispersal is through the gut of whatever animal feeds on the berries. Included here is the maidenhair tree (*Ginkgo biloba*), not strictly a conifer, but the sole survivor of a prehistoric division of plants.

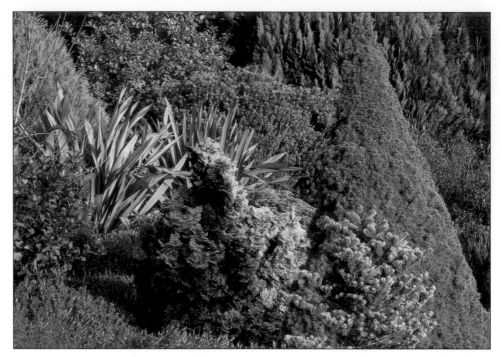

Dwarf conifers planted close will gradually merge with one another to create a living sculpture. A spiky phormium provides strong contrast.

What distinguishes conifers from other plants in most people's eyes are the leaves, which are usually needle-like (botanically, linear or acicular) or scale-like. Most are stiff and hard and have a waxy surface that stops water evaporating – essential to the survival of the plant in freezing conditions. The needles are usually mid- to dark green, but some are yellowish and others have a glaucous bloom that makes them appear blue (extreme cold usually intensifies the blue). The leaves can be carried in two ranks opposite each other on the stem in a comb-like arrangement; alternative arrange-ments include whorls (three or more arising from a single point), spirals or loose bundles. Spruces (*Picea*) have leaves that are set singly, but densely; some species have decidedly bristly branches.

Most conifers grow strongly upright, naturally forming tall, slim obelisks or cone shapes, good examples being the Serbian spruce (*Picea omorika*) and the Japanese cedar

(*Cryptomeria japonica*). A few, such as the Kashmir cypress (*Cupressus torulosa* 'Cashmeriana'), have pendulous, "weeping" branches. Many, such as the Scots pine (*Pinus sylvestris*), become spreading with age, developing a characteristic broad crown. A few conifers, however, are prostrate plants that hug the ground. Some dwarf forms make dense mounds or cone shapes.

Many conifers are resinous and have sticky, aromatic stems. Though some are so well-clothed with foliage that the central trunk is barely visible, if at all, others shed their lower branches as they mature. This can reveal striking bark. The black pine (*Pinus jeffreyi*), for instance, has black bark that is deeply fissured (split) and greyish shoots.

Changes in the names given to conifers down the years have resulted in some potential confusion. Certain common names have remained in use in spite of revisions to the botanical name. Not all conifers commonly referred to as cedars belong to the genus *Cedrus*: botanically, the Japanese cedar is *Cryptomeria japonica,* and the white cedar *Thuja occidentalis.* The swamp cypress belongs to the genus *Taxodium*, not *Cupressus*. Nor are all firs *Abies*: some belong to *Pseudotsuga*.

Conifers in the garden

These plants are – or can be – a mainstay of the garden, providing solid masses of colour (in rather subdued tones it is true) throughout the year. They earn their keep as a backdrop to showier but transitory spring- and summer-flowering plants, but come into their own when the earth is bare in winter and their shapes, textures and colours dominate. With heights ranging from 1m (3ft) or less for a dwarf conifer such as *Picea pungens* 'Globosa' to the 90m (300ft) of the giant redwood, there is a conifer for every garden. When choosing a small conifer, however, make sure that dwarf really does mean dwarf. Some varieties sold as dwarfs are actually better described as slow-growing: they stay reasonably compact for a number of years, but eventually make huge trees, and are a viable option only provided that you are prepared to discard them once they outgrow their allotted space.

Some of the bigger conifers make dramatic specimens provided there is adequate room for them. Many of the cedars (*Cedrus*) are excellent for this purpose, as also are the spruces (*Picea*) and cryptomerias. For a deciduous tree, the maidenhair tree (*Ginkgo biloba*) would take some beating, with its unique fanlike leaves that turn butter yellow in autumn, as well as its fissured bark.

Dwarf conifers planted close together will grow into each other, like a living sculpture, besides making excellent ground cover. Some

Conifers and heathers are a classic combination, and can provide welcome colour during the coldest months of the year.

form dense mats, particularly the prostrate junipers (*Juniperus*). In such plantings, they are often combined with heathers, a combination that should not be dismissed, despite its ubiquity: subtle effects can be achieved through a judicious mix of foliage and flower colours. Dwarf conifers are also excellent in rock gardens, providing height and structure among mat-forming alpines, and are also suitable for troughs and containers, either with other dwarf plants or on their own.

Certain conifers, such as yew (*Taxus*), *Thuja* and false cypress (× *Cupressocyparis*), make excellent hedging plants that provide thick, impenetrable screens. The deciduous larch (*Larix*), however, makes a very effective windbreak, filtering the wind when the branches are bare.

Dramatically lit by the winter sun, this group of conifers exhibit a great variety of subtle colours at a time when the showier plants have finished their display.

Abies amabilis 'Spreading Star'

Abies balsamea 'Nana'

Abies grandis

Abies koreana

ABIES
Silver fir

These trees are found in Europe, North Africa, Asia and North America. Most grow too large for the average garden, but there are some dwarf and slow-growing forms. *A. koreana* is very popular, and there are compact forms of that which can be planted in borders and rock gardens. Most silver firs are conical.

Cultivation Silver firs will grow in most fertile soils, but not in shallow chalk or excessively dry soil. They like a reasonably open situation as long as it is not exposed to harsh winds.

A. amabilis
Pacific silver fir, beautiful fir

The species is not widely grown, but the selection **'Spreading Star'** makes excellent ground cover, as its name implies. The glossy dark green needles smell of oranges when they are crushed, and the cones are deep purple. H 50cm (20in), S to 5m (16ft). Hardy/Z 6–8.

A. balsamea
Balsam fir, balm of Gilead

Although this, too, is unfamiliar in gardens, it has a number of notable cultivars. All are hardy/Z 4–7. Those classified as **Hudsonia Group** are dwarf trees, usually compact and rounded in form, although there is some variation. H to 60cm (2ft), S 1m (3ft). **'Nana'**, a good rock garden conifer, makes a dome-shaped

bush, which is tolerant of some shade. The aromatic, shiny green, needle-like leaves, shorter than those on the species, are arranged in two ranks on the stems; the cones are purplish-blue. H and S 1m (3ft).

A. cephalonica
Greek fir

This rare tree is, at 30m (100ft) in height, unsuitable for most gardens, but the selection **'Meyer's Dwarf'** (syn. 'Nana') is more manageable, forming a low, spreading, flat-topped, shade-tolerant mound that is good in a rock garden. The needle-like leaves are glossy green and are shorter than on the species; the cones are greenish-brown and resinous. H 50cm (20in), S 1.5m (5ft) or more. Hardy/Z 6–8.

A. forrestii
Forrest fir

This medium-sized to large conifer is from Yunnan, China, and it forms a narrow, cone-shaped tree. The needles, carried in a comb-like arrangement, are dark green above and silvery white beneath; the cones are violet blue. This is a quick-growing tree, but it can be unreliable in areas where prolonged cold spells occur. H 10–20m (33–65ft), S 3–6m (10–20ft). Hardy/Z 7.

A. grandis
Giant fir, grand fir

Native to western North America, this is one of the most majestic of the species, making a tall, slim, cone-shaped tree. The needle-like leaves smell of oranges when they are crushed; the cones ripen from green to reddish brown. Vigorous and quick-growing, this makes a handsome specimen tree. H to 80m (270ft), S to 8m (25ft). Hardy/Z 7–9.

A. koreana
Korean fir

This is one of the most attractive of the silver firs, notably for its impressive violet cones that age to brown, which are produced even by young specimens. The needles are dark green with white undersides. Use it as a specimen tree or in mixed planting; it associates well with a wide range of garden plants. H 10m (33ft), S 6m (20ft). Hardy/Z 6–8.

A. procera
(syn. *A nobilis*)
Noble fir

From the western United States, this forms a cone-shaped tree, which matures to a broader, irregular obelisk. The greyish-green needles, sometimes with a bluish cast, are arranged in

Abies cephalonica 'Meyer's Dwarf'

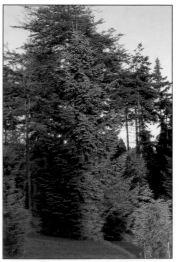

Abies procera

two ranks. Mature trees have silvery-grey, fissured bark; the cones are green. The noble fir makes an attractive specimen, particularly when young; it is sometimes used as a Christmas tree. It is wind-tolerant and reliable at high altitudes. H to 45m (150ft), S to 9m (30ft). Hardy/Z 6–8.

ARAUCARIA

The southern hemisphere is the main home of these striking trees, which have, triangular leaves that are larger than those of most conifers. Only *A. araucana* is in general cultivation, and mature specimens are often found in the gardens of Victorian houses, to which they bring an exotic flavour. Other species are well worth considering for a warm climate or as conservatory (porch) plants.
Cultivation Araucarias do well in a fertile soil in a sunny but sheltered position.

A. araucana
(syn. *A. imbricata*)
Chile pine, monkey-puzzle tree
This tree, which comes originally from Chile and Argentina, is slow growing at first but accelerates as it approaches maturity. It develops a broad, dome-shaped crown on a tall trunk. The female trees have impressive spiky cones, almost pineapple-like in appearance: large and rounded, they take up to three years to ripen. H 25m (80ft), S 10m (33ft). Hardy/Z 7–10.

A. heterophylla
(syn. *A. excelsa*)
Norfolk Island pine)
A good conservatory (porch) plant when young, this will eventually outgrow most conservatories. It has an appealing tiered habit and fan-like branches. It occasionally serves as a Christmas tree in Latin countries. H to 45m (150ft), S 8m (25ft). Tender/Z 9–10.

CALOCEDRUS
Incense cedar
Incense cedars are a small genus of large conifers from the Far East and parts of western North America. Only the species described is widely grown.

Cultivation Any good soil in sun or light shade is suitable, but avoid exposed positions.

C. decurrens
(syn. *Heyderia decurrens,* *Libocedrus decurrens*)
Native to the western United States, this tree tends to vary in habit in gardens. In Europe it forms a tall, elegant spire, whereas specimens in the wild are often more spreading, since the habit influenced by climatic differences. The needles are glossy dark green. The maroon bark is fissured and flakes off, and the cones are yellowish-brown, aging to red-brown. It is resistant to honey fungus. H 30m (100ft) or more, S 6m (20ft) or more. Hardy/Z 6–9.

CEDRUS
Cedar
A small genus, but perhaps containing the most magnificent of all conifers when mature. They are generally suitable only for large gardens but are worth considering if you are prepared to remove them once they start to get too large. They make ideal lawn specimens.
Cultivation Cedars are tolerant of most soils, including chalk (alkaline), and do best in a sunny open site.

C. atlantica
Atlas cedar
Originating from the Atlas Mountains in North Africa, this species is less common in gardens than some of the following selections. All are hardy/Z 7–9. 'Aurea' has bright, golden-yellow leaves. H 40m (130ft), S 10m (33ft). *C. atlantica* f. *glauca* (blue Atlas cedar) is one of the most handsome forms. Initially cone-shaped, it develops a more spreading crown. The needles, white when young but becoming bright glaucous blue, are arranged in clusters; the cones are light green. H to 40m (130ft), S to 10m (33ft). Plants in cultivation are normally sold under the name Glauca Group (indicating that they may vary). 'Glauca Pendula', also glaucous blue, has an arching leader and pendulous branches,

Cedrus atlantica 'Aurea'

Cedrus atlantica f. glauca

and it develops as a tent-like structure. It can be kept small by cutting back the central leader, which will persuade the horizontal branches to spread more widely (they may need support as a result). H and S to 15m (50ft), more or less.

C. deodara
Deodar cedar
This graceful, though potentially large, conifer originating from the Himalayas has a weeping habit. H 40m (130ft), S 10m (33ft). Hardy/Z 7–9. The more modestly sized 'Aurea' is an improvement, having the same broadly conical outline, with weeping branches,

but with the added distinction of bright yellow needles. A slow-growing tree, it is a good choice for a specimen in a small garden. H 5m (16ft), S 2.5m (8ft).

C. libani
Cedar of Lebanon
A tree for a stately home, this species originates from the near Middle East. It forms a conical tree that spreads with age, making a dramatic outline. The needle-like leaves are dark greyish-green; the cones are greyish-brown. Heavy snowfalls can cause problems to mature specimens, which may need surgery. H and S to 30m (100ft). Hardy/Z 7–9.

Cedrus atlantica 'Glauca Pendula'

Chamaecyparis lawsoniana 'Aurea Densa'

CHAMAECYPARIS
False cypress

This is a useful genus, from East Asia and North America, with a huge range of cultivars. There is a cypress for every garden, and the range includes giant forest trees as well as smaller forms that can be used as specimen trees, for hedging and as dwarf plants for the rock or scree garden.
Cultivation The soil should ideally be neutral to acid, but cypresses tolerate chalk. An open, sunny site is best.

C. lawsoniana
(syn. *Cupressus lawsoniana*)
Lawson cypress
Although this conical tree, native to North America, is too large for most gardens, it has given rise to a bewildering number of cultivars of widely diverging habits. All are hardy/Z 6–9. Among the best dwarfs is **'Aurea Densa'**, which is ultimately rounded and one of the outstanding golden-leaved cultivars. H 2m (6ft), S to 1m (3ft). **'Bleu Nantais'** is another good blue-green, slow-growing, cone-shaped, dwarf cultivar. H and S to 1.5m (5ft). Both these have needle-like leaves that become scale-like. Taller varieties include the conical **'Ellwoodii'**, which is one of the most popular grey-green varieties. H 3m (10ft).

Chamaecyparis obtusa 'Nana Gracilis'

'Fletcheri' forms a dense, greyish-green column. H to 12m (40ft). The weeping **'Pembury Blue'** has striking bluish-grey foliage. H to 15m (50ft).

C. obtusa
(syn. *Cupressus obtusa*)
Hinoki cypress
This Japanese species is less tolerant of lime than some species, and it is not widely planted, yielding to its many attractive cultivars. All are hardy/Z 4–8. **'Crippsii'** (syn. 'Crippsii Aurea') is a rich gold when grown in full sun,

Chamaecyparis lawsoniana 'Bleu Nantais'

making a fine specimen. H 15m (50ft), S 8m (25ft). **'Nana Gracilis'** is a dwarf, forming a rough pyramid. The scale-like, glossy green leaves are held in plates. H and S 2m (6ft) or more.

C. pisifera
(syn. *Cupressus pisifera*)
Sawara cypress
Seldom found in cultivation, this Japanese species has given rise to a number of useful cultivars, all of which are hardy/Z 5–8. **'Boulevard'** is a popular selection, which will thrive in moist soil, and has bright silver-blue, feathery leaves. H 10m (33ft), S 4m (12ft). **'Filifera Aurea'** is a delightful conifer, with elegant, drooping, whippy branches. It is a good choice for a small plot because it is too slow-growing to pose a problem in most gardens, despite its eventual height. H 12m (40ft), S 5m (15ft).

CRYPTOMERIA
Japanese cedar

Despite the common name, this monotypic genus (there is only one species) is found in China as well as Japan, albeit in two distinct forms. Unusually among the conifers, Japanese cedars will tolerate pruning and can even be coppiced or trained. They look good in a Japanese-style garden, especially when they are grown to develop a gnarled trunk. Japanese cedars are among the most beautiful of all conifers.
Cultivation These trees will grow in any well-drained, preferably fertile, soil in sun or light shade.

C. japonica
The species can reach a height of 25m (80ft) and is roughly columnar in shape. There are a huge number of cultivars available, suitable either as specimens or for use in rock gardens. All are hardy/Z 6–9. **'Bandai-Sugi'** is a slow-growing rounded dwarf form with blue-green foliage that bronzes well in cold winters. H and S 2m (6ft). The intriguing **'Cristata'** (syn. 'Sekka-sugi') has leaves that are curiously fused together, so that they resemble coral. H 8m (25ft), S 5m (15ft). **'Elegans'** is potentially large and

Cryptomeria japonica

will form a broad obelisk; the trunk is often attractively curved. The wedge-shaped leaves are soft and bluish-green when young, turning a rich, glowing bronze in autumn. Plants sold as **Elegans Group** may vary. H 20m (65ft), S 6m (20ft). **'Lobbii'** makes a handsome specimen in a large garden, forming a tall, slender, conical tree. The needle-like leaves are arranged in spirals. On mature specimens the thick, fibrous bark peels away. The cones age to brown. H 25m (80ft) or more, S to 6m (20ft).

Cryptomeria japonica 'Lobbii'

× *Cupressocyparis leylandii* 'Golconda'

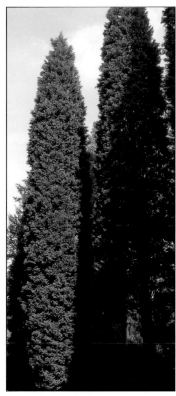

× *Cupressocyparis leylandii* 'Leighton Green'

× CUPRESSOCYPARIS

The chief value of this much maligned hybrid genus between *Chamaecyparis nootkatensis* and *Cupressus macrocarpa* lies in the trees' speed of growth. They are often planted as hedging where a pollution-resistant screen is needed quickly, and they do in fact make a splendid, tough, tight hedge, but only if cut regularly. Allowed to grow freely, they can soon get out of hand.
Cultivation Grow in any well-drained soil in sun or light shade.

× *Cupressocyparis leylandii*
Leyland cypress
This is the hybrid most common-ly sold as hedging, but it has a number of named varieties that can fulfil other purposes. All are hardy/Z 6–9. 'Golconda', one of the most decorative, forms a narrow cone shape. The scale-like leaves, carried in flattened sprays, are brilliant golden yellow; the cones are rounded. H to 35m (120ft), S to 5m (16ft), but tolerant of clipping. 'Leighton Green' develops as a tall, narrow, cone-shaped tree with bright green foliage. Although it is no less

suitable for hedging than other cultivars, it is perhaps best as a specimen because it produces a stronger central leader than the other cultivars and thus makes a slimmer, more elegant tree. The cones are freely produced. H to 35m (120ft), S to 5m (16ft).

CUPRESSUS
Cypress
The characteristic tree of the Mediterranean, these are among the stateliest of conifers. They are not always easy to grow away from their native habitat, but they can be used as fine specimens or for hedging. They resent transplanting, so always look for young specimens rather than mature trees. The broadly similar *Chamaecyparis* is more reliable.
Cultivation Grow in any fertile, well-drained soil in full sun.

Cupressus arizonica var. *glabra* (syn. *C. glabra*)
Smooth cypress
From the south-west United States, this is a good specimen where space in a garden is limited. It forms a regular cone shape. On young specimens the bark is

smooth, reddish-purple and flaking; it thickens and turns to greyish-brown on older trees. The scale-like leaves are glaucous bluish-grey and aromatic; the cones are dark brown. H to 15m (50ft), S to 5m (15ft). Hardy/Z 7–9.

C. macrocarpa
Monterey cypress
From Monterey Bay, California, this was once widely used for hedging, but it has largely been superseded by × *Cupressocyparis leylandii*. Excellent cultivars have been developed from the species, however. Both those listed here are borderline hardy/Z 7–10. 'Donard Gold' forms an elegant obelisk that gradually becomes conical. The bright yellowish-green leaves are aromatic when crushed; the cones are rounded and maroon- to dark-brown. H to 30m (100ft), S to 12m (40ft). 'Goldcrest' is a highly desirable smaller version. H 5m (16ft), S 2.5m (8ft).

GINKGO
Maidenhair tree
This deciduous tree is a living fossil, the sole survivor of a family of trees from 200 million years ago, once serving as a food source for dinosaurs during the Mesozoic era.
Cultivation Ginkgos are easy to grow in any moderately fertile soil in sun. They are also tolerant of urban pollution.

G. biloba
This long-lived, ornamental deciduous tree makes an eye-catching specimen. Initially upright in habit, it becomes more spreading on maturity. Its distinction lies in its unique, fan-shaped, light green leaves, which turn butter yellow before falling in autumn. The fruits (not cones) are plum-like. H to 30m (100ft), S to 8m (25ft). Hardy/Z 5–9. The selection 'Fastigiata' (sentinel ginkgo) is narrower and more column-like. H 30m (100ft), S 5m (16ft).

Cupressus arizonica var. *glabra*

Cupressus macrocarpa 'Donard Gold'

Juniperus chinensis 'Aurea'

JUNIPERUS
Juniper

Junipers are usually represented in gardens by the cultivars and hybrids rather than by the species. Many are rock garden plants, while others look good grouped in island beds. They also do well in troughs and containers. On female plants, berry-like fruits develop and are used in the production of gin or to flavour game dishes.
Cultivation Any well-drained soil in sun or light shade is suitable. Junipers tolerate pruning.

J. chinensis
Chinese juniper
The species is not notable in itself, but has given rise to many attractive cultivars. **'Aurea'** (Young's golden juniper), a slow-growing male selection that forms a narrow obelisk, has aromatic, dull golden-yellow leaves, which are wedge-shaped initially, but become scale-like as they mature. Many cones appear in spring, and the tree produces its best colour in sun. H to 20m (65ft), S 6m (20ft). Hardy/Z 5–9.

J. communis
Common juniper
This variable species is found throughout the northern hemisphere. Selections include **'Hibernica'** (Irish juniper), which makes a distinctive, narrow cone-shape, the foliage having a bluish-green cast; the berries, initially green, ripen to black over three years. H 3–5m (10–15ft), S 30cm (1ft). Hardy/Z 3–7.

J. 'Grey Owl'
(syn. J. virginiana 'Grey Owl')
This is a splendid, spreading conifer, with silver-grey leaves and violet berries. H 3m (10ft), S 4m (13ft). Hardy/Z 3–9.

J. horizontalis
Creeping juniper
A ground-hugging conifer from North America, the species forms a mat of greyish-green leaves, which are needle-like when young, becoming scale-like with age, with dark blue berries. H to 30cm (1ft), S 2m (6ft) or more. Hardy/Z 3–9. There are many attractive cultivars, all suitable for ground cover. **'Blue Chip'** (syn. 'Blue Moon') is glaucous blue. H 50cm (20in), S 3m (10ft). **'Douglasii'** is bluish-green, turning rich purple in autumn. H 30cm (1ft), S 3m (10ft). **'Golden Carpet'** is bright yellowish-green. H 30cm (1ft), spread 3m (10ft).

Juniperus × pfitzeriana
(syn. J. × media)
This dwarf conifer is a hybrid, probably between *J. chinensis* and

Juniperus communis 'Hibernica'

J. sabina (the hybrid is thought to occur wild in Inner Mongolia). The cultivars listed are hardy/Z 4–9. **'Pfitzeriana Glauca'** forms a spreading, flat-topped bush clothed in glaucous blue to silver foliage. The berries are dark purple initially, developing a paler bloom as they ripen. The natural habit develops best if the plant is given sufficient space. H 1m (3ft), S 2m (6ft). **'Sulphur Spray'**, which has yellowish-green

Juniperus horizontalis

foliage, can become table-like on maturity. The dark purple berries develop a bluish bloom as they ripen. This is one of several plants in this hybrid group that are more or less indistinguishable from one another, including the widely grown **'Pfitzeriana Aurea'**. H 1m (3ft), S 2m (6ft).

LARIX
Larch

A genus of deciduous conifers with often brilliant autumn colour. Larches are usually grown as forestry trees but are useful for windbreaks.
Cultivation Grow in any moist garden soil in an open situation.

L. decidua
European larch
As the common name implies, this is a European species, which develops a spreading crown with age. The pale green leaves turn red and yellow before falling in autumn. H to 30m (100ft), S to 6m (20ft). Hardy/Z 3–6.

L. kaempferi
Japanese larch
Largely similar to *L. decidua*, this has purplish-red shoots that are conspicuous in winter, making it more garden-worthy. Both have a number of cultivars. H 30m (100ft) or more, S to 6m (20ft). Hardy/Z 5–7.

METASEQUOIA
Dawn redwood

The genus consists of a single species, one of the few deciduous conifers. It is a remarkable tree, known until 1941 only from fossilized remains. It is best by water, appreciating damp conditions, but is also tolerant of drier soils. It can be used as a specimen in a lawn.
Cultivation Fertile, preferably moist soil, in sun or light shade, suits the dawn redwood. On drier soils it is usually less vigorous.

M. glyptostroboides
Native to China, this rapidly grows into a narrow cone-shaped, almost columnar tree. The feathery leaves are light green in spring, turning pink, red, then brown in autumn, the best colour

Metasequoia glyptostroboides

being produced on mature trees. H to 40m (130ft), S to 5m (16ft). Hardy/Z 5–10.

PICEA
Spruce

Found throughout the northern hemisphere, spruces are widely planted as Christmas trees, *P. abies* being the usual choice. There is a wide range of garden varieties, some with grey, yellow or blue foliage. Most are symmetrical in shape, and there are many dwarf forms suitable for rock gardens.
Cultivation Neutral to acid, slightly moist soil is the ideal, in an open site. Late frosts can cause damage.

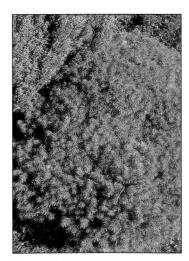

Picea abies 'Gregoryana'

P. abies
Christmas tree, Norway spruce

The species, which is native to Scandinavia, is a conical tree and the traditional choice for Christmas trees in Europe. H 40m (130ft), S 6m (20ft). Hardy/Z 3–8. **'Gregoryana'** is an attractive dwarf selection that makes an impenetrable mound of dark green foliage. It is one of the most compact of all dwarf conifers. H and S 60cm (2ft).

P. glauca
White spruce

Although the species, which comes from North America, is rarely grown in gardens, it is represented in cultivation by its many cultivars. Those listed here are hardy/Z 3–6. *P. glauca* var. *albertiana* **'Conica'** is a dwarf selection of a naturally occurring variant from the Canadian Rocky Mountains. As its name suggests, it makes a tight cone of bluish-green, seldom bearing cones. H to 4m (13ft), S 2m (6ft). The slow-growing **'Alberta Globe'** is another, even smaller clone, also bluish-green but making a dome. H and S 1m (3ft).

P. omorika
Serbian spruce

This large conifer comes from Bosnia and Serbia. Initially narrowly conical, it matures to a broad obelisk. The dark green foliage sometimes has a bluish cast; the bark cracks in squares on maturity. The cones are purple, ripening to brown. It tolerates alkaline soils and urban pollution. H 20m (65ft), S to 3m (10ft). Hardy/Z 5–8.

P. pungens
Colorado spruce

Originating in the United States, the species is the parent of many notable garden plants. All are hardy/Z 3–8. **'Globosa'** forms a dome or mound shape and has bristle-like, glaucous green foliage, arranged radially. H and S 1m (3ft). **'Montgomery'** is silver-blue, making a broad-based cone. Slow-growing, it should be among the first choices for a specimen tree in a small garden. H 1.5m (5ft), S 1m (3ft).

Picea pungens 'Globosa'

PINUS
Pine

Most of the straight species are unsuitable as garden plants, magnificent though they are, since they are nearly all too large for the average plot. Selection by nurserymen has produced a number of useful clones that are more manageable, however. The needles, which are sometimes quite long, are held in characteristic bundles. Dwarf pines associate well with heathers in a border display.
Cultivation Any well-drained soil in sun is suitable, but pines are not tolerant of pollution.

P. mugo
Dwarf mountain pine

This useful conifer from central Europe is less widely grown than its many garden-worthy clones, many of them dwarf and ideal for

Picea pungens 'Montgomery'

Pinus mugo 'Corley's Mat'

a rock garden. H to 3.5m (11ft), S to 5m (16ft). Hardy/Z 3–7. **'Corley's Mat'**, as its name suggests, makes a prostrate, spreading carpet. H 1m (3ft), S 2m (6ft). The slow-growing **'Mops'** is almost spherical. Resinous brown buds are borne in winter. H and S 1m (3ft).

P. sylvestris subsp. scotica
Scots pine

A majestic conifer, this is widely distributed throughout northern Europe and eastern Asia. It grows as a cone-shape but develops a characteristic spreading crown with age. A distinguishing feature is its grey-green, twisted needles. An exceptionally hardy conifer, it is effective when planted in stands in exposed sites. H to 30m (100ft), S to 9m (30ft). Hardy/Z 3–7.

Pinus sylvestris subsp. *scotica*

Sequoia sempervirens 'Adpressa'

SEQUOIA
Californian redwood

The single member of this genus is one of the tallest and oldest living things on the planet, with specimens dating back 2000 years and achieving heights of more than 100m (325ft). There are a few more modest selections, but even these need space.
Cultivation Well-drained, fertile soil is needed, in sun or light dappled shade. Growth is slower in shade.

S. sempervirens

This is a gigantic conifer from coastal California and Oregon. The smaller **'Adpressa'** develops a broadly conical habit, with horizontal upper branches and lower ones that sweep down to the ground. The foliage is creamy white at first, aging to grey-green. This selection is slow growing and may with time exceed the dimensions given here; it does best in a damp climate. H 9m (30ft) or more, S to 6m (20ft). Hardy/Z 7–9.

SEQUOIADENDRON
Giant redwood, big tree, Sierra redwood, wellingtonia

A close relative of *Sequoia*, the giant redwood is also a genus of one species. Although less tall than the Californian redwood, it is the world's largest tree by mass.
Cultivation Grow in fertile, well-drained soil in a sunny, open site.

S. giganteum

Native to California, this forms a cone shape, more spreading with age; the lower branches sweep down, then curve upwards. The scale-like leaves, arranged spirally, are awl-shaped, suffused with grey and aromatic when crushed. The bark is thick and fissured. A magnificent specimen tree, although it is obviously suitable for large gardens only, it can achieve a great age. H 80m (260ft) or more, S to 10m (33ft). Hardy/Z 6–9.

Sequoiadendron giganteum

TAXODIUM
Swamp cypress

Swamp cypresses are among the most beautiful and elegant of all conifers. Unfortunately, their eventual size rules them out for all but the largest gardens.
Cultivation These trees need reliably moist or even wet soil, ideally acid, and a shaded spot.

T. distichum
Swamp cypress, bald cypress

This large, deciduous (though sometimes semi-evergreen) conifer comes from the south-eastern United States. It forms a tall cone shape that becomes untidy as it matures. The needle-like leaves, which redden in autumn, are carried in two ranks, as on yew. Mature plants produce the best colour. Purple male cones hang down and are a feature in winter; the female cones are inconspicuous. Near water it produces special breathing roots, which look like knees emerging from the ground around the trunk. H to 40m (130ft), S to 9m (30ft). Hardy/ Z 5–10. The slender *T. distichum* var. *imbricatum* **'Nutans'** is more modest. H to 20m (70ft), S to 6m (20ft).

TAXUS
Yew

This is an extremely valuable genus of conifers for the garden, with a range of foliage colour and habit. Yew is widely used for

Taxodium distichum

hedging and topiary work, since, unlike most other conifers, it tolerates pruning and even seems to thrive on it. Even mature specimens will recover well if cut back hard. A further distinction is that these conifers produce fleshy berries (usually red) rather than woody cones, helping to brighten up the winter garden. All parts of the conifer are toxic; in some areas, there are restrictions on planting, particularly where cattle are grazed.
Cultivation These tolerant conifers can be grown in any but swampy ground, in sun or shade.

T. baccata
Common yew

A long-lived conifer, this is widely found in Europe and also in North Africa and Iran. Typically, it has blackish-green leaves, carried in a comb-like arrangement on the stems; male and female flowers are produced on separate plants, with berries, each containing a single seed, following on the females. Uncut, the yew forms a broad, spreading cone shape with dense horizontal branches. H to 20m (65ft), S to 10m (33ft), if unpruned. Hardy/Z 6–7. **'Fastigiata'** (Irish yew), a female (and hence berry-producing) selection, is a familiar graveyard tree, forming an obelisk, pointed at the crown, but spreading with age. The stems are

Taxus baccata 'Fastigiata'

Taxus baccata 'Repandens'

strongly upright. It can be kept within bounds by pruning and can also be wired into a narrower, more formal shape. H to 10m (33ft), S to 6m (20ft). The selection **'Fastigiata Aureomarginata'**, also strongly upright, is a golden-foliaged female, which forms a broad obelisk. The leaves are actually dark green; only the margins are yellow. H to 5m (16ft), S to 2.5m (8ft). **'Repandens'** does not produce a strong vertical leader but forms a mat of spreading branches near ground level. It makes good ground cover and is best without extensive pruning that might affect its natural habit.

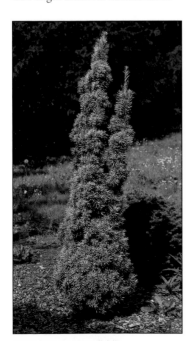

Taxus baccata 'Standishii'

H to 60cm (2ft), S to 5m (16ft). **'Standishii'** forms a slim, tightly packed column of yellowish-green, needle-like leaves carried on strongly upright stems. It is one of the most decorative of all yews and, due to its limited size, is an excellent choice for a small garden. It requires full sun and makes a good container plant. H 1.5m (5ft), S 60cm (2ft).

THUJA
Arborvitae

These excellent conifers are similar to *Chamaecyparis* and are often mistaken for them, a distinction being that *Thuja* has aromatic foliage. They are just as good for hedging. Varieties include a number of coloured foliage forms.
Cultivation Any but waterlogged soil is suitable, in full sun or light shade, although yellow forms are best in full sun.

T. occidentalis
Eastern thuja, northern white cedar

Although this species is not widely grown, it is the parent of a vast number of cultivars. **'Ericoides'** is a dwarf form, growing into a broad, sometimes rounded, obelisk. The spreading, scale-like leaves are green in summer, turning rich brown, sometimes purple, in autumn. As the name suggests, it combines well with heathers and is good in a rock garden. H and S 1.2m (4ft). Hardy/Z 3–8.

T. orientalis 'Aurea Nana'
(syn. *Platycladus orientalis* 'Aurea Nana')

This is an appealing dwarf selection of a much larger species from China and Iran. It makes an egg-shaped plant, with yellowish-green, scale-like leaves held in irregular, vertical, fan-like plates; they tinge bronze in cold weather in autumn. The cones are flagon-like and bluish-green, maturing to grey. An excellent choice for a small garden, it associates well with heathers and other yellow-leaved shrubs. H and S to 60cm (2ft). Hardy/Z 6–9. **'Sieboldii'** (syn. *Platycladus orientalis* 'Sieboldii') also makes an egg-shaped plant and holds its mid-green, aromatic leaves in similar fashion. It combines well with heathers or other low-growing conifers. H and S 2m (6ft).

T. plicata
Western red cedar

A large conifer originating from western North America, the species forms a cone-shaped tree, broadening at the crown with age. It is an excellent specimen for a large garden. The scale-like leaves are carried in two ranks on stems that hang downwards at their tips. The spread of the Western red cedar can exceed the dimensions shown because where the stems

Thuja orientalis 'Aurea Nana'

Thuja occidentalis 'Ericoides'

trail on the ground, they can self-layer, a habit that has produced some vast specimens in the wild. It is suitable for planting as a hedge. H to 35m (120ft), S 9m (30ft) or more. Hardy/Z 6–8. The conical **'Atrovirens'** is slightly slower growing than the species. H 8m (25ft), S 2m (6ft). **'Irish Gold'** usually stays fairly dwarf. The foliage is bright yellow-green with lighter patches. H and S 2m (6ft), although it can reach a height of 20m (65ft).

Thuja plicata 'Irish Gold'

Shrubs

Shrubs encompass a wide range, from tree-like plants (which can substitute for trees in small gardens) to more diminutive ones that can be used in rock gardens or as ground cover. Most are grown for their often spectacular flowers, but others have less obvious attractions – showy berries or good leaf colour in autumn, attractive winter stems, or an appealing habit. Judiciously chosen, shrubs give an air of permanence to any planting.

Shrubs are the mainstay of any garden and this large garden of trees and shrubs will virtually look after itself.

What is a shrub?

Shrubs are woody plants and can be evergreen or deciduous. That definition also applies to trees, but most gardeners would never confuse the two. In general, shrubs are usually compact plants with a height and spread no greater than 3m (10ft), and usually branching from the base. This habit, however, can also be observed in trees; equally there are some shrubs that can be grown with a single upright trunk and look to all intents and purposes like miniature trees. Some slow-growing plants, such as hollies (*Ilex*) and bay (*Laurus*), will be shrubby initially (and can be treated as shrubs in gardens) but will end up as trees in the fullness of time.

In the wild, shrubs are found in a huge range of habitats, from coastal areas to high altitudes, open plains to woodland: hence the need to consider carefully any plant's cultural preferences when making a choice. The different habits of growth represent a response to climate. Plants from coastal areas, for instance, tend to be tough,

Magnolias can be either be classified as trees or shrubs depending on the species. This *Magnolia × loebneri* 'Leonard Messel' in bloom is however a shrub, and here combines well with the flowers of a *Camellia japonica* hybrid.

stunted-looking and scrubby, the better to weather salt-laden winds, while woodland shrubs are more rangy, as they crane their necks towards the available light. You do not need to imitate nature slavishly in your garden, however, since many seem to perform well in a variety of conditions.

The shrubs grown in gardens today comprise both species and hybrids. Some genera have been extensively hybridized to produce a vast range of plants, most notably roses – dealt with in their own section in this book – and rhododendrons, which include dwarf plants suitable for a rock garden as well as others that end up as huge tree-like specimens. Shrubs such as *Fuchsia* and – to a lesser extent – *Hydrangea* and *Ceanothus* are other genera that have attracted the attention of hybridizers.

Shrubs in the garden

These useful plants are the backbone of many a planting, particularly in a small garden, where there is often

little or no space to grow trees. A shrub border can be a low-maintenance option for a driveway, or indeed any other area of the garden where there is space to be filled. A mixture of evergreens and deciduous shrubs will provide a shifting focus of interest; apart from the seasonal flowers and berries for which most shrubs are grown, variegated evergreens will provide year-round interest.

Be sure to include some winter-flowering shrubs, such as *Viburnum tinus*, *Mahonia × media* and *Lonicera fragrantissima*. There are too many spring-flowering shrubs to mention them all here, but for interest after midsummer, you could look to the hydrangeas, fuchsias, *Buddleja davidii* and *Ceratostigma willmottianum* (of modest size, but a real eye-catcher when starred with its sky blue flowers). *Parrotia persica* has vivid autumn leaf colour.

Many shrubs are utility plants and make ideal hedging material, the shrubby honeysuckle (*Lonicera nitida*) and privet (*Ligustrum*) both providing

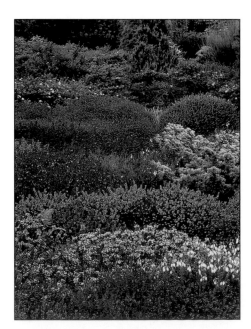

Massed heathers need little attention, and provide weed-suppressing ground-cover besides making a sea of colour.

good dense screens. *Aucuba* and Portugal laurel (*Prunus lusitanica*) have larger, more handsome leaves, but cannot be clipped quite so tightly. Some camellias make excellent flowering hedges, and it is also possible to mix plants for an informal look appropriate to rural gardens (such hedges will also attract wildlife).

There is a whole host of shrubs suitable for planting in light woodland. If you have acid soil, a rhododendron garden can be spectacular (perhaps also including other acid lovers such as *Pieris* and camellias), but there are plenty of lime-tolerant alternatives, such as *Photinia*, if you garden on alkaline soil. On a very open, windswept site, heathers are the obvious choice.

For a specimen, choose some architectural plants such as yuccas, or those with spectacular flowers, such as a tree peony (provided the site is reasonably sheltered from frost). Forms of *Viburnum plicatum*

Rhododendrons, combining well here with conifers and other evergreens, have flowers that range from small and delicate to magnificent and gloriously coloured, along with exquisite foliage.

have a striking tiered habit that is appealing even when the plant is bare of leaves in winter.

Prostrate shrubs can be used as ground cover, particularly those with stems that will root where they touch the ground. *Ceanothus*

thyrsiflorus var. *repens* would be a delight when smothered with its clear blue flowers in early summer, but is not so long-lived or as shade-tolerant as such humbler alternatives as cotoneasters and periwinkle (*Vinca*).

Some shrubs lend themselves to pruning and training, and these are ideal in a formal scheme, either to punctuate geometrically shaped borders or to line the edge of a path. Box is the classic choice for a low formal hedge, and larger specimens can be clipped to ball, cone or cube shapes. Rather faster growing is privet – a coarser plant, it is true, but of surprising elegance when trained as a standard. *Viburnum tinus* and *Prunus lusitanicus* are comparably stylish alternatives.

All of these shrubs are also excellent in containers, as are the spotted laurel (*Aucuba japonica* 'Crotonifolia') and hydrangeas. Many others will also thrive in pots, and this gives you the opportunity to grow any that would not thrive otherwise in the soil type in the open garden.

Pruning

Many woody plants benefit from pruning occasionally, but few actually need it regularly, and a good many are best with minimum intervention. You should be guided by the way the plant is performing in your garden.

If necessary, winter- and spring-flowering shrubs can be pruned immediately after flowering, which gives them ample time to produce sufficient new growth for flowering the following year. Summer-flowering shrubs (which generally flower on wood made in the current season) can be pruned in early spring. All deciduous shrubs can also be pruned in winter, often a good time, since the stems are bare then and it is easy to see what you are doing.

As a matter of routine, cut out all diseased, damaged or obviously dead wood. You should also remove entirely any plain green shoots on variegated shrubs. You can then trim the rest of the growth, but be selective. Cut out some of the older wood to the base (this is always less productive and more disease-prone than younger growth) and shorten the remaining stems, cutting weak shoots back hard, but vigorous ones only lightly. You will probably be able to leave some shoots unpruned.

In cold districts the topgrowth of some shrubs (for instance some fuchsias) will die in winter, and this should be cut back hard in spring. Certain other shrubs, notably *Buddleja davidii*, can also be cut back hard annually, though this is by no means essential.

Abelia × grandiflora

ABELIA

These evergreens are greatly valued for their graceful habit and late flowers, which last from summer to late autumn.
Cultivation Grow in any well-drained soil in full sun or light shade. In cold areas, they prefer a warm, sheltered site, ideally against a wall.

A. × grandiflora

Of garden origin, this shrub has slightly scented, white flowers from midsummer to autumn. H and S 2m (6ft). Borderline hardy/Z 6–9. **'Gold Spot'** (syn. 'Aurea', 'Gold Strike', 'Goldsport') has golden-yellow leaves. H and S 2m (6ft).

Abelia × grandiflora 'Gold Spot'

ABELIOPHYLLUM

There is only one species in the genus, and it is a real connoisseur's plant and something of a rarity in gardens. It is slow-growing, takes some years to settle down to reliable flower production and is difficult to propagate. Like wisteria, it is hardy but needs a hot spot to ripen the wood sufficiently for good flowering. Left to its own devices, it is a sprawling shrub, seen to best advantage when wall-trained. Frost can damage the flowers.
Cultivation Grow in fertile, well-drained soil in a sheltered site, ideally trained against a warm wall.

A. distichum

In late winter to early spring this deciduous Chinese species has dainty, sweetly fragrant white flowers, something like forsythia but much smaller. H and S to 1.5m (5ft). Hardy/Z 5–9.

ABUTILON
Flowering maple, Indian mallow

These elegant shrubs produce appealing lampshade-like flowers from late summer into autumn. They are sometimes trained as standards and used as dot plants in park bedding schemes. They are also good in containers, either on their own or as the central feature in a mixed planting.
Cultivation Grow in any fertile, well-drained soil in full sun in a

sheltered spot. In cold areas, wall-training is an effective way of improving their hardiness. The species described is a very lax grower, needing the support of wires or of other shrubs.

A. megapotanicum
Trailing abutilon

The evergreen or semi-evergreen species has orange-red and yellow, lantern-like flowers and maple-like leaves. H and S 2m (6ft). Borderline hardy/Z 8–9. The leaves of **'Variegatum'** are mottled with yellow. This makes a good standard.

ARTEMISIA
Wormwood

These aromatic subshrubs are ideal for mixed borders, white and grey gardens and herb gardens. They make excellent 'fillers' in rose gardens or, indeed, anywhere where you need to fill space in summer. The genus also includes a number of perennials.
Cultivation Artemisias will grow in poor, dry, well-drained soil in full sun. Prune in spring to keep plants neat.

Abutilon megapotanicum 'Variegatum'

A. abrotanum
Southernwood, lad's love, old man

This deciduous or semi-evergreen species is an effective filler in a number of situations. The aromatic, silvery-grey leaves are very finely divided. The grey-yellow flowers borne in late summer are insignificant. H 70cm (28in), S 50cm (20in). Hardy/Z 6–9.

Artemisia abrotanum

Aucuba japonica

AUCUBA

Tough, tolerant evergreens, aucubas thrive in quite deep shade and make excellent hedging. Female plants have red berries in autumn, but there are also self-fertile forms. It is easy to take them for granted, but few shrubs look so stylish in containers, which is, perhaps, the best way of growing them.
Cultivation Aucubas grow in any soil that is not waterlogged, in sun or shade.

A. japonica
Spotted laurel
To all intents and purposes, this is the only species grown, generally in one of its variegated

Ballota pseudodictamnus

forms. '**Crotonifolia**' (female) is the best, with leaves generously mottled with yellow. H and S 2m (6ft). The plain green *A. japonica* f. *longifolia* (female) is worth looking out for, however and has elegant, narrow, glossy leaves with wavy edges. H and S 2m (6ft). Hardy/Z 7–10.

BALLOTA

These often sub-shrubby plants are excellent in a Mediterranean-style garden or as an edging to a border, where they are a good foil to more flamboyant plants. They look their best in hot, dry conditions and revel in the reflected heat of a gravel garden.
Cultivation Grow in sharply drained soil in full sun.

B. pseudodictamnus
This woolly-leaved species is of greatest interest when it is in flower in summer. The individual flowers, tiny and lilac-purple, are not striking in themselves, but they are held in woolly, beige-green calyces in 'bobbles' on the stem and complement the grey-green evergreen leaves. H 45cm (18in), S 60cm (2ft). Borderline hardy/Z 7–9.

BERBERIS
Barberry
An important genus, tough and hardy, that includes both evergreens and deciduous species, all with spiny stems. Although some are almost too familiar as hedging, there are also some very choice species that are well worth seeking out. The forms with coloured leaves make excellent specimens.
Cultivation Any soil is suitable. The evergreens are shade-tolerant. Deciduous types grown for their leaf colour are best in sun or only light shade. Overgrown and straggly plants can be cut back hard in spring.

B. darwinii
This evergreen species from Chile is one of the best for hedging. Showers of rich orange flowers are produced in mid- to late spring, followed by blue-black fruits. H 2m (6ft), S 1.2m (4ft). Hardy/Z 7–9.

B. 'Goldilocks'
One of the best evergreens, this slow-growing hybrid has drooping racemes of glowing orange flowers in spring (and sometimes in mid-summer). The flowers are followed by blue-black fruits. H 4m (13ft), S 3m (10ft). Hardy/Z 7–10.

B. temolaica
A very handsome deciduous berberis, this slow-growing plant is difficult to propagate but is well worth looking out for. It has glaucous green leaves on whitened stems, lemon-yellow spring flowers and egg-shaped autumn fruits. Plants can be cut back hard annually or every two years for the interest of its winter stems. H and S 1.5m (5ft). Hardy/Z 5.

B. thunbergii
This variable deciduous shrub has a number of interesting selections, all of which do best in fertile soil. The purple leaves of *B. thunbergii* f. *atropurpurea* turn orange in autumn. H and S 1.5m (5ft). '**Aurea**' has soft yellow leaves and is best in some shade. H and S 1m (3ft). '**Helmond Pillar**' is a

Berberis temolaica

distinctive upright selection with dark purple-red leaves. H 1.5m (5ft), S 45cm (18in). The popular and distinctive '**Rose Glow**' has purple leaves swirled with pink and cream turning lipstick red in autumn. H 1.5m (5ft), S 1.2m (4ft). On '**Silver Beauty**', the leaves are mottled with creamy white. H 60cm (2ft), S 1m (3ft). Hardy/Z 5–9.

Berberis thunbergii f. *atropurpurea*

Buddleja alternifolia

BUDDLEJA

The heavily fragranced flowers of these medium-to-large deciduous shrubs are irresistible to butter-flies. *B. davidii* is almost a weed in some gardens, seeding itself freely even in cracks in walls, paving and gravel drives, but there are also other species, many beautiful. They are reliable plants for the back of a border.

Cultivation Grow in any, even poor, soil in full sun. Buddlejas thrive in alkaline soil. Some species can be pruned hard in late winter to early spring, but this is not essential.

B. alternifolia

This handsome plant, originally from China, has pendent racemes of deliciously scented mauve flowers in early summer. Its size is easily controlled by pruning. H and S 4m (13ft). Hardy/Z 6–9. The form **'Argentea'** is even more desirable. It has silver-grey

leaves and is very effective both as a standard and as a specimen. H and S 2.4m (8ft).

B. crispa
(syn. *B. sterniana*, *B. tibetica*)

This handsome Chinese species makes a fine subject for a warm wall, the additional heat enhancing the woolliness of its grey leaves. The lilac-coloured flowers are scented. H and S 3m (10ft). Borderline hardy/Z 9.

B. davidii
Butterfly bush

The most familiar of all the buddlejas, this bears long spikes of fragrant, usually mauve flowers in mid- to late summer. It is essential in a wild or ecological garden, because of its attraction to butterflies. H and S 3m (10ft), if unpruned. Hardy/Z 7–9. There are several selections, all of which can be pruned hard in late winter to early spring, including **'Black Knight'**, which has rich reddish-purple flowers; **'Nanho Blue'** with rich lavender-blue flowers; and **'Peace'**, which is a reliable white selection.

B. × weyeriana

A curious hybrid of *B. globosa* and *B. davidii*, this plant bears flowers that show the characteristics of both parents, being arranged in tapering, ball-shaped clusters. The flowers are a muted orange flushed with mauve, a refreshing addition to any mixed planting in high summer. H 4m (13ft), S 3m (10ft), but less if pruned hard annually. Hardy/Z 6–8.

BUXUS
Box

These are indispensable evergreen plants in the garden for dwarf hedging. New plants can be easily raised from cuttings. Box thrives in containers.

Cultivation Grow in any reasonable soil in full sun or light shade. Clip hedges in mid-spring and late summer.

B. sempervirens
Common box

The species most commonly used for hedging, this would eventually make a tree if left unpruned (albeit over several generations), although the plants seen in gardens are usually considerably smaller than the dimensions indicated. H and S 4m (13ft). Hardy/Z 6–9. **'Elegantissima'** is a delightful selection, with small leaves that are variegated with cream. H and S 1.5m (5ft). **'Suffruticosa'** is a very slow-growing dwarf form, also with small leaves and a tight habit. It is the traditional choice for knot gardens. H 1m (3ft), S 1.5m (5ft).

CALLISTEMON
Bottlebrush

Native to Australia, the evergreen bottlebrushes bring a quirky, exotic touch to gardens with their vivid, brush-like flowers. In general, callistemons are not reliably hardy and are best grown in only fairly mild climates or in sheltered spots in frost-prone gardens.

Cultivation Grow callistemons in lime-free, preferably acid, well-drained soil in full sun, against a warm wall in cold areas. They are suitable for growing in containers under glass.

C. citrinus
Crimson bottlebrush

This species has a profusion of spikes of red flowers from early to midsummer. H and S 5m (16ft). Half-hardy/Z 9–10. **'Splendens'** has flowers of a more vivid scarlet. H and S 2m (6ft).

C. viminalis 'Captain Cook'

This low-growing form produces an abundance of large red flowers from spring to summer. H and S 1.2m (4ft). Half-hardy/Z 10.

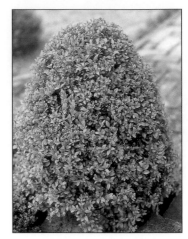

Buxus sempervirens 'Suffruticosa'

CALLUNA
Heather, ling

This genus of heathers consists of a single species, but there are a huge number of cultivars, all evergreen and producing their spikes of bell-shaped flowers between midsummer and late autumn (some have a shorter flowering season within that overall period). Some also have coloured foliage, which provides interest over a longer period. Grow them on their own in heather beds or combine them with dwarf conifers or the other heath genera, *Daboecia* and *Erica*. Heathers are good in containers.

Cultivation Grow in a sunny, open site in well-drained, humus-rich, acid soil. Clip after flowering.

C. vulgaris

The following selection indicates something of the scope of the hybrids now available. All are hardy/Z 5–7. **'Alba Rigida'**

Buddleja davidii 'Black Knight'

Buddleja davidii 'Nanho Blue'

Callistemon citrinus

Calluna vulgaris 'Alison Yates'

(syn. 'Rigida Prostrata') has white flowers. H 15cm (6in), S 30cm (12in). **'Alison Yates'** has white flowers and silver-grey foliage. H 45cm (18in), S 60cm (24in). **'Annemarie'** has double, rose pink flowers. H 50cm (20in), S 60cm (24in). **'Anthony Davis'** has white flowers and grey-green foliage. H 45cm (18in), S 50cm (20in). **'Arran Gold'** has purple flowers and bright golden-yellow foliage, which turns lime green flecked with red in winter. H 15cm (6in), S 25cm (10in). **'Beoley Gold'** has white flowers and bright golden-yellow foliage. H 35cm (14in), S 60cm (24in). **'County Wicklow'** has double, pale pink flowers. H 25cm (10in), S 35cm (14in). **'Dark Beauty'** has blood-red flowers and dark green foliage. H 25cm (10in), S 35cm (14in). **'Darkness'** has bright crimson flowers and dark green foliage. H 25cm (10in), S 35cm (14in). **'Elsie Purnell'** has double, pale

pink flowers and greyish-green foliage. H 40cm (16in), S 75cm (30in). **'Firefly'** has pinkish-lilac flowers and orange-red summer foliage, darkening to brick red in winter. H 45cm (18in), S 50cm (20in). **'Foxii Nana'** has mauve flowers. H 15cm (6in), S 30cm (12in). **'H.E. Beale'** (syn. 'Pink Beale') has double, pink flowers. H and S 60cm (24in). **'Hammondii'** has white flowers. H and S 75cm (30in). **'Hammondii Aureifolia'** has white flowers and foliage tipped with yellow in spring. H 30cm (12in), S 40cm (16in). **'J.H. Hamilton'** has double, dark pink flowers. H 10cm (4in), S 25cm (10in). **'Joy Vanstone'** has pink flowers and yellow-gold foliage, which turns orange in winter. H 50cm (20in), S 60cm (24in). **'Kerstin'** has mauve flowers and greyish-lilac foliage, the new growth tipped with light yellow and red in spring. H 50cm (20in), S 45cm (18in). **'Kinlochruel'** has double, white flowers. H 25cm (10in), S 40cm (16in). **'Mair's Variety'** (syn. 'Alba Elongata') has white flowers. H 40cm (16in), S 60cm (24in). **'Mullion'** has lilac-pink flowers and dark green foliage. H 20cm (8in), S 50cm (20in). **'Multicolor'** has mauve flowers and copper foliage flecked with orange and red. H 10cm (4in), S 25cm (10in). **'My Dream'** (syn. 'Snowball') has double, white flowers, which are good for cutting. H 45cm (18in), S 75cm (30in). **'Orange Queen'** has lavender flowers and golden-yellow foliage, which turns bronze in autumn and orange in winter. H 30cm (12in), S 50cm (20in). **'Peter Sparkes'** has double, pink flowers. H 25cm (10in), S 55cm (22in). **'Red Carpet'** (syn. 'Marinka') has mauve-pink flowers and golden-yellow foliage, reddening after hard frosts in winter. H 20cm (8in), S 45cm (18in). **'Red Favorit'** has double, crimson flowers and dark green foliage. H 20cm (8in), S 70cm (28in). **'Red Pimpernel'** has crimson flowers. H 20cm (8in), S 45cm (18in). **'Red Star'** has double, deep lilac-pink flowers and dark green foliage. H 40cm (16in), S 60cm (24in). **'Robert Chapman'**

Calluna vulgaris 'Dark Beauty'

has lavender flowers and golden-yellow summer foliage, which turns orange in autumn and red in winter and spring. H 25cm (10in), S 65cm (26in). **'Roland Haagen'** has mauve flowers and golden-yellow foliage, turning bright orange with darker tips in winter. H 15cm (6in), S 35cm (14in). **'Serlei Aurea'** has white flowers and yellowish-green foliage, tipped with yellow in summer and autumn. H 50cm (20in), S 40cm (16in). **'Silver Queen'** has pale mauve flowers and silver-grey foliage. H 40cm (16in), S 55cm (22in). **'Silver Rose'** has lilac-pink flowers and hairy, silver-grey foliage. H 40cm (16in), S 50cm (20in). **'Sir John Charrington'** has mauve-pink flowers and golden-yellow summer foliage, which turns orange and red in winter. H 40cm (16in), S 50cm (24in). **'Sister Anne'** has mauve flowers and grey-green foliage, turning bronze in winter. H 10cm

Calluna vulgaris 'Darkness'

(4in), S 25cm (10in). **'Spring Cream'** has white flowers and foliage tipped with cream in spring, and yellow in autumn and winter. H 35cm (14in), S 45cm (18in). **'Spring Torch'** (syn. 'Spring Charm') has mauve flowers and foliage tipped with cream orange and red in spring. H 40cm (16in), S 60cm (24in). **'Sunset'** has lilac-pink flowers and golden-yellow summer foliage, turning red in autumn and winter. H 20cm (8in), S 45cm (18in). **'Tib'** has cyclamen purple flowers and dark green foliage. H 30cm (12in), S 40cm (16in). **'White Coral'** has white flowers. H 30cm (12in), S 40cm (16in). **'White Lawn'** has white flowers. H 5cm (2in), S 40cm (16in). **'Wickwar Flame'** has mauve-pink flowers and flame-orange foliage, deepening to brilliant orange-red in winter. H 50cm (20in), S 60cm (24in).

Calluna vulgaris 'Arran Gold'

Calluna vulgaris 'Hammondii Aureifolia'

Calluna vulgaris 'Wickwar Flame'

Camellia 'Cornish Snow'

CAMELLIA

This is a large genus, containing about 250 species of superb evergreen shrubs and small trees, made larger by the number of hybrids. Unfortunately for many gardens, they must have acid soil. On the credit side, they thrive in containers, so it is possible to enjoy these aristocrats of spring whatever your soil type. There are an increasing number of autumn-flowering camellias, which have been bred from *C. sasanqua*. Few of the species are in general cultivation: on the whole, they are not very hardy and are too large for most conservatories (porches). Hybrids can be divided into two large groups, cultivars of *C. japonica* and of *C.* × *williamsii*, although from the gardener's point of view, there is no appreciable difference between the two. There are two smaller groups: cultivars of *C. sasanqua* (which flower in autumn) and of *C. reticulata* (which flower in late winter to spring). Use camellias as specimens or in shrub borders. All have lustrous green leaves, making them splendid backdrops to other plants when out of flower. Some camellias

Camellia 'Doctor Clifford Parks'

have flexible stems and can be wall-trained, to breathtaking effect once they are mature.

Cultivation Camellias must have lime-free soil (although they do not demand such a low pH as rhododendrons). The soil should be fertile and well-drained and, ideally, incorporate leaf mould. Camellias are best in light shade where early morning sun will not strike emerging flower buds in early spring. Make sure they do not dry out in late summer to early autumn, when plants are building the following season's flowers. They can be pruned after flowering.

C. 'Cornish Snow'
This medium-sized shrub produces dainty, single white flowers opening from pink-tinted buds from midwinter to late spring. It needs a sheltered spot. H 3m (10ft), S 1.5m (5ft). Hardy/ Z 7–9.

C. 'Doctor Clifford Parks'
This desirable camellia bears semi-double, loose peony- or anemone-form deep red flowers in mid-spring. H 4m (13ft), S 2.5m (8ft). Half-hardy/Z 7–9.

C. 'Inspiration'
A reliable, upright plant that has semi-double, deep pink flowers from midwinter to late spring. This is good when trained as a wall shrub. H 4m (13ft), S 2m (6ft). Hardy/Z 7–9.

C. *japonica* cultivars
The following flower from mid- to late spring unless otherwise indicated. All are hardy/Z 7–9 unless otherwise stated. '**Adolphe**

Camellia 'Inspiration'

Audusson' has semi-double, dark red flowers with white stamens in early to mid-spring. H 5m (16ft), S 4m (13ft). '**Akashigata**' (syn. 'Lady Clare') has very large, semi-double, deep salmon-pink flowers from early to late spring. It is suitable for wall training. H 1.5m (5ft), S 3m (10ft). '**Apollo**' (syn. 'Paul's Apollo') has semi-double, red flowers (sometimes marbled with white) with yellow stamens from early to late spring. H and S 3m (10ft). '**Ave Maria**' has formal double, pale pink flowers from early to late spring. This is a slow-growing plant, which is an excellent choice for a container. H and S 3m (10ft). '**Berenice Boddy**' has semi-double, pale pink flowers from late winter to late spring. It is exceptionally hardy and wind-tolerant. H and S 3m (10ft). '**Bob Hope**' has semi-double or peony-form blackish-red flowers. It is a good choice for a container. H and S 3m (10ft). The choice and unusual '**Bob's Tinsie**' has anemone-form flowers, the outer petals deep crimson, the inner petals crimson and white, from early to late spring. H 2m (6ft), S 1m (3ft). The compact and upright '**Doctor Tinsley**' has peony-form or formal double, pale pink flowers. H and S 3m (10ft). '**Elegans**' (syn. 'Chandler's Elegans') has anemone-form, soft pink flowers, sometimes spotted with white. It is slow-growing and best with minimal pruning. H and S 3m (10ft). '**Elizabeth Hawkins**' has anemone-form, bright red flowers in mid-spring. H and S 2m (6ft). '**Gloire de Nantes**' has semi-double, rich rose-pink flowers from late autumn to late spring, one of the longest flowering

Camellia japonica 'Ave Maria'

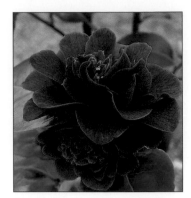

Camellia japonica 'Elizabeth Hawkins'

seasons of any camellia. H and S 3m (10ft). '**Grand Prix**' has semi-double, brilliant clear red flowers with yellow stamens. This looks magnificent when wall-trained. H and S 5m (16ft). '**Janet Waterhouse**' has semi-double or formal double, white flowers. H and S 3m (10ft). The reliably hardy '**Jupiter**' (syn. 'Paul's Jupiter') has single, bright red flowers with golden stamens. H 3m (10ft), S 2m (6ft). '**Kramer's Supreme**' has beautiful peony-form, bright red flowers in late autumn and in early to mid-spring. H 3m (10ft), S 2m (6ft). Borderline hardy/Z 8. '**Lady Loch**' has peony-form, pink flowers. H 3m (10ft), S 2m (6ft). '**Lavinia Maggi**' (syn. 'Contessa Lavinia Maggi') has formal double, white to pale pink flowers striped with pink and red from early to mid-spring. H and S 2m (6ft) or more. '**Nuccio's Jewel**' has peony-form, white flowers, flushed pink. This is a slow-growing camellia and a good choice for a container. H and S 3m (10ft). The dense and compact '**Rubescens Major**' has formal double or rose-form double, pinkish-crimson flowers with attractive darker veins in mid-spring. H and S 2.5m (8ft). '**Tricolor**' (syn. 'Sieboldii') has single or semi-double flowers striped in shades of red, pink or white in early spring. H and S 2m (6ft).

C. 'Leonard Messel'
Semi-double to peony-form, pink flowers, veined with darker pink, are borne in early to late spring. H 4m (13ft), S 3m (10ft). Hardy/Z 7–9.

Camellia × williamsii 'Jury's Yellow'

C. reticulata

This species has a number of desirable cultivars, suitable for training against a warm wall. H and S to 4m (13ft) or more. Half-hardy/Z 9–10. **'Captain Rawes'** has large, semi-double flowers in mid-spring. **'Mandalay Queen'** has deep, rose-pink, semi-double flowers.

C. sasanqua

This species is distinguished by its fragrant flowers, produced from late autumn to late winter. H and S to 3m (10ft). Borderline hardy/Z 7–9. The upright selection **'Narumigata'** has single, pink-tinted white flowers.

C. 'Spring Festival'

This charming camellia has dainty, formal double, pale pink flowers from mid- to late spring. H 4m (13ft), S 2m (6ft). Borderline hardy/Z 8.

C. × williamsii hybrids

The following is just a selection of the large number of fine hybrids available in this group. All are hardy/Z 7–9. The slow-growing **'Anticipation'** has very large, peony-form, deep rose-pink flowers from late winter to early spring. H 4m (13ft), S 2m (6ft). The exceptionally hardy **'Brigadoon'** has semi-double, soft silver-pink flowers with golden stamens in mid- to late spring. H 2.5m (8ft), S 2m (6ft). The prolific **'Debbie'** has peony-form, clear deep pink flowers from late winter to late spring. H 3m (10ft), S 2m (6ft). **'Donation'** has semi-double, pink flowers veined darker pink and with yellow stamens from late winter to late spring. It is deservedly one of the most popular of all camellias. H 5m (16ft), S 2.5m (8ft). One of the best whites, **'E.T.R. Carlyon'** has semi-double to rose-form white flowers in mid- and late spring. H 2.5m (8ft), S 2m (6ft). **'Golden Spangles'** has single, pinkish red flowers from mid- to late spring, but it is grown primarily for its leaves, which are generously splashed with yellow. H 2.5m (8ft), S 2m (6ft). **'J.C. Williams'** bears single, pale blush pink flowers in profusion in mid- to late spring. This is suitable for wall training. H and S 5m (16ft). **'Joan Trehane'** has rose-form, clear pink flowers from mid- to late spring. H 2.5m (8ft), S 2m (6ft). **'Jury's Yellow'** has anemone- to peony-form flowers, with creamy-white outer petals and creamy-yellow inner ones, from mid- to late spring. This is the nearest to a yellow camellia. H 2.5m (8ft), S 2m (6ft). **'Muskoka'** has semi-double, pink flowers veined darker pink, the number one camellia for a container. H 2.5m (8ft), S 2m (6ft). **'Rose Parade'** has formal double, rich deep rose pink flowers from early to late spring. H and S 3m (10ft). **'St Ewe'** has single, bright rose pink flowers with golden stamens in early to mid-spring. H 2.5m (8ft), S 2m (6ft).

CEANOTHUS
California lilac

No shrub has flowers of so true a blue as the *Ceanothus*. When the early forms burst into flower, it is a sure sign that summer is only just around the corner. There is also a valuable second group that flowers in late summer. There are deciduous and evergreen species, the evergreens being slightly more tender. In cold areas all are best grown as wall shrubs, but in more favoured spots they make truly spectacular specimens. The pink- and white-flowered types are of interest but less popular.
Cultivation Grow in any fertile, well-drained soil in full sun. They tolerate lime, but dislike shallow soils over chalk. In cold areas most do best as wall shrubs. Prune after flowering if necessary.

C. 'Autumnal Blue'

A late-flowering plant, with clusters of powder blue flowers from late summer to autumn. One of the hardiest evergreens and ideal for wall training. H and S 3m (10ft). Hardy/Z 8–9.

C. 'Cascade'

This evergreen is seen at its best when loosely tied to a wall, so that the arching stems, smothered in powder-blue flowers in late spring, can billow forwards. H and S to 2m (6ft). Half-hardy/Z 9.

C. 'Dark Star'

Dark purplish blue flowers are carried in spring on this arching evergreen. H 2m (6ft), S 3m (10ft). Half-hardy/Z 8.

C. 'Delight'

This evergreen variety, which has clusters of rich blue flowers in late spring, makes a good wall shrub. H and S 3m (10ft). Half-hardy/Z 9.

C. × delileanus 'Gloire de Versailles'

An open, deciduous ceanothus, this would make a fine specimen in a sheltered spot. The pale blue

Ceanothus 'Delight'

flowers appear from midsummer to early autumn. H and S 1.5m (5ft). Hardy/Z 7. **'Topaze'** is more compact and has richer blue flowers. H and S 1.5m (5ft). Hardy/Z 7.

C. × pallidus 'Marie Simon'

One of the few pink-flowered hybrids, this is a deciduous variety with pale pink flowers from midsummer to autumn. H and S 1.5m (5ft). Hardy/Z 9.

C. 'Puget Blue'

This evergreen hybrid has masses of brilliant blue flowers appearing in early summer. H and S 2.1m (7ft). Borderline hardy/Z 8–10.

C. thyrsiflorus var. repens
Blueblossom

The species, one of the hardiest evergreens, is usually grown in this prostate form, which is a wonderful carpeter for banks and large rockeries. Rich blue flowers cover the plant in late spring to early summer. It is shade-tolerant and looks splendid as groundcover under such airy, deciduous trees as gleditsias. H 1m (3ft), S 2.5m (8ft). Hardy/Z 8–9.

Camellia 'Leonard Messel'

Camellia 'Spring Festival'

Ceanothus 'Dark Star'

Ceratostigma willmottianum

Cestrum elegans

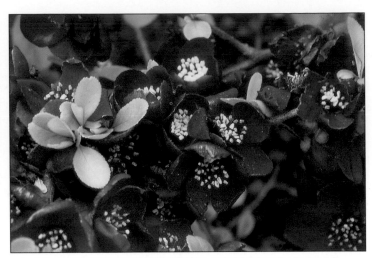

Chaenomeles × superba 'Crimson and Gold'

CERATOSTIGMA

A diminutive shrub, but of great significance, for this is probably the only late-flowering shrub that can provide flowers of this shade of blue. It tends to die back in hard winters but generally recovers. The species described should have a place in every garden. Its low habit makes it suitable for a mixed planting including perennials, annuals and grasses. The genus also includes the perennial *C. plumbaginoides*.
Cultivation Grow in any well-drained soil in full sun. In cold areas, cut back hard annually in spring.

C. willmottianum

This deciduous Chinese species, which makes a twiggy bush, has small, vivid blue flowers in late summer to early autumn. H and S 60cm (2ft). Hardy/Z 7–10.

CESTRUM

This small genus of generally tender plants contains one species that is hardy enough to be grown outdoors in cool gardens. The others make good conservatory (porch) plants in cold areas.
Cultivation Any fertile, well-drained soil is suitable. Grow in full sun, ideally in the shelter of a warm wall, and cut back hard annually in spring if the topgrowth dies back.

C. elegans
(syn. *C. purpureum*)
An evergreen species originally from Mexico, this has clusters of reddish-purple flowers that appear throughout summer. H 1.2m (4ft), S 1m (3ft). Tender/Z 10.

C. parqui
Willow-leaved jessamine
This deciduous species from Chile has pyramid-like clusters of lime-green, star-shaped flowers, unspectacular in themselves but releasing a unique bubblegum-like fragrance at night in late summer. H 1.2m (4ft), S 1m (3ft). Borderline hardy/Z 7–10.

CHAENOMELES
Ornamental quince, japonica
Essential shrubs for late-winter interest, these plants are charming as free-standing specimens and spectacular when trained against a wall. Selections with white, pink and red flowers are available, but the red-flowered types are the most popular.
Cultivation These plants are tolerant of any but waterlogged soil. They will grow in sun or shade and can be trained against north-facing walls.

C. × superba
This multi-stemmed, deciduous hybrid group is usually represented in gardens by its selections, all of which flower on the bare wood in late winter. H and S 1.5m (5ft). All are hardy/Z 5–8. '**Crimson and Gold**' has red flowers with eye-catching yellow stamens. '**Knap Hill Scarlet**', has large, bright red flowers. '**Nicoline**' has scarlet, sometimes semi-double flowers. '**Pink Lady**' has dark pink flowers.

CHOISYA
A small genus of evergreens that have a neat, rounded habit making them excellent for creating a topiary effect without pruning, though older plants can become untidy. The leaves are highly aromatic, and they also bear fragrant white flowers in spring.

Cultivation Grow in any fertile, well-drained soil. Choisyas will tolerate some shade and are good for growing against a wall, but flower best in full sun.

C. 'Aztec Pearl'
This compact shrub has fairly narrow, elegant dark green leaves

Choisya ternata

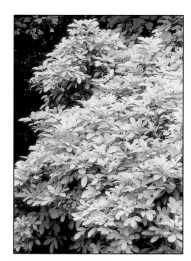

Choisya ternata 'Sundance'

and pink-tinged, white flowers that have a scent of almonds. H and S 1.5m (5ft). Hardy/Z 7.

C. ternata
Mexican orange blossom
A handsome evergreen with glossy green leaves, this flowers mostly in spring with, often, a second flush in late summer or autumn. H and S 2.4m (8ft). Hardy/Z 7–9. The selection **'Sundance'** (syn. 'Lich') has bright yellow leaves. H and S 2m (6ft).

CISTUS
Sun rose, rock rose
In Mediterranean countries these scrubby evergreen shrubs fulfil the same function as heathers in northern Europe. The flowers, which have a papery texture, like poppies, are short-lived, but

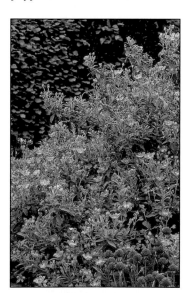

Cistus × skanbergii

follow one another in quick succession at the height of summer. A hot spot enhances the resinous quality of the stems, and hence the plant's aromatic property. They are perfect in a scree or gravel garden, basking in the reflected heat from the stones, combining well with shrubby herbs and *Genista*.
Cultivation Cistus need very well-drained soil of low to moderate fertility in full sun. Dead-head regularly to maintain flower production. In cold areas they may need winter protection.

C. × hybridus
(syn. C. coeris, C. × corbariensis)
This tough hybrid has crinkled, papery, white flowers with a yellow blotch at the base of each petal in summer. H 1m (3ft), S 1.5m (5ft). Borderline hardy/Z 7–9.

C. ladanifer
Gum cistus
This species has large white summer flowers, each petal of which is blotched with maroon at the base. H 2.4m (8ft), S 1m (3ft). Borderline hardy/Z 8.

C. × pulverulentus
A hybrid cistus with pale pinkish-purple flowers. H and S 60cm (2ft). Borderline hardy/Z 7–9. The compact, spreading **'Sunset'** has glowing magenta flowers. H 60cm (2ft), S 1m (3ft).

C. × skanbergii
A hybrid with small green leaves and pale pink flowers from early to midsummer. H and S 1m (3ft). Hardy/Z 8–9.

CORNUS
Dogwood, cornel
These mainly deciduous shrubs and trees, native to northern temperate areas around the world, are excellent in cold, damp sites, associating very well with water features. Many can be cut back hard annually, which not only keeps them well within bounds but improves their winter stem colour, for which most are grown. They are highly effective in groups, a feast for the eye when lit up by low shafts of winter sun.

Cistus × pulverulentus 'Sunset'

Cultivation Dogwoods are tolerant of most soil types. They prefer sun but will do reasonably well in shade.

C. alba
(syn. Swida alba, Thelycrania alba)
Red-barked dogwood
This suckering, deciduous species has clusters of small yellow-white flowers in early summer and good autumn leaf colour (red and purple). H and S 3m (10ft). Hardy/Z 2–7. **'Aurea'** has golden leaves and glowing red winter stems. H and S 3m (10ft).

'Sibirica Variegata' has leaves boldly variegated with creamy-white, excellent autumn leaf colour and red winter stems. H and S 3m (10ft).

C. stolonifera
Red osier dogwood
This deciduous species is mainly seen in the form **'Flaviramea'**, which has mustard-yellow winter stems. H and S 1.5m (5ft). **'Kelseyi'** is a dwarf form with blackish-red winter stems. H 75cm (30in), S 1.5m (5ft). Hardy/Z 2–8.

Cornus alba 'Sibirica Variegata'

Cotinus 'Grace'

COTINUS
Smoke bush

The two species of impressive deciduous shrubs in the genus are usually grown in their purple-leaved forms, which also have spectacular autumn colour. They make large, rangy shrubs, but can be cut back hard for larger leaves, albeit at the expense of the flowers. The flowers are tiny, but carried in large panicles, looking like smoke from a distance – hence the common name. They are produced reliably only in hot summers. In cold areas it is better to cut the plant back hard annually for an improved foliage display. The purple-leaved forms are indispensable in a red or purple border.
Cultivation Grow in reasonably fertile soil in full sun. Hard pruning in spring produces the best leaves, but this can be at the expense of good autumn colour.

C. coggygria
Smoke bush, smoke tree
The plain green species is seldom grown. Far better known is the selection **'Royal Purple'**, grown principally for its coin-like, dramatic purple leaves, which turn vivid red in autumn. H and S 1.2m (4ft). Hardy/Z 5–9.

C. 'Grace'
This familiar hybrid is similar to *C. coggygria* 'Royal Purple', but is larger and has oval leaves, which turn dark brownish-red in autumn. H 6m (20ft), S 5m (16ft). Hardy/Z 5–9.

Cotoneaster lacteus

COTONEASTER

This is one of the most important shrub genera, containing both evergreen and deciduous species. Cotoneasters are tough, hardy, tolerant plants, which make excellent foils to a huge range of other showier plants. Some have sufficient distinction to work as specimens, but on the whole it is best to think of these as companions to other plants. Bees appreciate their creamy-white flowers in that bloom in early summer, and birds enjoy their autumn berries.
Cultivation Cotoneasters will do well in any reasonable soil in sun or light shade (evergreens cope with deep shade) and are tolerant of pruning.

C. dammeri
This evergreen or semi-evergreen species is an outstanding ground-cover plant, carpeting the ground and thriving in many difficult garden situations. The plant flowers in early summer and bears scarlet berries in autumn. H 5cm (2in), S 1.2m (4ft). Hardy/Z 5.

C. frigidus
This semi-evergreen species has the outstanding cultivar **'Cornubia'**, a tree-like shrub, bearing bright red fruit in autumn, that is good enough to use as a specimen in a small garden. H and S 5m (16ft). Hardy/Z 7–8.

C. horizontalis
Fishbone cotoneaster
A versatile deciduous species, this can be grown as a wall shrub (or even up a tree trunk) or allowed to cascade over a bank, both of which methods display its unusual 'herringbone' habit, or it can be clipped to a table-like shape. It has excellent autumn leaf colour, along with an impressive display of vivid red berries. H 1m (3ft), S 2m (6ft). Hardy/Z 5–9.

C. lacteus
This evergreen or semi-evergreen species is a dense shrub with an abundant crop of early summer flowers followed by orange-red berries. It is excellent hedging material. H and S 1.5m (5ft). Hardy/Z 7–9.

Cytisus battandieri

C. salicifolius
Willowleaf cotoneaster
The species is seldom grown, but its excellent selections include **'Rothschildianus'**, a large evergreen notable for its abundant autumn crop of creamy-yellow berries. H and S 5m (16ft). Hardy/Z 7–8.

C. × suecicus 'Coral Beauty' (syn. C. 'Royal Beauty')
This small evergreen with arching branches is covered with masses of bright red fruits in autumn. It is good for groundcover. H 60cm (2ft), S 1.2m (4ft). Hardy/Z 6–8.

CYTISUS
Broom

The genus contains about 50 species, found mainly in Europe, but also northern Africa and western Asia. These desirable, if usually short-lived, deciduous shrubs seem to pour out their pealike flowers in late spring to early summer. These are fragrant, usually yellow, and are followed by green seedpods. The brooms are excellent in gravel gardens or on any hot, dry site.
Cultivation Full sun and well-drained soil is essential, as is wall-training in cold districts. Brooms do not respond well to pruning or being transplanted.

C. battandieri
Pineapple broom
A fascinating plant, this is beautiful in all its parts. The yellow flowers, which both look and smell like pineapples, appear in midsummer among the silky textured, silver-grey leaves. H and S 4m (13ft). Borderline hardy/Z 7–9.

C. × beanii
Golden-yellow, pea-like flowers smother this sprawling hybrid in late spring or early summer. H 30cm (1ft), S 60cm (2ft). Hardy/Z 7–8.

C. × praecox
This hybrid group has generally pale yellow flowers. H and S 1m (3ft). Hardy/Z 6–9. The form **'Warminster'** (Warminster broom) has masses of long-lasting, rich cream-coloured flowers.

Daboecia cantabrica 'Alba'

Daboecia cantabrica 'Rainbow'

Daphne bholua

DABOECIA
Heather

This genus contains two evergreen species, but only one is hardy, and most of the plants in cultivation are selected forms of this or hybrids with the other. They are best grown en masse in an open situation or in island beds with other heathers or conifers.
Cultivation Grow in preferably sandy, well-drained, acid soil in full sun. An open, scrubby site is preferable.

D. cantabrica
Cantabrian heath, St Dabeoc's heath

This plant is normally represented in gardens by one of its many cultivars, all producing their urn-shaped flowers from early summer to mid-autumn. The following are all hardy/Z 5–8. **'Alba'** has white

flowers; plants sold under this name can vary. H 40cm (16in), S 70cm (28in). **'Atropurpurea'** makes glowing colonies of bronze-tinged foliage and has dark pinkish-purple flowers. H 40cm (16in), S 70cm (28in). The flowers of **'Bicolor'** can be white, pink or beetroot red (or streaked), different colours appearing simultaneously on the same stem. H 25cm (10in), S 65cm (26in). The purple flowers of **'Hookstone Purple'** appear only from midsummer. H 25cm (10in), S 65cm (26in). **'Rainbow'** is less eye-catching for its purple flowers than its colourful foliage, variegated with red and yellow. H 25cm (10in), S 65cm (26in). **'Waley's Red'** (syn. 'Whaley') has deep magenta flowers. H 35cm (14in), S 50cm (20in).

D. × scotica

There are several outstanding members of this hybrid group. **'Silverwells'** has white flowers in summer and mid-green foliage. H 15cm (6in), S 35cm (14in). **'William Buchanan'** has purplish-crimson flowers which appear in mid- to late summer. H 35cm (14in), S 55cm (22in). Both are borderline hardy/Z 4–7.

DAPHNE

Evergreen, semi-evergreen or deciduous, these delightful shrubs bear flowers with an exquisite fragrance. Some are rock garden plants, but the ones described here work well in mixed or shrub borders. Winter-flowering types

are best sited near a door where their fragrance can be appreciated to the full without the need to go too far outdoors.
Cultivation Grow these plants in any moist but well-drained soil in sun or light shade, ideally in a sheltered spot.

D. bholua

This semi-evergreen species bears deliciously scented clusters of pink and white flowers in late winter. H 3m (10ft), S 1.2m (4ft). Borderline hardy/Z 8–9. The deciduous and hardiest variety **D. bholua** var. *glacialis* **'Gurkha'** bears purplish-pink flowers from mid- to late winter. Hardy/Z 8. **'Jacqueline Postill'** is evergreen and has deep purplish-pink flowers. H 3m (10ft), S 1.2m (4ft). Borderline hardy/Z 8–9.

D. mezereum
Mezereon

A deciduous species, which suits a woodland garden, this produces pink or reddish, highly scented flowers in late winter. The red summer berries are poisonous, but equally attractive. H 1.2m (4ft), S 1m (3ft). Hardy/Z 5–8.

D. tangutica

This small, evergreen species originates from western China. The fragrant white flowers, which are tinged with rose-purple, appear in late winter to early spring. H 60cm (2ft), S 45cm (18in). Hardy/Z 7–9.

DESFONTAINEA

This genus of evergreen shrubs is usually represented in gardens by the species described here. When they appear, the flowers are something of a surprise, because in all other respects the plant looks just like a holly. This is an excellent specimen.
Cultivation Any well-drained, fertile soil suits these plants, but they need light shade and a sheltered spot. They do well in a mild, damp, maritime climate and will not thrive in dry conditions. In cold areas, grow against a warm wall.

D. spinosa

Narrow, tubular scarlet and orange flowers hang among the branches in late summer. H and S 2m (6ft). Borderline hardy/ Z 9–10.

Daboecia cantabrica 'Atropurpurea'

Daphne tangutica

Desfontainea spinosa

Deutzia longifolia

Elaeagnus × ebbingei 'Limelight'

Erica carnea 'Eileen Porter'

DEUTZIA

These elegant deciduous shrubs are grown for their dainty flowers in late spring and early summer. They are ideal plants for a cottage garden-style planting or for a small garden.
Cultivation Grow in any moderately fertile soil in sun or light shade.

D. × elegantissima

This hybrid has fragrant pink flowers. H and S 1.5m (5ft). Hardy/Z 5–8. Selections include the upright **'Rosealind'**, which has deep carmine pink flowers; **'Rosea Plena'** with double flowers that open pink and age to white and **'Strawberry Fields'**, which has large deep red-pink flowers. H 2m (6ft), S 1.2m (4ft).

D. × hybrida

The hybrids in this group have clusters of star-shaped flowers. H 1.2m (4ft), S 1m (3ft). Hardy/Z 5–9. **'Mont Rose'** has deep pink flowers borne on arching stems. H 1.2m (4ft), S 1m (3ft).

D. longifolia

The straight species has white flowers (usually striped purple on the back) in early to midsummer, but is better known through the selected form **'Veitchii'**, which has purple flowers on purple stems. H 2m (6ft), S 3m (10ft). Hardy/Z 7–9.

ELAEAGNUS

The genus contains handsome evergreen and deciduous shrubs with a number of uses in the garden, either as specimens or as hedging. Some seem to prefer acid soil. Some also have the benefit of

late autumn flowers, which are inconspicuous and parchment-textured, but highly fragrant.
Cultivation They suit any well-drained soil except shallow soil over chalk (alkaline soil).

E. × ebbingei

A good plant for coastal gardens, this has evergreen leaves that seem to tolerate salt-laden winds, making it excellent hedging material. The leaves appear speckled with pewter grey. The autumn flowers are inconspicuous but ravishingly scented. H and S 3m (10ft). Hardy/Z 7–9. **'Limelight'** has leaves that are marked golden yellow in the centre. H and S 3m (10ft).

E. pungens

This large evergreen species is seldom seen and is usually represented in gardens by **'Maculata'**, an excellent shrub for the winter garden, with leaves that are splashed with bright yellow. It has a tendency to revert to the plain green of the species. H and S 3m (10ft). Hardy/Z 7–9.

Elaeagnus 'Quicksilver'

E. 'Quicksilver'

A truly outstanding deciduous hybrid, in time virtually a tree, this has narrow, silvery leaves, which are especially striking in spring. H and S 1m (3ft), ultimately larger. Hardy/Z 2–9.

ERICA
Heath

Also known as heathers, these are the familiar heaths, scrubby plants that can be used to carpet large tracts of land. They form the largest genus of heaths (the other two are *Calluna* and *Daboecia*), with some 700 or more evergreen species, and are particularly valued in the winter garden, although there are species that flower at other times of year. In smaller gardens ericas are excellent in island beds, either on their own (or with *Calluna* and *Daboecia*) or with dwarf conifers, with which they associate happily. They are also ideal container plants.
Cultivation Most heaths need acid soil, preferably sandy and well-drained, but *E. vagans* will tolerate alkaline conditions. If necessary, clip plants lightly after flowering. Tree heathers withstand hard pruning.

E. australis
Spanish heath

These are the shrublike tree heaths, straggly in growth but outstanding in flower. The species has lilac-pink flowers from mid- to late spring. H 2m (6ft), S 1m (3ft). Borderline hardy/Z 7–10. Selections include the more compact **'Riverslea'**, which has bright pinkish flowers, mostly in clusters of four. H 1.2m (4ft), S 1m (3ft).

E. carnea
Alpine heath, winter heath

This is an important species of carpeting heaths. The flowering season is from late autumn to mid-spring, with plants in milder climates being as much as two months earlier than those in colder areas. Generally they are in flower for six to eight weeks. The following selection of cultivars are all hardy/Z 5–8. **'Adrienne Duncan'** has lilac-pink flowers and dark green foliage tinged bronze. H 15cm (6in), S 35cm (14in). **'Ann Sparkes'** has rose-pink flowers deepening to lilac-pink from late winter to late spring and orange, bronze-tipped foliage, which turns crimson in winter. H 15cm (6in), S 25cm (10in). **'Aurea'** has pink flowers and gold foliage tipped with orange in spring. H 15cm (6in), S 35cm (14in). **'Challenger'** has magenta and crimson flowers and dark green foliage. H 15cm (6in), S 45cm (18in). The slow-growing **'Eileen Porter'** has magenta flowers. H and S 20cm (8in). **'Golden Starlet'** has white flowers and glowing yellow foliage, which turns lime green in winter. H 15cm (6in), S 40cm (16in). **'King George'** has pink flowers and dark green foliage. H 15cm (6in), S 25cm (10in). **'Myretoun Ruby'** (syn. 'Myreton Ruby') has pink flowers, which turn magenta then crimson, and dark green foliage. H 15cm (6in), S 45cm (18in). **'Praecox Rubra'** has lilac-pink flowers and foliage that is sometimes tinged with brown. H 15cm (6in), S 40cm (16in).

Erica carnea 'Rosy Gem'

'**Rosy Gem**' has lilac-pink flowers and dark green foliage. H 20cm (8in), S 45cm (18in). The vigorous '**Springwood White**' has white flowers. H 15cm (6in), S 45cm (18in). '**Vivellii**' (syn. 'Urville') has lilac-pink flowers, which deepen to magenta, from late winter to early spring and dark green, bronze-tinged foliage. H 15cm (6in), S 35cm (14in). '**Westwood Yellow**' has shell-pink flowers initially that darken to lilac-pink, and yellow foliage throughout the year. H 15cm (6in), S 30cm (12in).

E. cinerea
Bell heather, twisted heather
These are the summer-flowering heathers, although some will continue well into autumn. The bell heather is typical of the genus and requires acid soil. The cultivars listed are all hardy/ Z 6–8. '**Alfred Bowerman**' has magenta flowers. H 35cm (14in), S 45cm (18in). '**Blossom Time**' has also magenta flowers. H 30cm (12in), S 55cm (22in). '**C.D. Eason**' has bright magenta-pink flowers and dark green foliage. H 25cm (10in), S 50cm (20in). '**C.G. Best**' (syn. 'Graham Thomas') has salmon pink flowers. H 30cm (12in), S 70cm (28in). '**Champs Hill**' has dusky rose-pink flowers. H 35cm (14in), S 45cm (18in). Hardy/Z 5. '**Eden Valley**' has lavender-pink flowers with white bases. H 20cm (8in), S 50cm (20in). '**Fiddler's Gold**' has lilac-pink flowers and bright golden-yellow foliage, which is best in spring. H 25cm (10in), S 45cm (18in). '**Golden**

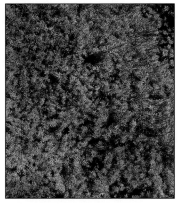
Erica cinerea 'Golden Drop'

Drop' has lilac-pink flowers and bright golden-yellow foliage, which is tinged copper in spring and turns copper red in winter. H 20cm (8in), S 60cm (24in). '**Golden Hue**' has amethyst flowers and pale yellow foliage, tipped with orange in winter. H 35cm (14in), S 70cm (28in). '**Golden Sport**' has deep carmine pink flowers and bright golden-yellow foliage. H 15cm (6in), S 30cm (12in). '**Heidebrand**' has flaming pink flowers. H 20cm (8in), S 30cm (12in). '**Hookstone White**' has white flowers. H 35cm (14in), S 65cm (26in). '**Lady Skelton**' has ruby red flowers. H 10cm (4in), S 15cm (6in). '**P.S. Patrick**' has bright reddish-purple flowers and dark glossy green foliage. H 30cm (12in), S 45cm (18in). '**Pentreath**' has rich reddish-purple flowers. H 30cm (12in), S 55cm (22in). '**Pink Ice**' (syn. 'Pink Lace') has rose-pink flowers and foliage that is tinged bronze when young and in winter. H 20cm (8in), S 35cm (14in). '**Stephen Davis**' has luminous red flowers. H 25cm (10in), S 45cm (18in). '**Summer Gold**' has magenta-pink flowers and bright golden-yellow foliage. H 30cm (12in), S 45cm (18in).

E. × darleyensis
Darley heath, Darley Dale heath
These easy-to-grow hybrids have coloured young foliage and a long flowering period, usually from midwinter (sometimes earlier) until well into spring. Darly Dale heaths tolerate lime reasonably. The following selection of cultivars are all hardy/Z 7–8.

Erica × darleyensis 'Kramer's Rote'

'**Archie Graham**' has lilac-pink flowers. H 50cm (20in), S 60cm (24in). '**Arthur Johnson**' (syn. 'Dunwood Splendour') has pink flowers, which deepen to lilac-pink, and foliage tipped with cream in spring. H 60cm (24in), S 75cm (30in). '**Jack H. Brummage**' has lilac-pink flowers and foliage that is yellow-orange throughout the year. H 30cm (1ft), S 60cm (2ft). '**Kramer's Rote**' has magenta flowers and bronze-tinged foliage. H 35cm (14in), S 60cm (24in). '**Silberschmelze**' (syn. 'Molten Silver') has ash-white flowers and foliage faintly tipped with cream in spring. H 35cm (14in), S 80cm (32in). '**White Perfection**' has pure white flowers. H 40cm (16in), S 70cm (28in).

E. lusitanica
Portuguese heath
This has the longest flowering period of any tree heath. The straight species has pink buds opening to white flowers from midwinter to late spring. H 1m

(3ft), S 70cm (28in). Borderline hardy/Z 8–10. The selection '**George Hunt**' is smaller, with white flowers in mid-spring. Its chief merit lies in its yellow foliage, which lasts all year, making it an outstanding specimen plant. It is a frost hardy heath but needs a sheltered position. H and S 60cm (24in).

E. vagans
Cornish heath, wandering heath
A vigorous, evergreen, bushy species that provides flowers in autumn (some selections coming into flower in late summer). Tolerates some lime and responds well to pruning. The faded flowers (if left on the plant) turn an attractive russet brown in winter. All are hardy/Z 6–8. '**Birch Glow**' has glowing rose-pink flowers. H 30cm (12in), S 50cm (20in). '**Hookstone Rosea**' has pale rose-pink flowers. H 35cm (14in), S 70cm (28in). '**Kervensis Alba**' has white flowers. H 30cm (12in), S 50cm (20in). '**Lyonesse**' has white flowers. H 25cm (10in), S 50cm (20in). '**Mrs D.F. Maxwell**' has deep rose-pink flowers and dark green foliage. H 30cm (12in), S 45cm (18in). '**Saint Keverne**' has bright pink flowers. H 30cm (12in), S 50cm (20in). '**Summertime**' has shell-pink flowers. H 15cm (5in), S 35cm (14in). '**Valerie Proudley**' has sparse, white flowers and bright lemon-yellow foliage. H 15cm (6in), S 30cm (12in). '**Viridiflora**' has small bluish-green or mauve flowers encased in green bracts. H 30cm (12in), S 55cm (22in).

Erica cinerea 'Alfred Bowerman'

Erica lusitanica 'George Hunt'

Erica vagans 'Valerie Proudley'

Euonymus fortunei 'Emerald and Gold'

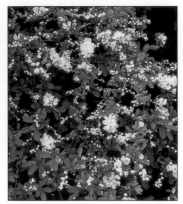
Exochorda × macrantha 'The Bride'

Fremontodendron 'California Glory'

EUONYMUS
Spindle tree
This is a large genus of about 175 species of deciduous, semi-evergreen and evergreen shrubs, trees and climbers. The evergreen shrubs make excellent ground-cover and some can even be persuaded to climb walls. Deciduous types are among the best plants for autumn interest, having both spectacular leaf colour and showy fruits.
Cultivation Grow these shrubs in any reasonable garden soil, including chalk (alkaline soil). The evergreens tolerate shade.

E. alatus
Winged spindle tree
The autumn fruits are the distinguishing feature of this deciduous shrub: bluish-purple, they split to reveal bright orange seeds, at the same time as the leaves redden but persisting on the branches for a while after the leaves have fallen. It is suitable for a wild garden or can be used in a hedgerow-type planting and will ultimately make a fine specimen. H 2m (6ft), S 3m (10ft). Hardy/Z 4–9.

E. fortunei
This evergreen is exclusively grown in its variegated forms, of which there are a great many. The following are all hardy/Z 5–9. 'Emerald and Gold' has leaves edged yellow. H 1m (3ft), S 1.5m (5ft). 'Harlequin' is a dwarf plant, with mottled white and green leaves, useful as ground-cover if planted in groups. H and S 1m (3ft). Most handsome of all is 'Silver Queen', which has

leaves broadly edged with creamy white. It is slow-growing but worthwhile and spectacular as a climber. H and S 1.5m (5ft), more if wall-trained.

EXOCHORDA
Pearl bush
A genus usually represented in gardens in the form described here, a lovely, fresh-looking plant for late spring, associating happily with late-flowering white or cream daffodils.
Cultivation This is tolerant of all except waterlogged soils in sun or light shade.

E. × macrantha 'The Bride'
The deciduous hybrid is only ever seen in this form, which is wreathed in white flowers in late spring, as its name implies. H and S 1m (3ft). Hardy/Z 5–9.

FORSYTHIA
Indispensable spring-flowering shrubs, these deciduous plants bear bright yellow flowers before the leaves appear. They can be grown as specimens, and are also

Forsythia suspensa

excellent in a shrub or mixed border, especially with spring bulbs. The stems are good for cutting, which is a good method of keeping plants within bounds. Eye-catching when in full flower, but of less interest the rest of the time, plant them as unobtrusive backdrops to perennials or as a support for summer-flowering climbers such as clematis.
Cultivation Grow in any reasonable soil in sun or light shade. Remove older wood after flowering if necessary and shorten the previous year's growth by about one-third.

F. × intermedia 'Lynwood'
This ungainly shrub is the best-known form, with rich yellow flowers on arching stems in early to mid-spring. H to 3m (10ft), S 1.5m (5ft). Hardy/Z 5–9.

F. suspensa
Golden bell
An arching shrub with branches covered in bright yellow flowers in early to mid-spring. H and S 2m (6ft) or more. Hardy/Z 6–8.

FOTHERGILLA
This small but interesting genus, containing only two deciduous species, is related to *Hamamelis*.
Cultivation Fothergillas need neutral or lime-free soil in sun or light shade.

F. major
The pussywillow-like, fragrant flowers are a delight in early spring. Good leaf colour in autumn provides a second season of interest. H and S 2m (6ft). Hardy/Z 5–9.

FREMONTODENDRON
Flannel bush
A superb plant for a favoured spot in the garden, these Californian plants will reward you with a magnificent display of gleaming yellow flowers in summer. Contact with the stems and leaves can cause allergies.
Cultivation Fremontodendrons tolerate all soil types (except those that are waterlogged) but need a very warm position, such as against a heat-reflecting wall in cold areas. Some winter protection may also be necessary.

F. 'California Glory'
This hybrid, which is evergreen in all but the hardest winters, covers itself with gleaming buttercup-yellow flowers in summer. It is a fast-growing plant, but can be short-lived. H 3m (10ft), S 2m (6ft). Borderline hardy/Z 8–9.

FUCHSIA
Thousands of hybrids have made this deservedly popular genus of evergreen or deciduous shrubs huge. They flower over a long period (from summer until the first frosts). Some have small, dainty flowers, like the species, but others are more flamboyant. They have a number of uses: in beds and borders, as wall shrubs, and in containers and hanging baskets (particularly pendent varieties). So-called hardy types can be cut back by hard frosts but will recover. From the gardener's point of view, fuchsias can be divided into two broad groups: hardy and tender. Hardy varieties (here defined as those that tolerate temperatures of -5°C/ 23°F or below) are excellent for cool borders. Smaller ones work well as edging plants and in rock gardens. Larger types can be used as specimens, trained against a wall or used for an informal flowering hedge, *F. magellanica* being especially effective for all these purposes. Tender varieties can be used as summer bedding and in containers planted for seasonal interest; those with trailing stems are ideal for hanging baskets. All are suitable for training as standards (trailing fuchsias will produce weeping standards). Most can be

Fuchsia 'Army Nurse'

Fuchsia 'Prosperity'

Fuchsia 'Dark Eyes'

Fuchsia 'Igloo Maid'

successfully overwintered if allowed to dry off at the end of summer before storage in a cool, bright, frost-free place. (The beautiful triphylla types, however, cannot always be relied upon to regenerate the next year.)
Cultivation Grow fuchsias in any well-drained soil in sun or light shade in not too cold a position. Protect hardy types over winter with a dry mulch. Cut back to ground level in spring.

F. magellanica
Lady's eardrops
This elegant species comes from South America and is one of the most reliable of all the fuchsias. From late summer until well into autumn, the red and bluish-purple flowers hang from the stems in a most appealing way. H 1.2m (4ft), S 45cm (18in), but considerably more where it overwinters successfully. Borderline hardy/Z 7–8. Desirable selections include *F. magellanica* var. *gracilis*, which is more slender in all its parts, with leaves daintily margined with

cream; *F. magellanica* var. *molinae*, which has smaller, pale pink flowers; and **'Versicolor'**, which has the advantage of beautiful leaves, coppery pink on emergence in spring, becoming grey-green.

Hardy hybrids
These hybrids are all frost hardy/Z 7–9. **'Army Nurse'** has semi-double, blue-violet and deep carmine red flowers. It makes an excellent standard. H 1.5m (5ft), S 1m (3ft). **'Brutus'** is vigorous and has single, rich dark purple and cerise-red flowers. H and S 1m (3ft). The upright and bushy **'Genii'** has single violet-purple and cerise-red flowers among yellow-green leaves. H 1.5m (5ft), S 75cm (30in). **'Hawkshead'** is a popular cultivar, with single, pinkish-white flowers, which are tinged green. H 60cm (2ft), S 45cm (18in). **'Mrs Popple'** has single, deep violet and scarlet flowers. It is good as a hedge. H and S 1m (3ft). **'Prosperity'** has double, pale rose-pink and crimson flowers. H 1.5m (5ft),

S 1m (3ft). **'Riccartonii'** (syn. *F. magellanica* 'Riccartonii'), a good hedging fuchsia, has small purple and red flowers. H and S 1m (3ft). **'Tom Thumb'**, a compact form and good for a rock garden, produces masses of small, single, mauve-purple and carmine-red flowers. H and S 50cm (20in).

Tender hybrids
These are all half-hardy to frost tender/Z 9–10. **'Alf Thornley'** has double, white and rose-pink flowers. H and S 1m (3ft). **'Chang'** has unusual, single, orange-red flowers, the sepals tipped green. H 1m (3ft), S 75cm (30in). **'Cotton Candy'** is an upright form with double, pale pink and blush-white flowers. H 1m (3ft), S 60cm (2ft). The trailing **'Dark Eyes'** has an abundance of perfectly formed, double, deep violet-blue and red flowers. H and S 1m (3ft). The trailing **'Frosted Flame'** produces large, single, barrel-shaped, bright red and white flowers over a long period. H 30cm (1ft), S 1m

(3ft). **'Gay Parasol'** has dramatic, dark red-purple and ivory-white flowers that open like a parasol. H 1m (3ft), S 45cm (18in). **'Golden Eden Lady'** has single, violet and pink flowers among yellow-green leaves. H 1m (3ft), S 75cm (30in). The trailing **'Igloo Maid'** is initially upright, then spreading, with double, white, pink-tinged flowers among yellow-green leaves. H 1m (3ft), S 60cm (2ft). **'Lord Lonsdale'** is unique, with single, salmon-orange and apricot-pink flowers and curled and crinkled foliage. H 1.5m (5ft), S 1m (3ft). **'Mantilla'**, a trailing, triphylla type, has long, single, rich carmine-pink flowers among bronze-tinged leaves. H 15cm (6in), S 75cm (30in). **'Monterey'** has elegant, long, single, salmon-orange flowers. H and S 1m (3ft). **'Royal Velvet'** has large, double, luminous deep purple and crimson flowers. H 75cm (30in), S 1m (3ft). **'Thalia'** is a triphylla type, with long, single, rich orange-red flowers among velvety leaves. H 45cm (18in), S 1m (3ft).

Fuchsia 'Brutus'

Fuchsia 'Chang'

Fuchsia 'Golden Eden Lady'

Fuchsia 'Mantilla'

Genista aetnensis

× *Halimiocistus sahucii*

GENISTA
Broom

These largely deciduous, airy plants, native to the Mediterranean, have showers of yellow pea flowers in spring or summer. The stems are leafless, giving a twiggy, even dead appearance in winter. They are not long-lived but are easily raised from seed. Essential plants for a Mediterranean garden or any planting in gravel. *G. aetnensis* can be a tree.
Cultivation Brooms thrive in well-drained soils of low fertility in full sun. They do not respond well to hard pruning.

G. aetnensis
Mount Etna broom

A delightful deciduous shrub or small tree for a hot, dry garden, showering golden-yellow flowers over lower plants in mid- to late summer. H and S 6m (20ft). Borderline hardy/Z 9–10.

G. lydia

This deciduous species produces a mass of twiggy branches that are covered in deep yellow flowers in late spring and early summer. H 30cm (12in), S to 1m (3ft). Hardy/Z 6–9.

× HALIMIOCISTUS

A group of usually evergreen hybrids, crosses between the genera *Halimium* and *Cistus*, both of which hybridize naturally in the wild. They have papery flowers that are saucer-shaped, and are excellent in a Mediterranean garden.
Cultivation Grow in any free-draining soil, ideally gritty and of low fertility, in full sun.

× H. sahucii

A shrub with a long flowering season. The chalk-white flowers can be produced from early summer into autumn. H 45cm (18in), S 1m (3ft). Hardy/Z 7–9.

× H. wintonensis

A compact shrub, with white flowers marked with yellow and maroon at the base of the petals. H 60cm (2ft), S 1m (3ft). Borderline hardy/Z 7–9.

HAMAMELIS
Witch hazel

The genus contains some of the finest winter-flowering shrubs, which would no doubt be more widely grown were it not for their specific cultivation needs. Propagation is also difficult, and plants are slow-growing, so those offered for sale tend to be small and expensive. Besides their spidery, scented winter flowers, they also have outstanding autumn leaf colour.
Cultivation Witch hazels need rich, ideally lime-free soil in a sunny site that is sheltered from strong winds.

H. × intermedia

This is a group of variable hybrids. H and S 4m (13ft), but only after many years. Hardy/Z 5–9. Selections include **'Arnold Promise'**, which has bright yellow winter flowers and splendid autumn leaf colour; **'Diane'**, which has red flowers and rich autumn tints; and the rare **'Vesna'**, with pale copper-coloured flowers and superb autumn leaf colour.

H. mollis
Chinese witch hazel

One of the best of the witch hazels, this slow-growing species has scented yellow flowers in mid-winter. H and S 4m (13ft), for mature plants. Hardy/Z 5–9.

HEBE

The large genus of scrubby evergreen plants from Australia and New Zealand contains about 100 species. They are grown for their (mainly) summer flowers, which are highly attractive to bees, and for their foliage. All hebes are excellent in seaside areas. Some have small leaves that cling to the stems almost like scales; these are the so-called whipcord hebes. The species with large, fleshy leaves are less hardy than others. Compact types are good in containers.
Cultivation Grow in any reasonable soil in full sun. Some of the taller hebes are remarkably tolerant of dry shade. The larger-leaved species can be pruned hard.

H. 'Blue Clouds'

This excellent hybrid has long spikes of bluish-mauve flowers from early summer until well into autumn. H 1m (3ft), S 1.2m (4ft). Hardy/Z 8.

H. cupressoides

This whipcord hebe has grey-green leaves and pale lilac-blue

Genista lydia

Hamamelis mollis

Hebe 'Blue Clouds'

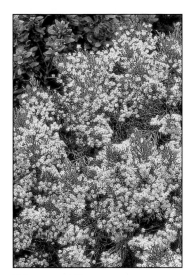

Hebe cupressoides

flowers which appear in early summer. H and S 1.2m (4ft). Borderline hardy/Z 8–9. The selection **'Boughton Dome'** is unique. It looks like a conifer, seldom if ever flowers and makes a neat bun shape without pruning. H 30cm (12in), S 60cm (24in). Hardy/Z 8–9.

H. 'Great Orme'
An elegant hybrid, this has narrow green leaves and spikes of pale pink flowers, aging to white, from summer to autumn. H 1.5m (5ft), S 1m (3ft). Borderline hardy/Z 9–10.

H. hulkeana
A species quite unlike any other, this has red-edged, toothed leaves and lilac-like flowers, which may be white, blue or mauve, in early

summer. H and S 60cm (2ft). Borderline hardy/Z 9–10.

H. 'Mrs Winder'
(syn. *H.* 'Waikiki', *H.* 'Warlyensis')
This hebe has violet-blue flowers in autumn. The leaves often flush purple in cold weather. H and S 1m (3ft). Borderline hardy/Z 8.

H. pinguifolia 'Pagei'
A dainty, spreading shrub, this has thick, silver-grey leaves and spikes of white flowers towards the end of spring. H 20cm (8in), S 60cm (2ft). Hardy/Z 8–9.

H. rakaiensis
This small, green-leaved species grows in a compact bun-shape and produces its white flowers in early to midsummer. H 60cm (2ft), S 1m (3ft). Hardy/ Z 8–10.

H. speciosa 'La Séduisante'
This upright hybrid is aptly named. The rich, purplish-red flowers, carried on stems of the same colour, open from mid-summer to late autumn. The leaves also have a purplish finish. H and S 60cm (2ft). Borderline hardy/Z 8.

HELIANTHEMUM
Rock rose, sun rose
The genus contains about 110 species of evergreen or semi-evergreen shrubs and subshrubs with brightly coloured flowers

Hebe pinguifolia 'Pagei'

from late spring to summer. *Cultivation* Grow in any free-draining soil in full sun. They thrive on soils of low fertility.

H. hybrids
Most rock roses are of garden origin, varying in habit but generally hummock-forming. The following are hardy/Z 6–8. 'Ben Nevis' has yellow flowers with red centres. H and S 20cm (8in). **'Rhodanthe Carneum'** (syn. 'Wisley Pink') has pink flowers. H 25cm (10in), S to 45cm (18in). **'Wisley White'** has white flowers with yellow stamens. H 25cm (10in), S 45cm (18in).

HIBISCUS
Rose mallow
These shrubs have mallow-like flowers in late summer. The

deciduous types described here are among the last woody plants to come into leaf, which happens in late spring. The genus also includes perennials and annuals. *Cultivation* Grow in any well-drained soil in a sunny, sheltered position.

H. syriacus
A large number of cultivars have been developed from this upright deciduous species. The following are all hardy/Z 6–9. H 2.5m (8ft), S 2m (6ft). **'Oiseau Bleu'** (syn. 'Blue Bird') is among the best known. It has violet-blue flowers with darker eyes. **'Totus Albus'** is a rarity in having pure white flowers. It will add late interest to a white border. **'Woodbridge'** has warm rose-pink flowers.

Hebe 'Great Orme'

Helianthemum 'Rhodanthe Carneum'

Hibiscus syriacus 'Oiseau Bleu'

Hydrangea arborescens 'Annabelle'

Hydrangea macrophylla 'Ayesha'

Hydrangea quercifolia 'Snow Flake'

HYDRANGEA

The genus contains medium to large, mainly deciduous shrubs. Late-flowering shrubs are few, and hydrangeas fill the gap nicely. They are also some of the few deciduous shrubs that thrive in containers. Planted in half-barrels, they give distinction to any garden. Hydrangea flower heads take a number of forms: lacecaps have a central mass of tiny fertile flowers surrounded by larger sterile flowers; mopheads (hortensias) have domed heads of sterile flowers only; others have flowers in conical panicles. *Cultivation* All hydrangeas need rich, moisture-retentive soil. The larger, soft-leaved varieties need shelter from strong winds and hot sun, thriving in woodland conditions. Soil pH affects the colour of some hybrids: acid soil enhances blue flowers, while alkaline soil enhances pink flowers. Some selected forms of *H. paniculata* can be pruned hard annually for larger flowers.

H. arborescens
Sevenbark
The species is less widely grown than its named selections, the loveliest of which is **'Annabelle'**, which produces large, cream-coloured flowerheads in late summer. H and S 1.5m (5ft). Hardy/Z 4–9.

H. aspera
A rangy shrub, this has velvety stems and blue and white flowers in late summer. Best in lime-free soil in light woodland. H 3m (10ft), S 1.5m (5ft). Hardy/Z 7–9. The **Villosa Group** (syn. *H. villosa*) hybrids are characterized by pale purple flowers and make more rounded shrubs. H and S 1.2m (4ft) or more.

H. macrophylla
Common hydrangea
The Japanese species is rarely seen in cultivation, but it is widely represented by many selected forms. The following are all hardy/Z 6–9. **'Altona'** (mophead) is a stiffly growing shrub, with flowers that are cerise pink on alkaline soils and mid-blue on acid soils. H and S 1m (3ft). **'Ayesha'** (mophead) has pale mauve or pale blue flowers. H and S 1.5m (5ft). **'Mariesii Perfecta'** (syn. 'Blue Wave'; lacecap) has blue (or mauve, depending on the soil pH) outer flowers surrounding pink central ones. H and S 2m (6ft).

H. paniculata
This species makes an upright, vase-shaped shrub and has conical flowerheads. It can be pruned annually to keep it within bounds. H 2m (6ft), S 1.2m (4ft), less if pruned annually. Hardy/Z 4–8. There are a number of fine cultivars, including **'Burgundy Lace'**, which has white flowers, aging to dull pink; **'Kyushu'**, which has pure white flowers; and **'Limelight'**, which has cool lime green flowers, the best colour being in shade.

H. quercifolia
This species has conical flowerheads, like those of *H. paniculata*, but is distinguished by its oak-like leaves. H 2m (6ft), S 1.5m (5ft). Hardy/Z 5–9. **'Snow Flake'** has pure white flowers.

H. serrata
(syn. *H. macrophylla* subsp. *serrata*)
The straight deciduous species seldom finds a place in gardens, but the named forms include some splendid plants for late summer-autumn interest, all hardy/Z 6–9. **'Bluebird'** (syn. 'Acuminata'; lacecap) has pale pink, pale purple or rich blue flowers and leaves that assume rich red autumn tints. H 80cm (32in), S 1m (3ft). **'Grayswood'** (lacecap) produces mauve central flowers surrounded by large white flowers that redden as they age. H and S 2m (6ft). **'Preziosa'** (syn. *H.* 'Preziosa'; hortensia) is outstanding, with rich red, mauve or blue flowers, depending on the soil pH. H ans S 1.5m (5ft). **'Rosalba'** (lacecap) has a row of white sterile flowers surrounding the central pink ones. H and S 1.2 m (4ft).

Hydrangea aspera

Hydrangea macrophylla 'Altona'

Hypericum 'Hidcote'

HYPERICUM
St John's wort

These valuable shrubs can be difficult to place in the garden because of the uncompromising yellow of the flowers. Try growing them in association with white groundcover roses. *H. olympicum* makes good groundcover.
Cultivation Grow hypericums in any well-drained soil in sun or light shade.

H. 'Hidcote'

This is probably the most significant member of the genus. It has large, shining yellow flowers from midsummer onwards. H and S 1m (3ft). Hardy/Z 6–9.

H. olympicum

The best species for groundcover, this is a sprawling shrub with golden-yellow flowers from midsummer onwards. Trim it with shears. It can also be grown in rock gardens. H 25cm (10in), S 30cm (12in). Hardy/Z 6–8.

H. 'Rowallane'

This elegant hybrid needs a sheltered spot. Large, golden-yellow flowers are produced from early summer to autumn. H 2m (6ft), S 1.2m (4ft). Borderline hardy/Z 7–9.

ILEX
Holly

Hollies become trees eventually, but they are slow-growing plants and can be treated as shrubs in the garden, particularly if they are cut back regularly, a practice to which they generally respond well. Male and female flowers are carried on separate plants, so if

Hypericum olympicum

you are growing hollies for berry production, make sure there is a male nearby. Conversely, if you grow only males, don't expect any berries. Hollies make excellent hedges (given time) and can be clipped to shape.
Cultivation Hollies are tolerant of most sites and soils and will grow in sun or light shade.

I. × altaclerensis

This is a large hybrid group. The heights and spreads shown are the ultimate size if plants are not pruned, but all can be controlled by regular pruning. Hardy/Z 7–9. The female **'Belgica Aurea'** has leaves that are irregularly variegated with creamy yellow.

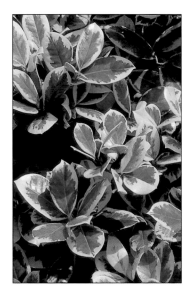

Ilex × altaclerensis 'Golden King'

H and S 3m (10ft). **'Camelliifolia'** is a handsome plain green, free-berrying form. It has smooth leaves that develop a bronze hue in cold weather, and it is one of the best for hedging. H and S 5m (16ft). **'Golden King'**, a female form, bears large red berries and has gold-edged leaves. H and S 6m (20ft). **'Lawsoniana'**, a female, is unusual in that the leaf edges are green and the centres are splashed with yellow. H 2.4m (8ft), S 1m (3ft). **'Wilsonii'** is a female that is grown for its abundant scarlet berries, rather than its plain green leaves. It will eventually reach tree proportions. H to 9m (29ft), S 5m (16ft).

I. crenata
Japanese holly

The species has small, rounded leaves, similar to those of box, and plants can be used for the same purposes. H 2.5m (8ft), S 2m (6ft). Hardy/Z 6–8. **'Mariesii'**, a female form, is very slow-growing, with black berries. H and S 1m (3ft).

ITEA

These elegant rather than showy shrubs have fragrant flowers and handsome leaves. The species described here repays careful cultivation and makes a superb wall shrub.
Cultivation Grow in fertile, well-drained but not too dry soil in a sunny, sheltered site.

Itea ilicifolia

I. ilicifolia

This beautiful evergreen shrub from China has shining, holly-like leaves and racemes of greenish flowers in late summer. It is an excellent support for yellow-flowered clematis. H and S 3m (10ft). Borderline hardy/Z 7–9.

KALMIA

The genus contains seven species of hardy, evergreen shrubs for an acid site. Kalmias are excellent used in conjunction with heathers or in light woodland.
Cultivation Grow in reliably moist, lime-free soil in either sun or light shade.

K. latifolia
Calico bush, mountain laurel

The species bears white, pink, purple or red flowers in midsummer, which provide a fine contrast to the glossy leaves. H and S 3m (10ft). Hardy/Z 5–9.

Kalmia latifolia

KERRIA
Jew's mallow

These spring-flowering, deciduous shrubs, bearing desirable yellow flowers, have a curious, upright, suckering habit. Not the most winsome plants, they are tough and reliable, equally good with daffodils and in a shrub border. There is only one species.
Cultivation Kerrias are tolerant of all but waterlogged soils in sun or light shade.

K. japonica

The species from China and Japan is seldom seen in gardens. It has single yellow flowers from mid- to late spring. H and S 2m (6ft). Hardy/Z 5–9. **'Golden Guinea'** is a rare but worthwhile single form with larger flowers than the species. H 1.5m (5ft), S 1m (3ft). Much more often grown is **'Pleniflora'**, which has double, button-like flowers. H to 2m (6ft), S 1m (3ft).

KOLKWITZIA
Beauty bush

The single species in the genus was given its common name for good reason. Its beautiful pink flowers make a stunning sight.
Cultivation Kolkwitzias are suitable for all except waterlogged soils in sun or light shade.

K. amabilis

This elegant, arching deciduous shrub is normally seen in the selected form **'Pink Cloud'**, which

Kerria japonica 'Pleniflora'

is festooned with pink, bell-shaped flowers in late spring to early summer. H 3m (10ft), S 4m (12ft). Hardy/Z 5–9.

LAVANDULA
Lavender

Lavenders are well-known herb garden plants, but they have a number of other uses, principally as flowering hedging. When they are in flower, these evergreen shrubs and subshrubs will be alive with bees. They make a classic combination with old roses and can also be trained as standards.
Cultivation Lavenders will grow in all soil types but must have good drainage and a position in full sun. Clip hedging lightly in spring.

L. angustifolia
(syn. *L. officinalis*)
Old English lavender

The species has grey-green leaves and scented blue-grey flowers all summer long. H and S 60cm (2ft). Hardy/Z 6–9. There are many selections, including **'Hidcote'** (syn. *L.* 'Hidcote Blue'), which has rich deep lavender-blue flowers; **'Munstead'**, which has soft, lilac-blue flowers; and the strong-growing **'Rosea'**, with pink flowers. H and S 60cm (2ft).

L. stoechas
French lavender

Essential in any herb garden, this species has distinctive flower spikes, with bright purple, erect bracts at the top of each flower-head. It has a long flowering period. H and S 45cm (18in). Borderline hardy/Z 7–9.

LAVATERA
Tree mallow

A genus of evergreen, semi-evergreen and deciduous shrubs, perennials and annuals, which are highly valued for their late-season flowers. The species described is widely grown but is rather harsh in colour. The various hybrids are all improvements on the species and integrate better into mixed borders planned for late-summer interest.
Cultivation Grow lavateras in any well-drained soil in full sun.

L. 'Barnsley'

One of the best-known hybrids, this semi-evergreen plant bears very pale pink mallow flowers with warm pinkish-red eyes towards the end of summer. It has a tendency to revert to type over time. H and S 2m (6ft). Hardy/Z 8.

L. thuringiaca
Tree lavatera

The species bears deep pink flowers in profusion in late summer to autumn. H 2m (6ft), S 1.5m (5ft). Hardy/Z 8. The superior selection **'Ice Cool'** is similar to 'Barnsley', but the flowers do not have the red maskings. H and S 1.5m (5ft).

× LEDODENDRON

This hybrid genus consists of a single shrub, which is a cross between *Rhododendron trichosomum* and *Ledum glandulosum* var. *columbianum*.
Cultivation Grow in acid, well-drained soil in partial shade.

Kolkwitzia amabilis 'Pink Cloud'

Lavandula stoechas

Lavandula angustifolia 'Hidcote'

× *Ledodendron* 'Arctic Tern'
(syn. *Rhododendron* 'Arctic Tern')
This compact, vigorous, evergreen
shrub bears white flowers in late
spring to early summer. H and S
60cm (2ft). Hardy/Z 8.

LEPTOSPERMUM
Tea tree
The genus contains about 80
species of evergreen trees and
shrubs from Australia, New
Zealand and South-east Asia
grown for their foliage and small
flowers. Not for all gardens, these
plants are not reliably hardy and
have specific soil requirements,
although in the right conditions
they make charming specimens.
Cultivation Grow in lime-free,
reliably moist, well-drained soil in
full sun with some shelter,
particularly in cold areas.

L. lanigerum
Woolly tea tree
This erect species from Australia
has white flowers in early summer.
H 1.5m (5ft), S 1m (3ft).
Borderline hardy/Z 8.

L. scoparium
Manuka, New Zealand tea tree
This is a variable species, which
is rarely seen in cultivation, but
there are many cultivars. The
following are half-hardy/Z 9–10.
The dwarf **'Kiwi'** has pinkish-red
flowers and reddish-purple leaves.
H and S 1m (3ft). The rarer
'Lyndon' has white flowers. H
and S 3m (10ft).

Lavatera 'Barnsley'

LEUCOTHOE
These compact and dainty shrubs
are grown for their evergreen
foliage and flowers. They are not
reliably hardy in all situations and
have specific soil requirements.
They are good in peat beds or in
light woodland.
Cultivation Grow in fertile, acid
soil in sun or light shade, with
shelter from cold winds. They will
not tolerate dry conditions.

L. 'Scarletta'
(syn. *L. axillaris* 'Scarletta',
L. 'Zeblid')
This evergreen shrub bears small,
white, pitcher-shaped flowers in
late spring. The foliage reddens in
late summer, but is not shed. H
and S 60cm (2ft). Hardy/Z 5.

L. walteri
(syn. *L. fonanesiana*)
The form of the species most
generally seen is **'Rainbow'**, a
spreading evergreen with striking
leaves variegated with pink and
cream. The white, lily-of-the-
valley-like flowers seem incidental
when they appear in summer. H
and S 60cm (2ft). Hardy/Z 5–8.

LEYCESTERIA
These sombre, deciduous shrubs
are grown for their late-summer
flowers and autumn fruits.
The genus, which contains six
species, is generally represented in
cultivation by the single species
described here.
Cultivation It is suitable for most
soils in sun or light shade.

L. formosa
Pheasant berry, Himalayan honeysuckle
The first common name derives
from the appeal of the dark
purple autumn fruits to
pheasants. These follow the
drooping panicles of white and
claret-purple summer flowers.
H 2m (6ft), S 1m (3ft).
Borderline hardy/Z 7–9.

LIGUSTRUM
Privet
An unnecessarily maligned genus,
Ligustrum is usually seen in
gardens as hedging, for which
purpose it is inferior to some
other plants. It is put to best use
in a mixed or shrub border as an

Leucothoe 'Scarletta'

unassuming backdrop to other
more flamboyant plants, but
privets are also surprisingly good
as specimens. Variegated forms
are highly effective when trained
as standards.
Cultivation Privets are tolerant
of any ordinary garden soil in sun
or shade.

L. ovalifolium
This is the privet most widely used
as hedging, when it is clipped to
keep it to size. The species, which
is usually evergreen, has plain green
leaves and white flowers in summer.
H and S 4m (13ft). Hardy/
Z 6–10. The selection **'Aureum'**
(syn. 'Aureomarginatum') is
variegated with yellow and is less
vigorous. H and S 3m (10ft).

Leptospermum scoparium 'Lyndon'

Leycesteria formosa

Ligustrum tschonoskii

L. tschonoskii
This handsome deciduous species is a rarity in gardens. The leaves and flowers are somewhat larger than those of most other privets. H and S 2m (6ft), but eventually tree-like. Hardy/Z 6.

LONICERA
Honeysuckle
Most honeysuckles are climbers, but the genus also includes the following shrubs, many of them excellent for the winter garden and extremely hardy. The deciduous species described here can be wall-trained if you choose, which can sometimes lead to more abundant flowering. *L. nitida* is useful for hedging and also for small-scale topiary.

Cultivation Honeysuckles will grow in any, preferably humus-rich, soil in sun or light shade. Cut back some of the oldest stems every year after flowering.

L. fragrantissima
A good plant for winter interest, this deciduous or semi-evergreen Chinese species has small, fragrant, white and pink flowers in midwinter. Unfortunately, it is rather dull the rest of the time, unless used as a support for annual climbers, such as sweet peas. H and S 1.5m (5ft). Hardy/ Z 5–8.

L. nitida
This dense evergreen shrub has neat, oval, dark green leaves. Both the species and the cultivar described below are ideal for hedging and may be easily controlled by pruning. H 2m (6ft), S 1.5m (5ft). Hardy/Z 7–9. The form usually seen is 'Baggesen's Gold', which has yellow-green leaves.

L. × purpusii
This deciduous hybrid produces fragrant, white flowers on the bare stems in winter. Both this and the selected form described here are almost indistinguishable from *L. fragrantissima*, leading to confusion in the nursery trade. H and S 1.5m (5ft). Hardy/Z 7–9. 'Winter Beauty' has creamy-white flowers from early winter until spring. H and S 1.2m (4ft).

Lonicera nitida 'Baggesen's Gold'

MAGNOLIA
Many magnolias are trees, but there are a few shrubs in the genus that are delightful and easy to cultivate, if a little slow to get into their stride. The deciduous spring-flowers make ideal central features in spring borders planted with dwarf narcissi, *Anemone blanda*, species tulips and crocuses.
Cultivation Grow in fertile, well-drained soil in sun, although in frost-prone areas early flowering magnolias benefit from some shade from morning sun at flowering times.

M. × loebneri 'Leonard Messel'
This delightful deciduous hybrid has pale pink, spidery flowers in mid-spring. H 3m (10ft), S 2.5m (8ft). Hardy/Z 5–9.

M. stellata
Star magnolia
This slow-growing, deciduous species is indispensable, with masses of spidery white flowers in mid-spring. It requires a sheltered spot. H 1.2m (4ft), S 1.5m (5ft). Hardy/Z 5–9.

MAHONIA
The genus contains about 70 species of evergreen shrubs, which are rather similar to *Berberis* – in fact, some botanists would like to unite the genera. Most have deliciously scented flowers, but their prime use is to fill inhospitable sites.

Magnolia × loebneri 'Leonard Messel'

Cultivation Mahonias are happy in all well-drained soils, including chalk (alkaline soil). Large-leaved species benefit from shelter from strong winds. Pruning plants when young can encourage bushiness, but some forms are naturally rangy.

M. aquifolium
Mountain grape holly, Oregon grape
The species has glossy green leaves and yellow flowers in late winter to early spring. H 1m (3ft), S 1.5m (5ft). Hardy/Z 6–9. There are a number of cultivars, including the vigorous and low-growing 'Apollo'; and 'Smaragd', which has bronze, netted foliage. H 60cm (2ft), S 1m (3ft).

Magnolia stellata

Mahonia trifolia

Mahonia aquifolium

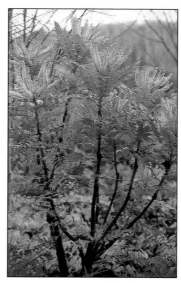

Mahonia × media 'Lionel Fortescue'

M. japonica

This erect species produces its arching racemes of scented yellow flowers from late autumn to early spring, followed by blue-purple berries. H 2m (6ft), S 3m (10ft). Hardy/Z 7–9. The selection '**Bealei**' has more compact flower spikes.

M. lomariifolia

This elegant species is one of the parents of M. × media (the other is M. japonica), which it resembles in some respects, though it is more rangy in habit and slightly less resistant to extreme cold. The racemes of flowers, which smell like lily-of-the-valley, appear from autumn to late winter and are followed by bluish, grape-like fruits. H 3m (10ft), S 2m (6ft). Hardy/Z 8–10.

M. × media

This hybrid group includes a number of notable named garden selections, all similar and equally effective and all with long racemes of fragrant yellow flowers in winter. Leggy specimens can be pruned hard in spring. They include '**Charity**', which has slender, upright, later-spreading spikes of very fragrant yellow flowers; '**Lionel Fortescue**', which has upright plumes of bright yellow, slightly less fragrant flowers; and '**Winter Sun**', which has dense clusters of yellow flowers. H 2m (6ft), S 1.2m (4ft). Hardy/Z 7–9.

M. trifolia
(**syn.** M. eutriphylla)

This unusual species is variable, existing in both prostrate and more upright forms. The short spikes of yellow flowers appear in spring, and the leaves flush purple-red in cold weather. H and S 2m (6ft). Hardy/Z 7.

M. × wagneri

This hybrid group contains a number of excellent garden plants. The notable '**Undulata**' (syn. M. 'Undulata') bears yellow flowers in spring and has hollylike leaves that, in addition to having wavy edges, turn rich plum-purple in cold weather. The rich yellow flowers appear in spring. H and S 2m (6ft). Hardy/Z 8–9.

MYRTUS
Myrtle

Myrtles are rich in historical associations and were traditionally used in royal wedding bouquets. In cold areas, they need to be tucked under a sheltering wall.
Cultivation They will grow in most soils, including chalk (alkaline), but they need a warm, sunny site. Young plants benefit from some protection in winter until they are well established.

M. communis
Common myrtle

This slow-growing evergreen bushy shrub has dark green foliage and fragrant white flowers in summer, followed by purple-black berries. H and S 3m (10ft).

Borderline hardy/Z 9–10. The more compact and wind-resistant **M. communis** subsp. *tarentina* (syn. 'Jenny Reitenbach', 'Microphylla', 'Nana') has pink-flushed, white flowers and white berries. H and S 2m (6ft).

NANDINA
Sacred bamboo, Heavenly bamboo

The only species in the genus is this elegant evergreen or semi-evergreen shrub, which is grown for its overall appearance and summer flowers. Although related to *Berberis*, it looks nothing like it. The sacred bamboo combines well with grasses and is a good choice where a true bamboo would be too large.
Cultivation Grow in any well-drained but not too dry, reasonably fertile soil in sun, preferably with some shelter. Young plants may need winter protection in cold areas.

N. domestica

The large panicles of white, starry, summer flowers are followed by red autumn berries. The leaves start purplish-red when young, turn dark green, redden again in autumn and hold their colour into winter. H 2m (6ft), S 1m (3ft). Borderline hardy/Z 7–10. '**Fire Power**' is a more compact form. H 1.2m (4ft), S 60cm (2ft). '**Richmond**' bears a mass of scarlet berries in autumn. H 2m (6ft), S 1.2m (4ft).

Myrtus communis

Nandina domestica 'Fire Power'

Nerium oleander 'Roseum Plenum'

Osmanthus delavayi

Olearia 'Waikariensis'

NERIUM
Oleander

This is a typical plant of the Mediterranean (although it also appears in China), where it is widely planted as a kerbside shrub. Not hardy enough to be grown outdoors in frost-prone climates, it makes an excellent conservatory (porch) plant. There is only one species, of which all parts are poisonous.
Cultivation Grow in moderately fertile, well-drained soil in full sun. Conservatory plants can be pruned hard to keep them compact.

N. oleander
Rose bay

The evergreen species has fragrant, pink, red, apricot, yellow

or white flowers throughout the summer among the upright, lance-shaped leaves. When grown in a container it will be smaller than the dimensions indicated. H to 3m (10ft), S 2m (6ft). Tender/Z 10. Selections include **'Peach Blossom'**, which has pink flowers; **'Roseum Plenum'**, which has double, pink flowers; and **'Variegatum'**, which has variegated leaves and pink flowers. H and S to 2m (6ft).

OLEARIA
Daisy bush

The daisy bushes, mainly from Australia and New Zealand, are fine shrubs, valued for their daisy-like summer flowers and evergreen foliage. They are good in island beds and also make very good wind-resistant shelter.
Cultivation Grow olearias in any well-drained, reasonably fertile soil in full sun.

O. × haastii

This hybrid has clusters of flowers in mid- to late summer and makes a dense, rounded bush. H 2m (6ft), S 3m (10ft). Hardy/Z 8–10.

O. macrodonta
New Zealand holly

This species is one of the most impressive of the genus, with large, pewter grey, holly-like leaves and daisy-like flowers in summer. H 6m (20ft), S 5m (16ft). Borderline hardy/Z 9–10.

O. 'Waikariensis'
(syn. *O. oleifolia*)

This hybrid has felted stems and the characteristic grey leaves and daisy-like summer flowers. H and S 2m (6ft). Hardy/Z 8.

OSMANTHUS

These shrubs with handsome, evergreen leaves are related to the olive. Plant in mixed or shrub borders or in light woodland. They also make an unusual hedge.
Cultivation Almost any soil is tolerated in sun or shade, but some shelter from cold winds is desirable to avoid leaf scorch.

O. decorus
(syn. *Phillyrea decora*)

This fine species from western

Asia is grown for its overall appearance. The white flowers, which appear in spring, are small but sweetly scented. It takes kindly to pruning. H 3m (10ft), S 4m (13ft). Hardy/Z 6–9.

O. delavayi
(syn. *Siphonosmanthus delavayi*)

A slow-growing species from China, this has tiny leaves and fragrant, white flowers in mid-spring. H 2m (6ft), S 2.4m (8ft). Hardy/Z 7–9.

OZOTHAMNUS

The genus of summer-flowering, evergreen shrubs, which look like *Rosmarinus*, contains about 50 species. They are good in mixed or shrub borders but are not

Olearia × haastii

Ozothamnus rosmarinifolius 'Silver Jubilee'

Paeonia suffruticosa subsp. *rockii*

Paeonia delavayi var. *lutea*

Philadelphus 'Belle Etoile'

hardy enough for all gardens. They are excellent in summer borders.
Cultivation Grow in any well-drained soil in sun. Some protection may be necessary in cold winters.

O. rosmarinifolius
(**syn.** *Helichrysum rosmarinifolium*)
This species has an erect habit and dark green foliage. Pinkish buds open to heads of white flowers in early summer. H 3m (10ft), S 1.5m (5ft). Borderline hardy/Z 8–9. The leaves of **'Silver Jubilee'** are silvery green. H 2m (6ft), S 1.2m (4ft).

PAEONIA
Peony
This is a genus primarily of perennials, but it also includes some magnificent deciduous shrubs, the so-called tree peonies. The hybrids are usually expensive, but the outlay should not put off the committed gardener, for these are long-lived plants that reward careful cultivation. All tree peonies make splendid specimens, while the species are probably best grown in light woodland.
Cultivation Tree peonies need rich, fertile soil in sun or light dappled shade. Some protection from late frost, which can damage leaves and flowers, is desirable.

P. delavayi
This species has rich dark red, bowl-shaped flowers in late

spring. H 2m (6ft), S 1m (3ft). Hardy/Z 5–8. The variety *P. delavayi* var. *lutea* (syn. *P. lutea*) has golden-yellow flowers and deeply divided glossy foliage.

P. suffruticosa
Moutan
This is the species that has engendered the huge range of hybrids (many of Japanese origin). All are hardy/Z 4–8. **'Banksii'** has double, carmine flowers; **'Reine Elizabeth'** has double, salmon-orange flowers with ruffled margins; and **'Renkaku'** (syn. 'Flight of Cranes') has dense, double, white flowers. *P. suffruticosa* subsp. *rockii* (syn. 'Joseph Rock', 'Rock's Variety') is the ultimate connoisseur's plant, with huge, double white flowers marked with maroon at the base. This rare plant is not variable in cultivation. H 2m (6ft), S 1.5m (5ft).

PEROVSKIA
Russian sage
A good shrub for late-summer flowers, this tough plant comes

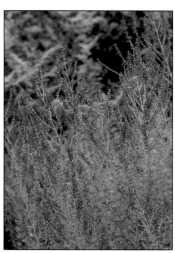

Perovskia 'Blue Spire'

from Siberia. It produces a sheaf of whitened stems covered in small, mauve-blue flowers. It is excellent in a Mediterranean or gravel garden, hot sun only enhancing its aromatic properties. The genus is normally represented in gardens by hybrids.
Cultivation Grow perovskias in any free-draining soil in full sun. They tolerate stony soil. Prune hard each year in spring.

P. 'Blue Spire'
This hybrid has silver-blue, deeply cut leaves and spires of rich blue flowers in late summer. H and S to 1m (3ft). Hardy/Z 6–9.

PHILADELPHUS
Mock orange
The scent of the mock orange is unmistakable and almost cloyingly sweet when it hangs in the air in early summer. Most of the plants in cultivation are hybrids of garden origin. Grow them as a fragrant backdrop to a mixed border. *P. coronarius* 'Aureus' can be grown exclusively for its foliage.
Cultivation Mock oranges do well in most reasonable garden soil in sun or light shade.

P. 'Avalanche'
This aptly named plant has masses of scented white flowers. H and S 1.5m (5ft). Hardy/Z 5–8.

P. 'Beauclerk'
The flowers of this distinctive, arching shrub are characterized by

central cerise blotches. H and S 1.5m (5ft). Hardy/Z 5–8.

P. 'Belle Etoile'
This hybrid has delicious, fragrant single white flowers. H 1.5m (5ft), S 1.2m (4ft). Hardy/Z 5–8.

P. coronarius
The species is grown less than its lovely cultivars, which are hardy/Z 5–9. **'Aureus'** has soft gold-green leaves. It needs shelter from hot sun, but lights up a dark corner when the light strikes it. Pruning just before flowering results in a fresh crop of lime-green leaves (at the expense of the flowers). **'Variegatus'** (syn. 'Bowles Variety') has leaves that are edged in cream and white flowers. H and S 1.2m (4ft).

P. 'Manteau d'Hermine'
One of the daintiest of the mock oranges, this hybrid smothers itself in double, creamy-white flowers. H and S 45cm (18in). Hardy/Z 5–8.

P. microphyllus
This elegant species produces a mass of fragrant, single, pure white flowers. H and S to 1m (3ft). Hardy/Z 6.

P. 'Virginal'
This well-known and justly popular cultivar has double, white flowers. This is a grand plant. Old specimens tend to become bare at the base. H to 3m (10ft), S 2m (6ft). Hardy/Z 5–9.

Philadelphus 'Manteau d'Hermine'

Phillyrea angustifolia

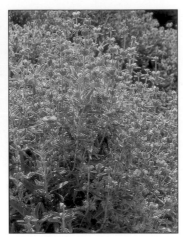

Phlomis italica

PHILLYREA
Jasmine box

This classy evergreen shrub was widely grown in the 17th century but is nowadays increasingly rare. It is a good alternative to box and rather faster-growing. It is suitable for a maritime garden. On the debit side, it is difficult to propagate, so stocks tend to be low.
Cultivation They will grow in any fertile, well-drained soil in sun or light shade.

P. angustifolia
The flame-like, hard, dark green leaves always excite comment. The flowers, produced in spring, are insignificant. This species responds well to pruning. H and S to 3m (10ft), but usually less in gardens. Hardy/Z 7–9.

PHLOMIS

These evergreen shrubs and perennials have woolly grey leaves. They are well-suited to a Mediterranean border, grown in association with plants such as *Cistus* and *Halimium* and woody herbs such as rosemary and lavender.
Cultivation Phlomis need very well-drained, only moderately fertile soil and a position in full sun.

P. fruticosa
Jerusalem sage
The best-known species, with whorls of sulphur-yellow flowers appearing in summer among the grey leaves. H and S 1.2m (4ft). Hardy/Z 8–10.

P. italica
Daintier than *P. fruticosa*, this choice species has pink or pale purple flowers. H and S 60cm (2ft). Borderline hardy/Z 8–9.

PHOTINIA

These excellent shrubs are grown mainly for the brilliance of their spring foliage. They suit a mixed or shrub border and make a good alternative to *Pieris* in gardens with alkaline soil.
Cultivation Grow in any well-drained soil in sun or light shade.

P. davidiana
(syn. *Stranvaesia davidiana*)
This handsome shrub, semi-evergreen in all but the coldest areas, has as its main feature long-lasting crimson berries, which ripen in autumn. Some of the leaves turn bright red at the same time, while others remain green. H and S 2.4m (8ft). Hardy/Z 7–9.

P. × fraseri
This hybrid group includes a number of excellent selected forms. Hardy/Z 8–9. The new growth of the spreading form **'Birmingham'** is deep coppery red. **'Red Robin'** has spectacular bright red young stems and leaves in vivid contrast to the glossy green older leaves. H and S 1.5m (5ft).

PHYGELIUS

The subshrubs in this genus will be evergreen in mild winters, but may die back in periods of prolonged cold, although they often reshoot from ground level. In cold areas, they are best in the lee of a wall.
Cultivation Phygelius need well-cultivated, rich soil and a warm, sheltered site. Cut back hard annually in spring if the top-growth is killed by frost.

P. aequalis
The species, a compact shrub, has dusky red-pink tubular flowers. H 1m (3ft), S 60cm (2ft). Borderline hardy/Z 7–9. The species is less often seen than the cultivar **'Yellow Trumpet'**, which has light green leaves and, as the name suggests, yellow flowers. H 1m (3ft), S 60cm (2ft).

P. × rectus
A group of hybrids normally represented in gardens by one of the several available cultivars, such as **'African Queen'**, which has red flowers; and **'Moonraker'**, which has creamy yellow flowers. H 1m (3ft), S 60cm (2ft). Borderline hardy/Z 8–9.

Phygelius × rectus 'Moonraker'

PIERIS

These elegant evergreen woodland shrubs bear racemes of lily-of-the-valley-like flowers in spring. Some forms have eye-catching young foliage as well.
Cultivation Acid soil, preferably enriched with leaf mould, is essential. Shelter from early morning sun and strong winds is also desirable. They do best in dappled light or a site with afternoon sun only.

P. 'Forest Flame'
This fine hybrid is grown for its foliage rather than for its flowers, which are not reliably produced. The flush of young leafy growth in spring is brilliant red, fading to green. H 2.2m (7ft), S 1m (3ft). Borderline hardy/Z 7–9.

Photinia x fraseri

Phygelius × rectus 'African Queen'

Pieris 'Forest Flame'

Pieris japonica

Potentilla fruticosa 'Medicine Wheel Mountain'

Potentilla fruticosa 'Abbotswood'

P. formosa

The young leaves are red, turning bronze and maturing to dark green. Sprays of white flowers are borne in spring. H and S 2m (6ft). Borderline hardy/Z 7–9. The species is normally represented in gardens in the form *P. formosa* var. *forrestii* 'Wakehurst', which has vivid red young leaves and sprays of white flowers that open from red buds.

P. japonica
Lily-of-the-valley bush

This bushy shrub has glossy green leaves and cascading sprays of white flowers in spring. H and S 3m (10ft). Hardy/Z 6–8. Selected forms include 'Pink Delight', which has masses of pink flowers; 'Valley Rose', which has pale pink flowers; and the prolific 'Valley Valentine', which has cherry red flowers.

PITTOSPORUM

These evergreen shrubs are grown for the interest of their leaves. Not only do some forms have coloured foliage, but the leaves also have wavy edges. Most thrive in coastal areas.
Cultivation These plants are suitable for most well-drained soil in sun, but they will not tolerate very cold spots.

P. tenuifolium

This, the most popular species, is usually grown in its coloured leaf forms, which all make excellent container plants. Borderline hardy/Z 9–10. 'Irene Paterson' has very pale green leaves heavily

marked with white. It is slower growing than the species. H 1.2m (4ft), S 60cm (2ft). The young leaves of 'Purpureum' are green but age to purple. H 1.2m (4ft), S 60cm (2ft). The leaves of the dwarf 'Tom Thumb' turn rich purple in cold weather. H and S 1m (3ft).

POTENTILLA

These neat, very hardy, deciduous shrubs bear masses of rose-like flowers in summer. They are a good choice for the front of a border or to mark the turn in a path. They can also be grown in rock gardens.
Cultivation Potentillas will grow in most well-drained soils is sun or light shade.

P. 'Blazeaway'

This hybrid has dark green leaves and fiery orange-red flowers. H and S to 1m (3ft). Hardy/Z 5–8.

Potentilla 'Blazeaway'

P. fruticosa
Shrubby cinquefoil

This is the best-known species, and a huge range of garden varieties have been developed from it, including 'Abbotswood', which has white flowers over a long period; 'Medicine Wheel Mountain', which has yellow flowers; 'Pretty Polly', which has pink flowers; and 'Snowbird', an unusual variety, which has double, pure white flowers. H 1m (3ft), S 1.2m (4ft). Hardy/Z 3–8.

PRUNUS
Ornamental cherry

This genus contains over 200 species and ornamental cherries are well known, but the genus also includes a couple of fine ever-green shrubs, which are good for hedging and for clipping to formal shapes or as standards.
Cultivation These grow in most soils but may not do well on shallow soil over chalk (alkaline soil).

P. laurocerasus
Cherry laurel

This useful evergreen shrub is much used for hedging, the large glossy leaves making a welcome contrast to most other hedging plants. Spikes of white flowers in spring and black autumn berries are bonuses. It can easily be kept under control by pruning. H 3m (10ft), S 2m (6ft). Hardy/Z

7–9. 'Camelliifolia' has curiously twisted leaves. H 3m (10ft), S 4m (13ft). The diseased-looking 'Marbled White' (syn. 'Castlewellan') has leaves that are heavily mottled with creamy white. H and S 5m (16ft). The well-known 'Otto Luyken' is a low-growing form with handsome, narrow leaves. H 1m (3ft), S 1.5m (5ft).

P. lusitanica
Portugal laurel

Less familiar, but more refined than *P. laurocerasus*, this evergreen species carries glossy leaves and spikes of white flowers in early to midsummer. It makes a beautiful large standard. H 2.7m (9ft), S 2m (6ft). Borderline hardy/Z 7–9.

Prunus laurocerasus 'Marbled White'

Rhamnus alaternus 'Argenteovariegata'

PYRACANTHA
Firethorn

An important genus of tough, hardy, spiny, evergreen plants that tolerate exposure. The cream-coloured flowers cascading from the branches in summer are followed by equally impressive yellow, orange or red berries that last all winter. An unexpected but highly effective use for pyracanthas is as a hedge.

Cultivation Grow in any fertile, well-drained soil in sun or shade.

P. coccinea 'Red Column'

This upright shrub has reddish shoots and vivid red berries in autumn, and shows good resistance to fireblight. H 1.5m (5ft), S 1m (3ft). Hardy/Z 7–8.

P. 'Knap Hill Lemon'

An unusual variety, worth growing for its clear yellow berries in autumn. H 1.5m (5ft), S 1m (3ft). Hardy/Z 7.

P. 'Soleil d'Or'

This popular hybrid has hawthorn-like white flowers in late spring succeeded by golden-yellow berries in autumn. H and S 1.5m (5ft). Hardy/Z 7.

RHAMNUS
Buckthorn

Fine foliage plants, sometimes evergreen, these shrubs are excellent as hedging or in a shrub border. The berries are poisonous.
Cultivation Grow in any reasonable garden soil in sun or light shade.

R. alaternus 'Argenteovariegata' (syn. R. alaternus 'Variegata')

Probably the most familiar of the genus, the leaves of this evergreen are handsomely variegated with grey marbling and irregular white leaf margins. It appreciates a warm, sheltered site. H and S 1.5m (5ft). Borderline hardy/Z 7–9.

RHODODENDRON

This large and complex genus includes plants that range from huge, tree-like shrubs to diminutive specimens for a rock garden or alpine trough. There would be a rhododendron for every garden were it not for the fact that they must have acid soil, which rules them out for some gardeners. Some are happy in containers, however, bringing them within reach for gardeners on alkaline soil. Essentially, most are wood-landers and look good in that setting, but modern varieties (especially those related to *R. yakushimanum*) are compact, dwarf plants that cope with more open situations. Rhododendrons combine well with other acid-loving shrubs, such as pieris and camellias, as well as with heathers. Deciduous rhododendrons, which are often more rangy and open in habit, are good with spring bulbs.
Cultivation Rhododendrons must have acid soil that is high in nutrients and well-drained. Most prefer light, dappled shade.

Species and selected forms
R. augustinii Electra Group

An evergreen shrub with funnel-shaped, violet-blue flowers in mid-spring. H 4m (13ft), S 2.5m (8ft). Hardy/Z 7–8.

Rhododendron decorum

R. charitopes

This compact evergreen species, which is good in a rock garden, comes from southern Tibet. Trusses of waxy, bell-shaped, pale pink or violet flowers are borne in late spring to early summer. H and S 1m (3ft). Hardy/Z 6–8.

R. cinnabarinum subsp. cinnabarinum Roylei Group

These evergreen hybrids have deep coppery plum to crimson, funnel-shaped flowers, which appear between mid-spring and early summer. H to 6m (20ft), S 2m (6ft). Hardy/Z 7–8.

R. decorum

This tree-like evergreen species from China bears loose trusses of fragrant, white or pink flowers in early summer. It tolerates warm dry conditions. H to 6m (20ft), S 2.5m (8ft). Hardy/Z 6–8.

R. impeditum

This dwarf evergreen, which is ideal for a rock garden or trough, comes from the mountains of Yunnan and Sichuan. The scaly leaves are aromatic. The blue-purple flowers open almost flat,

Rhododendron impeditum

like stars, in mid- to late spring. H and S to 60cm (2ft). Hardy/Z 6 8.

R. luteum

A dazzling deciduous species, this elegant rhododendron bears highly fragrant, clear yellow flowers in late spring and early summer. It is the parent of many more compact hybrids. H and S to 4m (13ft). Hardy/Z 6–9.

R. hybrids

There are a huge number of hybrid rhododendrons of garden origin of widely diverging size. The following gives an indication of the range available; all are evergreen unless otherwise stated. Hardy/Z 4–9. Plants of the **Alison Johnstone Group** have dainty, peach-pink flowers in late spring to early summer. H and S 2m (6ft). **'Bashful'** (Yakushimanum hybrid) has pink flowers aging white in spring; sun-tolerant. H and S 2m (6ft). The deciduous **'Berryrose'** has salmon-pink flowers with yellow flares in late spring; sun-tolerant. H and S 1.5m (5ft). **'Blue Peter'** has lavender-blue, frilled flowers in late spring and early summer;

Rhododendron charitopes

Rhododendron luteum

Rhododendron 'Bruce Brechtbill'

Rhododendron 'Cary Ann'

Rhododendron 'Dopey'

Rhododendron 'Exbury White'

Rhododendron 'Persil'

sun-tolerant. H and S 3m (10ft). **'Bruce Brechtbill'** has a dense habit and pale pink flowers in late spring and early summer. H 2m (6ft), S 2.5m (8ft). **Carita Group** rhododendrons have trusses of pale lemon-yellow flowers in mid-spring; they are best with some shelter. H and S 2.5m (8ft). **'Cary Ann'**, which is good for small gardens, has coral pink flowers in late spring to early summer. H and S 1.5m (5ft). The deciduous **'Cecile'** has salmon pink flowers over a long period in late spring. H and S 2m (6ft). **'Chanticleer'** has spectacular maroon-purple flowers in late spring and early summer. H and S 1.5m (5ft). The old deciduous cultivar **'Corneille'** has double, creamy-pink flowers in early summer. H and S 1.5–2.5m (5–8ft). **'Curlew'** has large, pale yellow flowers in mid-spring; it does best in a cool spot. H and S 60cm (2ft). **'Cynthia'**, an old, sun-tolerant cultivar, bears huge trusses of rich crimson pink flowers in late spring. H and S 6m (20ft). The deciduous **'Daviesii'** has scented cream flowers in late spring to early summer and good autumn leaf

colour. H and S 1.5m (5ft). The compact and upright **'Dopey'** (Yakushimanum hybrid) bears rounded trusses of satiny orange-red flowers in late spring. H and S 2m (6ft). The deciduous **'Exbury White'** has large white flowers with yellow eyes in late spring and early summer and good autumn leaf colour; it makes an elegant specimen. H and S 2m (6ft). **'Fastuosum Flore Pleno'** has deep mauve flowers in late spring and early summer. H and S 4m (13ft). The free-flowering **'Golden Torch'** has pale yellow flowers fading to cream in late spring and early summer. H and S 1.5m (5ft). **'Grace Seabrook'** is a robust and vigorous form bearing conical trusses of deep pink flowers in early to mid-spring. H and S 2m (6ft). The dwarf and compact **'Hatsugiri'** bears masses of funnel-shaped, glowing crimson flowers in spring. H and S 60cm (2ft). **'Hinomayo'** has clear pink flowers in mid-spring and early summer. H and S 60cm (2ft). The deciduous **'Homebush'** has trusses of rose pink flowers in late spring. H and S 1.5m (5ft). **'Hydon Dawn'** has globular trusses of pale pink

flowers in mid-spring and early summer. H and S 1.5m (5ft). **'Hydon Hunter'** has deep pink flowers spotted with orange in mid-spring and early summer; sun-tolerant. H and S 1.5m (5ft). The robust, vigorous and sun-tolerant **'Loder's White'** gives a sumptuous display of fragrant white flowers in midsummer. H and S 3m (10ft). **'May Day'** has funnel-shaped, glowing red flowers in late spring; sun-tolerant. H and S 1.5m (5ft). **'Mrs Charles E. Pearson'** has pale mauve-pink flowers spotted with brown in late spring and early summer. H and S 2m (6ft). **'Naomi'**, which has lilac-mauve flowers in mid-spring, is the parent of **'Naomi Exbury'** (yellow-tinted flowers) and **'Naomi Pink Beauty'** (deep satin pink). H and S 5m (16ft). The deciduous **'Narcissiflorum'** has fragrant soft-yellow flowers in late spring and early summer. H and S 2.5m (8ft). **'Palestrina'**, which has pure white flowers in late spring, is an excellent choice for a small garden. H and S 1.2m (4ft). **'Penheale Blue'** has star-like, glowing deep violet flowers in early spring; sun-tolerant. H

and S 1.2m (4ft). The compact and hardy **'Percy Wiseman'** has peach-pink flowers fading to white in late spring and early summer. H and S 2.5m (8ft). The deciduous **'Persil'** has glistening white flowers with golden-orange central blotches. H and S 2m (6ft). **'Pink Pearl'** has huge trusses of soft pink flowers in mid- to late spring; sun-tolerant. H and S 4m (13ft). **'Polar Bear'** produces headily scented, lily-like, white flowers in mid- to late summer, produced freely only once the plant is mature. H and S 5m (16ft). **'Sappho'** has funnel-shaped, white flowers liberally sprinkled on the inside with dark purple-maroon in early summer. H and S 3m (10ft). The deciduous **'Strawberry Ice'** has strawberry pink flowers in mid- to late spring. H and S 2m (6ft). **'Vuyk's Rosy Red'**, which has deep rose-pink flowers in mid-spring, is excellent for a sunny rock garden. H 75cm (30in), S 1.2m (4ft). **'Wombat'**, which has small pink flowers in profusion in early summer, makes excellent groundcover, even in sun. H 25cm (10in), S 1.2m (4ft).

Rhododendron 'Curlew'

Rhododendron 'Fastuosum Flore Pleno'

Rhododendron 'Narcissiflorum'

Rhododendron 'Strawberry Ice'

Rosmarinus officinalis

ROSMARINUS
Rosemary

The evergreen, aromatic rosemary is an essential element of any herb garden, but prostrate forms make good groundcover and also work well when planted at the tops of walls. There are also some suitable for hedging, and all can be clipped to shape. Rosemaries are not long-lived but are easily raised from cuttings.
Cultivation Rosemary does best in free-draining, light soil in full sun. Trim hedges after flowering.

R. officinalis
To all intents and purposes this is the only species widely cultivated. It has dark green, narrow leaves and mauve-blue flowers in summer. H and S to 1.5m (5ft). Borderline hardy/Z 7–9. There is a huge range of cultivars. **'Lady in White'** has white flowers. H and S 1m (3ft). **'Miss Jessop's Upright'** (syn.

'Fastigiatus') is an upright form with light purplish-blue flowers. H 2m (6ft), S 60cm (2ft). Plants in the **Prostratus Group** are spreading, and less hardy than the straight species. H 60cm (2ft), S 1m (3ft). **'Sissinghurst Blue'** is upright with deep blue flowers and one of the best for culinary purposes. H 1.2m (4ft), S 1m (3ft).

RUBUS
Bramble

In addition to a huge range of soft fruits (raspberries, blackberries and a number of hybrids), this genus also includes a few ornamental plants.
Cultivation Grow in well-drained, fertile soil in sun or partial shade.

R. 'Benenden'
(syn. *R. tridel* 'Benenden')
This beautiful deciduous hybrid has masses of large, saucer-shaped, white flowers in late spring to early summer. H and S 2m (6ft). Hardy/Z 5–9.

R. cockburnianus
Glistening white stems make this one of the finest of deciduous winter plants, an effect improved by annual hard pruning in spring. H 2m (6ft), S 1.2m (4ft). Hardy/Z 5–9.

R. odoratus
Flowering raspberry
An erect, vigorous deciduous species with fragrant, pinkish-purple flowers in summer followed by orange-red fruits. H and S 2m (6ft). Hardy/Z 4–9.

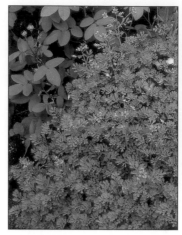

Ruta graveolens

R. thibetanus
This semi-erect species has small, purplish-red summer flowers and furry leaves, but it is grown principally for the winter interest of its stems, which are covered in a whitish bloom. Cut back hard annually for the best display. H and S to 2.4m (8ft), less with regular pruning. Hardy/Z 7–9.

RUTA
Rue

These subshrubs have aromatic, glaucous blue leaves. Only the species described is widely grown. Contact with the plant can cause allergic reactions in some people.
Cultivation Grow in well-drained soil in a sunny site. Clip plants in summer for a fresh crop of leaves.

R. graveolens
Common rue
This evergreen species has bluish-green, much divided leaves. Yellowish flowers appear in

Salvia officinalis Purpurascens Group

summer. H 1m (3ft), S 75cm (30in). Hardy/Z 5–9. The form generally found in gardens is **'Jackman's Blue'**, which has leaves of a more pronounced bluish-grey and is more compact. H and S 30cm (12in).

SALVIA
Sage

This large genus contains annuals and perennials as well as a number of shrubby plants, which are the familiar sages, widely used as a culinary herb. They are also good enough to use in borders, with roses or in a mixed planting.
Cultivation Grow in any well-drained soil in full sun.

S. officinalis
Common sage
The species has dull pewter-green leaves and blue and purple flowers. H 60cm (2ft), S 1m (3ft). Hardy/Z 6–9. Attractive selections include **'Icterina'**, which

Rubus odoratus

Rubus thibetanus

Salvia officinalis 'Icterina'

Santolina chamaecyparis

Skimmia japonica 'Tansley Gem'

has leaves marked with yellow and gold; **Purpurascens Group**, which has soft purple leaves; and 'Tricolor', with leaves marked with pink, cream and purple.

SANTOLINA
Curry plant

The species described is a useful evergreen, which can be used in the rock garden, as dwarf hedging or in combination with other plants, to which it offers a good foil. It is ideal for filling gaps in a border.
Cultivation Grow santolinas in any well-drained soil in full sun.

S. chamaecyparis
(syn. S. incana)
Cotton lavender
This is the best-known species, a mound-forming shrub with finely dissected silvery leaves. It has lemon-yellow flowers in mid-summer, but is principally valued as a foliage plant. Clip over in

spring to neaten, if necessary, but old, straggly plants are best replaced. H and S 60cm (2ft). Borderline hardy/Z 6–9.

SARCOCOCCA
Christmas box, sweet box

These choice plants for the winter garden have small but highly scented flowers among the shiny evergreen leaves. Use them with snowdrops, *Arum italicum* subsp. *italicum* 'Marmoratun' and early hellebores. They make excellent groundcover under deciduous trees, and flowering stems can be cut for use in winter flower arrangements.
Cultivation Grow in any fertile, well-drained soil in sun or light shade. They tolerate deeper shade.

S. confusa
This is an excellent dwarf shrub, which is useful as groundcover if planted en masse. Very fragrant, creamy white flowers are produced in midwinter. H and S 1m (3ft). Hardy/Z 6–9.

S. hookeriana var. dignya
This naturally occurring form has deliciously scented white flowers with pink stamens in winter. H and S 1.2m (4ft). Hardy/Z 6–9.

SKIMMIA

This small genus includes several attractive shrubs, which bear scented flowers in spring and (on female plants) crops of red berries in autumn, a fine contrast to the handsome, evergreen leaves. They are excellent in shrub or mixed borders and also work well in

containers. Young specimens of the male *S. japonica* 'Rubella' can be used in winter windowboxes.
Cultivation Most soils in sun or shade are suitable, but some yellowing of the older leaves can occur in alkaline conditions because of magnesium deficiency.

S. × confusa 'Kew Green'
This male selection has fragrant, cream flowers in early spring among the narrow leaves. H and S to 1m (3ft). Hardy/Z 7.

S. japonica
This, the most widely grown species, has distinctive narrow, glossy foliage and panicles of cream buds throughout winter that open to fragrant creamy-white flowers in spring. H and S to 1.2m (4ft). Hardy/Z 7–9. 'Rubella' is a male form with clusters of red buds through winter that open to dingy white flowers in early spring. 'Tansley

Gem' is a female form, with a good crop of red berries. **'Wakehurst White'** (syn. 'Fructo-alba'), a female form, has creamy-white berries. H 50cm (20in), S 1m (3ft).

SPIRAEA

These easy deciduous shrubs are cultivated for their flowers and leaves. Most stay reasonably compact and are suitable for small gardens. For maximum impact plant in groups of three or more, but solo plants work well with a wide range of perennials in mixed borders.
Cultivation These shrubs are easy to grow in most soils, in sun or light shade.

S. japonica
The species is usually grown in one of the following forms, both of which are hardy/Z 4–9. H and S 1m (3ft). **'Anthony Waterer'** is a charming selection, with dark leaves and rich pink flowers from mid- to late summer. **'Goldflame'** has yellowish-green leaves, which are sometimes marked with red. The dull pink summer flowers make a strange combination, but pleasing when positioned next to a purple-leaved plant.

S. nipponica 'Snowmound'
This outstanding form is smothered in creamy-white flowers in late spring or early summer. The plant tolerates hard pruning and can be kept smaller than the dimensions indicated. H and S 2m (6ft). Hardy/Z 4–9.

Sarcococca confusa

Skimmia japonica 'Rubella'

Spiraea japonica 'Goldflame'

Syringa emodi

Syringa vulgaris 'Firmament'

Viburnum × bodnantense 'Dawn'

SYRINGA
Lilac

Late spring can almost be defined as 'lilac time': a season easily recognized by that unmistakable scent in the air. Unfortunately, most of the hybrids, which are so impressive in flower, end up as unwieldy, rangy shrubs of small interest during the rest of the year. If you have the space, grow them in stands in a rough part of the garden. In a restricted area, choose from the species, many of which are more compact, with daintier flowers.
Cultivation Lilacs will grow in any well-drained soil and are especially useful on chalk (alkaline soil). They prefer sun but tolerate light shade. They can be pruned back hard.

S. emodi
Himalayan lilac
This vigorous species with dark green oval leaves has very pale flowers in late spring to early summer. H 5m (15ft), S 4m (13ft). Hardy/Z 7–8.

S. meyeri var. spontanea 'Palibin' (syn. S. palibiana, S. patula of gardens)
A most rewarding small lilac, this has very fragrant, pale lilac-coloured flowers, produced freely in late spring to early summer. H and S 1.5m (5ft). Hardy/Z 4–7.

S. vulgaris
Common lilac
This is the parent of a huge range of garden forms, all heavily scented, and including **'Andenken an Ludwig Späth'**, which has wine red flowers; **'Charles Joly'**, which has double, purplish-red flowers; 'Congo', with rich pink flowers opening from darker buds; **'Firmament'**, which has pink buds opening to lilac-coloured flowers; **'Madame Lemoine'**, with double, white flowers; and **'Primrose'**, the closest to yellow, with rich cream-coloured buds opening to creamy-white flowers. H and S 3.5m (12ft). Hardy/Z 3–9.

TEUCRIUM
Germander

These evergreen shrubs or subshrubs have aromatic foliage. Germanders are often included in herb gardens, but are also effective as rock garden plants or in mixed borders.
Cultivation Grow in free-draining, light soil in full sun. Winter protection may be necessary in cold areas. Prune lightly in spring to keep plants in shape.

T. chamaedrys
This species has glossy, holly-like leaves and purple flowers in summer. H and S 30cm (12in). Borderline hardy/Z 5.

T. fruticans
This elegant plant has pale blue summer flowers, making a cool complement to the pewter-green leaves, which are covered in a soft silvery down. It looks beautiful billowing out at the front of a border. H 1.2m (4ft), S 4m (13ft). Borderline hardy/Z 7–10. 'Azureum' is even more desirable, with darker blue flowers.

VIBURNUM

This large and important genus consists of both evergreen and deciduous shrubs that, between them, provide interest throughout the year. Some are grown for their flowers (winter or spring), others for their berries, and some for both. They are essential plants. Native species are excellent in wild gardens, providing food for birds in winter. Others are good in winter gardens or mixed borders. A select few make good specimens. *V. tinus* can be trained as a standard.
Cultivation Grow viburnums in any reasonably fertile, well-drained soil in sun or light shade.

V. × bodnantense 'Dawn'
One of the stars of the winter garden, this upright, deciduous, vase-shaped shrub has richly scented, pink flowers opening in mild spells from autumn to spring. H 2m (6ft), S 1.2m (4ft). Hardy/Z 7–9.

V. carlesii
This deciduous species from Japan and Korea is almost unmatched for the scent of its white spring flowers, pink in bud and carried in rounded clusters.

Teucrium fruticans

Viburnum carlesii 'Diana'

Viburnum plicatum 'Mariesii'

Viburnum tinus 'Eve Price'

Weigela 'Candida'

YUCCA

These dramatic, architectural evergreens add a touch of the exotic to any garden. They are often sold as houseplants, but the species described here are hardy enough to survive (and flower) outdoors. In their native habitat (North American desert) yuccas become trees. In gardens they are excellent when planted as focal points or sited at the corner of a border, and they make splendid permanent plantings for large containers.
Cultivation Grow in any well-drained soil in full sun.

H and S 1.5m (5ft). Hardy/Z 6–9. **'Diana'** has purplish-pink flowers that fade to white.

V. plicatum
Japanese snowball bush
A grand deciduous shrub with an architectural, tiered habit that makes a breathtaking specimen when in flower. Hardy/Z 5–8. **'Mariesii'** (syn. *V. mariesii*) is one of the most distinctive selections, with tabulated branches carrying flattened lacecap heads of white flowers in late spring. H 3m (10ft), S 4m (13ft). *V. plicatum* **f. tomentosum** produces blue-black berries in autumn as the leaves redden. H 3m (10ft), S 4m (13ft).

V. tinus
Laurustinus
An important winter shrub, this evergreen has a rounded habit and white flowers in late winter or early spring. Bluish-black berries follow the flowers. H and S 3m

(10ft). Hardy/Z 7–9. The flowers of **'Eve Price'** open from rich eye-catching pink buds.

VINCA
Periwinkle
These valuable trailing evergreen subshrubs make excellent ground-cover, particularly in the dry soil under trees. They are also good in containers. A large pot planted solely with *V. major* 'Variegata' will provide material for flower arranging throughout the year.
Cultivation Grow in any well-drained soil in sun or shade. Mulching in dry soils will accelerate growth. Stems can root wherever they touch the ground.

V. major
The species is not worth growing, but it has several worthy cultivars, the best of which is probably **'Variegata'** (syn. 'Elegantissima'), which has leaves with pale yellow margins. The periwinkle-blue flowers are produced mainly in early summer but never in sufficient quantities to smother the plant. H 20cm (8in), S indefinite. Hardy/Z 7–9.

V. minor
This species, which has small leaves, is more worthwhile than *V. major* and has many more cultivars, including **'Aureovariegata'**, which has leaves edged with creamy yellow and blue summer flowers; **'Burgundy'**, which has wine-purple flowers; and **'Gertrude Jekyll'**, which has white flowers. H 15cm (6in), S indefinite. Hardy/Z 4–8.

WEIGELA
The genus contains 12 species of deciduous shrubs with interesting leaves and trumpet-shaped flowers in early summer. They work well in a shrub border or a mixed planting, where, after flowering, they make effective backdrops to later-flowering perennials, annuals and bulbs.
Cultivation They do well in most soils, in sun or light shade.

W. 'Candida'
This is an unusual garden form with pure white flowers. H and S 1.5m (5ft). Hardy/Z 5–9.

W. florida
This is one of the less-appealing species in its wild form, but some of the selections are of great value. The following are hardy/Z 5–9. **'Aureovariegata'** is one of the prettiest. The leaves are edged with white in spring, making a fine combination with the pink flowers. The variegation deepens to yellow later on. H and S 1.2m (4ft). **'Foliis Purpureis'**, which needs careful siting, has rich purple leaves and deep pink flowers. H and S 1m (3ft).

W. 'Looymansii Aurea'
This hybrid has yellowish-green leaves and pink flowers. It needs shelter from strong, hot sun. H and S 1.5m (5ft). Hardy/Z 5–9.

W. middendorffiana
This superior species has sulphur-yellow flowers marked with dark orange in mid- to late spring. H and S 1.5m (5ft). Hardy/Z 5–9.

Y. filamentosa
Adam's needle
The species forms a rosette of stiff, upright, lance-shaped leaves. The distinguishing feature is the curly threads on the edges of the leaves. Established plants produce upright spikes, to 2m (6ft) tall, of white, tulip-shaped flowers in late summer to autumn, but not necessarily every year. H and S 1m (3ft). Hardy/Z 5–10. The leaves of **'Bright Edge'** have broad yellow edges.

Y. gloriosa
Spanish dagger
This plant has a thick stem topped by a rosette of hard, spiny, upright blue-green to dark-green leaves, through the middle of which the flowering spikes emerge in late summer (the flowers are similar to those of *Y. filamentosa*). Mature plants are multi-stemmed. H and S 2m (6ft) or more. Hardy/Z 7–10.

Vinca minor 'Aureovariegata'

Yucca filamentosa

Roses

As a garden plant, the rose is unrivalled. Few other plants have attracted so much attention from breeders and down the ages they have epitomized the summer garden. From the uncomplicated charm of the species to the sophistication of the hybrid teas, there is a rose for virtually every purpose, as hedging, to give weight and substance to borders, as specimens or to provide cut flowers. The climbers provide magnificent cover for walls and pergolas, while nowadays the range has been extended to include tough, compact, disease-resistant plants that are excellent as ground cover or for growing in containers.

Elegant hybrid tea roses are esssential plants for any cottage garden scheme, here combining well with phlox and other border perennials.

What is a rose?

Roses are a breed apart. No other plant genus has been so extensively hybridized to produce the wide range of plants that we enjoy in gardens today.

Roses are shrubs, mainly deciduous ones. In the wild, some make huge plants, colonizing vast areas and finding their way into trees, hooking themselves into the bark by means of their thorns.

Rose classification

The classification of roses represents an attempt to bring some order to a vast and diverse range of plants. However, in many cases, the distinctions are far from clear cut. Roses are generally classified as follows:

Wild roses

These comprise the species, their selections and certain hybrids. They usually have one flush of single flowers in early summer, often followed by decorative hips in autumn.

Old roses

● *Bourbon roses* are vigorous, and are usually repeat-flowering. They are often suitable for training as short climbers. *Portland roses* are similar, but repeat more reliably and generally make smaller plants.
● *Centifolia roses* (sometimes also called cabbage, Provence or Holland roses) make lax shrubs with large, many-petalled flowers that weigh down the arching canes. *Moss roses* are a closely allied group, distinguished by the characteristic mossy growth on their stems and calyces.
● *China roses* are dainty, repeat-flowering shrubs with small flowers and leaves. *Tea roses*, also repeat-flowering, are thin-stemmed with slender, pointed flower buds. Few are hardy enough to be grown outdoors in cold areas.

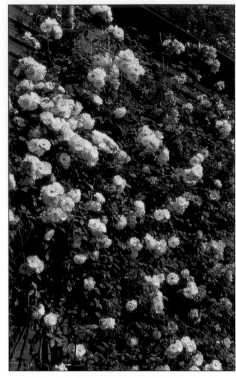

Correctly supported, many a climbing rose will reach the eaves of a house and be smothered in flowers in summer.

● *Damask roses* are lax, spreading shrubs, usually with fragrant flowers in clear colours. The leaves are typically greyish green and are downy underneath.

Flower shapes

Flat flowers are single (five petals) or semi-double (ten petals) and open flat.
Cupped flowers are single to fully double, with curving petals.
Rounded flowers have a rounded outline formed by overlapping petals.
Rosette flowers are low-centred and flat, with many short, crowded petals.
Quartered rosette flowers are similar to rosettes, but the petals are arranged in distinctive quarters.
Pointed and urn-shaped flowers, characteristic of Chinas, teas and hybrid teas, are high-centred and open from slender, elegant buds.
Pompon flowers are small and ball-like with many short petals, and are usually carried in clusters.

● *Gallica roses* are usually upright, compact shrubs with coarse leaves and flowers in shades of pink, rich crimson and purple. The group includes some striped roses.
● *Hybrid perpetuals* are vigorous and usually repeat-flowering. They tend to be leggy but this is a problem that can be overcome by pegging down the lax shoots.
● *Scotch roses* are dense shrubs with *R. pimpinellifolia* in their make-up.

Modern roses

● *Climbing roses* usually have long, stiff stems that make them suitable for training. The flowers, similar to those of hybrid teas and floribundas in appearance, are produced in one or – more usually – two flushes.
● *Floribunda* or *cluster-flowered roses* are repeat-flowering, with single to fully double flowers in clusters.
● *Ground-cover roses* have a lax, trailing habit, rather like miniature climbers. They typically have clusters of small flowers, produced over a long period.
● *Hybrid tea* or *large-flowered roses* are characterized by large, high-centred flowers carried singly (but sometimes in small clusters) that open from pointed buds. They are repeat-flowering. Some are of stiff, ungainly habit.
● *Miniature roses* are compact plants, usually under 30cm (12in) high, with sprays of tiny, usually scentless flowers. They are repeat-flowering.
● *Patio* or *dwarf cluster-flowered bush roses* are similar to floribundas but are much smaller, making them ideal container plants.
● *Polyanthas* are now more or less obsolete. Tough and repeat-flowering, with trusses of small flowers, they are the forebears of the modern floribundas.
● *Rambler roses* are large shrubs of exceptional vigour, with long flexible,

often trailing stems. Typically they flower early in the season on the previous season's wood.

● *Rugosa roses* are tough, hardy shrubs with characteristically wrinkled leaves and single to double flowers in succession throughout summer and autumn. Some have showy autumn hips.

● *Shrub roses* comprise a vast group of plants that do not fit into any of the above categories. They are usually larger than other modern roses and thus less suitable for bedding. Flowers can be single to double and can appear in one or two flushes. This group includes the so-called *English roses*, bred by David Austin, which combine the flower shape of the old roses with the repeat-flowering habit of modern roses.

Roses in the garden

Many people associate roses with bedding, and while it is true that many of the floribundas and hybrid teas are outstanding in a massed planting, the genus as a whole is much more versatile than that.

Many of the shrub roses are stylish plants that can be planted either as specimens or as elements of a mixed planting, combining happily with a range of other shrubs and perennials. The old roses earn their place in the garden largely on the merits of their sumptuous, usually deliciously scented flowers, as well as the romantic associations of their names – 'Cardinal de Richelieu', 'Duchesse de Montebello', 'Souvenir de la Malmaison', to mention just three.

A surprising number of roses are also excellent for hedging (though not providing an evergreen screen), thorny types making good barrier or boundary hedges. The rugosas are well suited for this purpose.

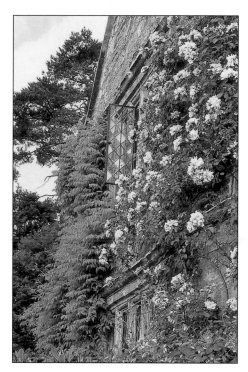

'Albertine' is an enduring favourite for its incomparable scent, trained here to allow the fragrance to waft through open windows.

The obvious way to grow the climbers and ramblers is by training them against a house wall, fence or over a pergola, but they can also be trained against trellis panels to screen one part of the garden from another. Shorter types can be grown over trellis obelisks or pillars to give height to a border. One of the most dramatic ways of growing climbers and ramblers is into the arms of a tree, but here you must make sure that the host is sturdy enough to bear the weight of the rose – some are vigorous plants that can swamp the tree. Among the most effective are those that bear a close resemblance to the species, such as 'Albéric Barbier' and 'Rambling Rector'.

Many of the more recent introductions make splendid ground cover, not just those defined as "groundcover roses". They are tough plants, handsome even when out of flower. Having been bred to be compact, to suit the modern garden, which tends to be smaller, they are also ideal plants for containers. Excellent health and length of flowering season only add to their merits.

Training the fragrant and long-flowering 'Dublin Bay' to climb up the wooden trellis is an effective and attractive way of screening one part of the garden from another.

'Agnes'

An upright, healthy rugosa of undoubted distinction, this bears double, scented, pale yellow flowers in summer, with only a few following in autumn. It combines the toughness of the rugosas with an old-rose look to the flowers. H 2m (6ft), S 1.2m (4ft). Hardy/Z 2–9.

R. × alba 'Alba Maxima'
(syn. R. × alba 'Maxima')

This alba rose dates from the 15th century, or even earlier, and is sometimes assumed to be the white rose of York. It is also a beauty, with untidy, double, very fragrant flowers that are tinged pink on opening in summer, then fade to creamy white. Red hips follow. It is also known as the great white rose, the Jacobite rose or the Cheshire rose. H 2.1m (7ft), S 1.5m (5ft). Hardy/Z 4–9.

R. × alba 'Alba Semiplena'
(syn. 'Semiplena')

An alba rose, this has been grown in gardens since the 16th century or before. It is a graceful shrub with clusters of semi-double, very fragrant, milky white flowers in summer. These open flat to display prominent golden stamens, with red hips making a second display in autumn. 'Alba Semiplena' is usually held to be the white rose of York, competing for that title with R. × alba 'Alba Maxima'. H 2.1m (7ft), S 1.5m (5ft). Hardy/Z 4–9.

'Alba Meidiland'
(syn. 'Meiflopan')

This is a groundcover rose, and unusually for a rose in this group, the pure white, fully double flowers are good for cutting. H 1m (3ft), S 1.2m (4ft). Hardy/Z 4–9.

'Albéric Barbier'

This vigorous rambling rose is a good choice for brightening up a shady wall or a dull tree. In early to midsummer, masses of double, rosette, creamy white, scented flowers cover the plant. To compensate for the lack of further flowers, the glossy leaves often hang on through the winter. H 5m (16ft), S 3m (10ft). Hardy/Z 4–9.

'Albertine'

A vigorous rambling rose, this has fully double, light pink flowers, which appear in a single flush in midsummer, opening from copper-tinted buds; they become untidy as they age. The rich, distinctive scent of this rose has assured its continuing popularity, despite its all too obvious drawbacks: its talon-like thorns and propensity to mildew. Thinning the growth after flowering to improve air circulation can help the latter problem. H 5m (16ft), S 4m (12ft). Hardy/Z 4–9.

'Alec's Red'
(syn. 'Cored')

This is a bushy hybrid tea with fully double, heavily scented, rich red flowers that open from pointed buds throughout summer and into autumn. A versatile rose, it is suitable for cutting, bedding and as a hedge, but blackspot can be a problem. H 1m (3ft), S 60cm (2ft). Hardy/Z 4–9.

'Alexander'
(syn. 'Harlex')

An upright hybrid tea, this has double, luminous red flowers opening from pointed buds from summer to autumn. The leaves are glossy dark green and show good resistance to disease. The flowers are produced on long stems, which means that this is a good rose for cutting as well as for planting as a tight hedge with little sideways spread. H to 2m (6ft), S 75cm (2ft 6in). Hardy/Z 4–9.

'Allgold'

A compact floribunda and an ideal bedding rose, this bears a succession of double, lightly scented, bright yellow flowers from summer to autumn. H 75cm (2ft 6in), S 50cm (20in). Hardy/Z 5–9.

'Aloha'

This climbing rose bears a succession of cupped, fully double, sweetly scented, light pink flowers from summer to autumn. The leaves are dark green, leathery and healthy. This is a rain-resistant variety, which is also good in a container. H 3m (10ft), S 2.5m (8ft). Hardy/Z 4–9.

Rosa 'Alec's Red'

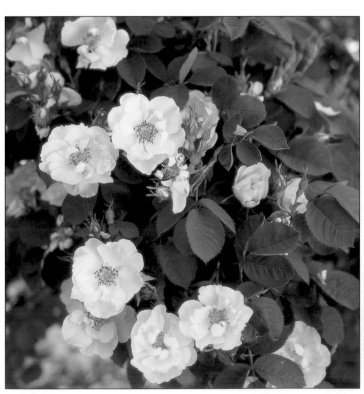

Rosa × *alba* 'Alba Semiplena'

Rosa 'Albertine'

Rosa 'Anna Ford'

Rosa 'Apricot Nectar'

Rosa 'Avon'

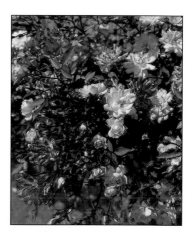

Rosa 'Baby Masquerade'

'Amber Queen'
(syn. 'Harroony', 'Prinz Eugen van Savoyen')

A neat-growing floribunda, this rose bears clusters of fully double, heavily scented, rich amber-yellow flowers, which open from rounded buds. Its compact habit makes it a good choice for bedding, hedges and containers. H and S 50cm (20in). Hardy/Z 4–9.

'Anna Ford'
(syn. 'Harpiccolo')

This is a dense, low-growing patio rose. The warm orange-red flowers, produced freely from summer to autumn, open flat from pointed buds to reveal yellow centres. One of the earliest of its type, this remains a popular bedding or container rose. H 45cm (18in), S 38cm (15in). Hardy/Z 4–9.

'Anne Harkness'
(syn. 'Harkaramel')

An upright, branching floribunda, this bears large clusters of pointed, urn-shaped, double, soft buff-yellow flowers from late summer to autumn. Spectacular when in full flower, This is a disease-resistant rose that is suitable for bedding, hedging and cutting. H 1.2m (4ft), S 60cm (2ft). Hardy/Z 4–9.

'Apricot Nectar'

This bushy floribunda bears tight clusters of large, fully double, sweetly scented, pinkish-buff-apricot flowers from summer to autumn. It is a good hedging rose, but it can be susceptible to mildew from midsummer. H 80cm (32in), S 65cm (26in). Hardy/Z 4–9.

'Arthur Bell'

An upright, branching floribunda, this bears clusters of semi-double to double, bright yellow flowers that pale as they age. The scent is outstanding for a rose of this type. This is a versatile rose, suitable for bedding, hedging and containers; the autumn flowering is especially good, making it a good companion for annuals and late-flowering perennials and bulbs. H to 1m (3ft), S 60cm (2ft). Hardy/Z 4–9.

'Avon'
(syn. 'Fairy Lights', 'Poulmulti', 'Sunnyside')

From summer to autumn this compact, spreading groundcover rose bears clusters of small, semi-double, fragrant, pinkish-white flowers, which open flat to reveal golden stamens. Besides its obvious uses for massed planting and as a low hedge, this rose can also be grown successfully in containers. H 30cm (1ft), S 1m (3ft). Hardy/Z 4–9.

'Baby Masquerade'
(syn. 'Baby Carnival', 'Tanba', 'Tanbakede')

Many people believe that this miniature rose is more attractive than its full-sized equivalent. From summer to autumn it carries clusters of tiny, double, rosette-shaped flowers, which open yellow and fade to pink then to deeper red, so that all the colours are present at any one time. The rose is probably seen at its best when grown as a miniature standard. H and S 40cm (16in). Hardy/Z 4–9.

Rosa 'Anne Harkness'

Rosa 'Arthur Bell'

'Belle de Crécy'

The quartered-rosette, sweetly scented flowers of this gallica rose are produced in abundance in midsummer. They open rich purple-pink then fade to a greyish pale pink. It has a laxer habit than most other gallicas and its arching stems may require some support; alternatively, simply allow them to trail into neighbouring shrubs. It does not flower as well in poor, light soil. H 1.2m (4ft), S 1m (3ft). Hardy/Z 5.

'Blairii Number Two'

In midsummer, this strangely named bourbon, first raised in 1845, carries an abundance of large, cupped, fully double, sweetly scented flowers, which are pale silvery pink with deeper pink centres. However, unlike some other bourbon roses, it produces only a few further blooms in autumn, if any. Untrained, it will grow into an arching shrub about 2.1m (7ft) high and across. Its vigour and flexible canes make it suitable for growing as a pyramid, on a pergola or against a wall, where it can reach 5m (16ft). H 4m (12ft), S 2m (6ft). Hardy/Z 4–9.

'Blue Moon'
(syn. 'Blue Monday', 'Mainzer Fastnacht', 'Sissi', 'Tannacht')

An intriguing hybrid tea, this is not one of the best overall, but is worth growing for the individual

Rosa 'Belle de Crécy'

flowers. Borne in summer and autumn, they are not blue, as the name implies, but silvery lilac, a colour associated with the old roses. However, the flower form is modern: high-centred and shapely. It is also one of the most sweetly scented of modern roses. 'Blue Moon' needs careful placing in the garden because of its curious colouring; it is perhaps best grown in isolation under glass. H 1m (3ft), S 60cm (2ft). Hardy/Z 4–9. The climbing form is also worth considering, but it needs good cultivation and a site where the flowers will not be bleached by too much sun.

'Bobbie James'

One of the most vigorous of ramblers, this rose looks like its wild antecedents. In summer it is covered with clusters of small, white, semi-double flowers that are also sweetly scented. It is a

Rosa 'Blue Moon'

good choice for growing into a large tree, and although it would be just as dramatic over a large pergola, its vigour could cause problems. H 10m (33ft), S 6m (20ft). Hardy/Z 5–9.

'Buff Beauty'

This is an excellent modern shrub rose or hybrid musk. The name refers to the colour of the cupped, fully double, sweetly scented flowers, which are pale buff-apricot, fading to creamy white in hot sun. They are carried in clusters in two distinct flushes, the autumn flowering being less profuse than the summer. 'Buff Beauty' can be used for hedging but needs the support of horizontal wires, since the canes are often bent down low by the weight of the flowers. Mildew may be a problem in late summer but need not deter you from growing this rose. H and S 1.5m (5ft). Hardy/Z 6–9.

'Cardinal de Richelieu'

This grandly named gallica – and one of the most sumptuous – was produced in 1840. It makes a

Rosa 'Buff Beauty'

compact bush and will exceed its usual size if the flexible stems are supported. The clusters of scented, dark maroon flowers appear in midsummer; the petals are velvety in texture and reflex as the flowers age to form a ball shape. The stems are well-covered with healthy, dark green leaves. This rose needs fertile, well-drained soil and regular thinning of the old wood to give of its best. H 1m (3ft), S 1.2m (4ft). Hardy/Z 4–9.

'Cécile Brünner'

Sometimes identified as the sweetheart rose or Maltese rose, this is a dainty, airy cultivar, which is classified as either a China rose or a polyantha. It flowers over a long period from early summer to mid-autumn, when clusters of elegant, pointed buds open to urn-shaped, delicately scented, pale pink flowers, which become more untidy as as they age. H and S 1m (3ft). Hardy/Z 5–9. A climbing form is available, which is less restrained and easily reaches 6m (20ft) in all

Rosa 'Blairii Number Two'

Rosa 'Cardinal de Richelieu'

Rosa 'Cécile Brünner'

Rosa 'Céleste'

Rosa 'Charles de Mills'

Rosa 'Chinatown'

Rosa 'Complicata'

directions; it is ideal for growing into a tree. The white-flowered bush form 'White Cécile Brünner' is rare.

'Céleste'
(syn. *R.* × *alba* 'Celestial')
The date of the introduction of this Alba rose is unrecorded, but it is certainly a very old cultivar, perhaps dating back to ancient times. The semi-double, sweetly scented, shell-pink flowers, with petals that seem almost transparent, are borne in summer and open flat to reveal prominent golden stamens. Red hips succeed them in autumn. H and S 2m (6ft). Hardy/Z 4–9.

R. × *centifolia* 'Cristata'
(syn. 'Chapeau de Napoléon', 'Crested Moss')
This distinguished centifolia rose is sometimes included among the moss roses, though incorrectly, since only the calyces and not the stems are mossed. It makes a graceful, slender-stemmed shrub. In summer it produces drooping, cupped, fully double, richly scented, deep silvery-pink flowers that open flat and are sometimes quartered. The alternative name, 'Chapeau de Napoléon' (Napoleon's hat), refers to the unopened buds, which look like a tricorn hat. H 1.5m (5ft), S 1.2m (4ft). Hardy/Z 4–9.

'Charles de Mills'
(syn. 'Bizarre Triomphant')
This is a gallica rose of unknown origin. The fully double, quartered-rosette, moderately scented, rich crimson flowers, which appear in summer, fade with grey and purple tones as they mature. The

abundant foliage is matt dark green. It makes a compact shrub, but the slender stems may need staking to support the large flowers as they open. H 1.2m (4ft), S 1m (3ft). Hardy/Z 4–9.

'Chinatown'
(syn. 'Ville de Chine')
A floribunda rose, this is probably unmatched for size and overall vigour; indeed, it is sometimes justifiably classified as a shrub rose. The fragrant clusters of fully double, bright golden-yellow flowers are freely produced throughout summer and into autumn among glossy dark green leaves. It is ideal grown at the back of a border as a backdrop for smaller plants, as a hedge or as a specimen plant. H 1.5m (5ft), S 1m (3ft). Hardy/Z 5–9.

'City of London'
(syn. 'Harukfore')
A spreading floribunda, this shows some of the characteristics of one of its parents, 'New Dawn', notably its continuity (it flowers from summer to autumn), its scent and its appealing soft pink colour. More versatile than some other members of this group, if it is pruned fairly hard it can be used for bedding, but with minimum pruning it can also be treated as a specimen or trained as a short climber. It also associates well with old roses. H to 2m (6ft), S to 1.2m (4ft). Hardy/Z 4–9.

'Compassion'
From summer to autumn this climbing rose produces shapely, rounded, fully double, sweetly scented, warm apricot-pink flowers. It is an excellent choice

for a pillar or a sturdy garden fruit tree. H 3m (10ft), S 2.5m (8ft). Hardy/Z 4–9.

'Complicata'
(syn. *R. gallica* 'Complicata')
Although this is a gallica rose, it has few of the characteristics normally associated with the group and is of uncertain origin, its pedigree possibly including the vigorous species *R. canina*. Its name also implies double flowers; in fact, they are single but are produced in abundance all along the arching canes in summer. Bright porcelain pink, they are sweetly scented and open wide to reveal white centres and golden stamens. Unusually for a gallica, the matt greyish-green leaves are rather pointed. 'Complicata' tolerates light, sandy soils and can be used as a rambler among trees and shrubs in a wild garden

or it can be trained on a pillar; H and S 2.5m (8ft) if supported, probably more as a climber. Hardy/Z 4–9.

'Constance Spry'
(syn. 'Autance')
This was one of the first of David Austin's 'English' roses, and it is still one of the best, although it flowers once only, in midsummer. The large, cupped, fully double, peony-like flowers of this shrub rose are rich pink and heavily scented. It can also be grown as a climber on a pillar or against a wall, where it will tolerate some shade. Even as a shrub it is best given some support or pruned hard to keep it compact. Untrained, it will grow into a large, lax shrub. H and S to 2m (6ft), though the spread can sometimes exceed the height. Hardy/Z 4–9.

Rosa 'Constance Spry'

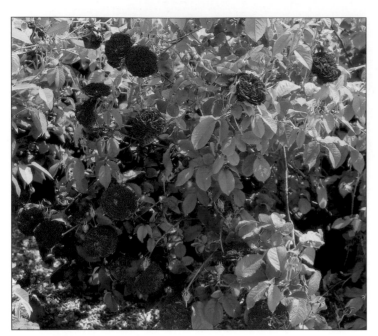

Rosa 'Duc de Guiche'

'Danse du Feu'

A stiffly branched climbing rose that, as far as the flower colour – luminous red – is concerned has not been surpassed, and it has retained its place in catalogues in spite of its tendency towards blackspot. The rounded, double flowers appear from summer to autumn, but the scent is not strong. H and S 2.5m (8ft). Hardy/Z 4–9.

'Desprez à Fleurs Jaunes'
(syn. 'Jaune Desprez')

This exquisite, vigorous climbing rose, introduced in 1830, should be planted more widely. The double flowers, borne throughout summer, are an unusual creamy buff-yellow and are also sweetly scented. The lax, flexible canes make this an excellent choice for training against a wall, preferably a sunny one. H and S 5m (16ft). Hardy/Z 6–9.

'Du Maître d'Ecole'

The date of origin of this gallica rose is in dispute, but some authorities say it was introduced in 1840. It makes a compact plant, and in summer the weight of blossom makes the stems arch over. The fragrant, fully double, quartered-rosette, carmine-pink flowers open flat and fade to lilac-pink and grey. H and S 1m (3ft). Hardy/Z 4–9.

'Dublin Bay'
(syn. 'Macdub')

A valuable red climber, this has almost fluorescent flowers. Double and lightly scented, they are carried in clusters from summer to autumn among glossy, healthy leaves. It is a good choice if space is limited, in a border on a tripod, for instance, since the growth tends to be upright. H and S 2.2m (7ft). Hardy/Z 4–9.

'Duc de Guiche'

The fully double, highly scented flowers of this outstanding gallica change colour as they age. Rich crimson initially, they develop purple veining before finally flushing purple. H and S 1.2m (4ft). Hardy/Z 4–8.

'Duchesse de Montebello'

This spreading gallica was bred before 1829. The open-cupped, fully double, sweetly fragrant flowers are soft blush pink. The foliage is light green. It is one of the daintiest and neatest growing of the gallicas. H and S 1.2m (4ft). Hardy/Z 4–8.

'Elina'
(syn. 'Dicjana', 'Peaudouce')

A bushy hybrid tea, this has fully double, lightly scented, creamy white flowers, which open to reveal lemon-yellow flushed centres. The flowering season lasts from summer to autumn. A versatile rose and easy to grow, it is generally healthy and can be used for bedding and cutting. H 1m (3ft), S 75cm (2ft 6in). Hardy/Z 4–9.

'Escapade'
(syn. 'Harpade')

This elegant floribunda has a freely branching habit, and it is also something of a novelty in being an outstanding garden plant. The semi-double, sweetly scented flowers, which are borne in clusters throughout summer into autumn, are of unusual coloration: they are soft lilac-pink, opening flat to reveal white centres and golden stamens. Unlike some other roses, it blends easily with other plants; it occasionally produces pure white flowers within the cluster, which adds to its charm. Shiny, light green foliage is borne in abundance. H to 1.2m (4ft), S 60cm (2ft). Hardy/Z 4–9.

Rosa 'Fantin-Latour'

'Fantin-Latour'

A centifolia rose, this makes a handsome, vase-shaped shrub, which is ideal as a specimen. The many-petalled, cup-shaped flowers are delicately scented. They are blush-pink and are borne in profusion over a long period in summer, their petals reflexing to reveal a green button eye. 'Fantin-Latour' was named in honour of the French painter, admired for his flower pieces, some of which include roses. Spraying against mildew may be necessary in summer. H and S to 2.2m (7ft). Hardy/Z 4–9.

'Félicité Parmentier'

This compact Alba rose bears a single crop of cup-shaped, highly scented, quartered, pale blush-pink flowers, which open from primrose yellow buds in midsummer. The densely packed petals fade to almost white in hot sun and reflex to form a ball

Rosa 'Du Maître d'Ecole'

Rosa 'Duchesse de Montebello'

Rosa 'Escapade'

Rosa 'Félicité Parmentier'

shape. The leaves are healthy and grey-green. One of the daintiest of its type, this is suitable for the smallest garden. H and S 1.2m (4ft). Hardy/Z 4–9.

'Fred Loads'

A strongly upright floribunda, this rose is ideal for the back of a border. Its generous clusters of semi-double, pleasantly scented, soft orange-vermilion flowers are produced from summer to autumn, making it invaluable for a long display in a mixed planting. Hard pruning can keep it in bounds, or it can be used for hedging. The flowers last well in water. H 2m (6ft), S 1m (3ft). Hardy/Z 5–9.

'Fru Dagmar Hastrup' (syn. 'Frau Dagmar Hartopp')

This compact, spreading rugosa rose bears single, pale pink summer flowers, which open almost flat to reveal prominent golden stamens; large, tomato-red hips develop in autumn as a second, sparser flush appears. This makes an excellent low hedge and can also be used for ground cover, possibly in light woodland. H 1m (3ft), S 1.2m (4ft). Hardy/Z 3–9.

'Frühlingsgold'

A Scotch hybrid rose, sometimes classified as a modern shrub rose, this makes a vigorous shrub, each arching cane reaching up to 2.2m (7ft) in length. The large, cupped, semi-double, fragrant, primrose-yellow flowers cover the stems in late spring to early summer, opening flat from long, pointed buds to display golden stamens. Its toughness and thorniness suggest that it might be used as a barrier plant at the end of the garden rather than in the border. H 2.5m (8ft), S 2.2m (7ft). Hardy/Z 4–8.

R. gallica var. *officinalis* (syn. *R. officinalis*)

This is a bushy gallica rose, which has been recorded in gardens since the 13th century. In summer it produces an abundance of large, semi-double, sweetly fragrant, light crimson flowers, which open flat and reveal golden stamens. Rich in historical association both as the red rose of Lancaster and the medieval apothecary's rose, this remains a superb garden plant in its own right. H and S 1.2m (4ft). Hardy/Z 5–9.

Rosa 'Graham Thomas'

R. gallica 'Versicolor'

An eye-catching gallica rose, this old rose was first recorded in the 16th century but is probably much older. The lightly scented flowers, produced in midsummer, are semi-double, opening flat to reveal golden stamens. The pale pink petals are dramatically splashed and striped with red and crimson. The common name, Rosa Mundi, reputedly commemorates Fair Rosamund, the mistress of Henry II of England. H and S 1.2m (4ft). Hardy/Z 5–9.

'Gentle Touch' (syn. 'Diclulu')

Neat and upright, this patio rose bears clusters of double, slightly fragrant, pale salmon-pink flowers, opening from urn-shaped buds, from summer to autumn. In addition to its suitability for containers and as groundcover, 'Gentle Touch' is excellent as a cut flower. H and S 40cm (16in). Hardy/Z 4–9.

'Gloire de Dijon'

One of the oldest climbing roses still in cultivation, this was introduced in 1853 and is usually one of the first climbers to flower. The striking, fully double, fragrant, quartered-rosette, buff-apricot flowers are produced over a long period from late spring to late summer. Its early flowering makes it susceptible to frosts, so grow it against a warm wall in cold areas. H 5m (16ft), S 4m (13ft). Hardy/Z 5–9.

'Golden Showers'

This climbing rose is a perennial favourite for many gardeners. It produces clusters of double, lightly scented, yellow flowers from summer to autumn. The flowers lack distinction, having few petals, but the reliability of this rose in a variety of situations, including light shade, has ensured its longevity. H 3m (10ft), S 2m (6ft). Hardy/Z 4–9.

'Graham Thomas'

A vigorous modern shrub or 'English' rose, this is one of the best of its type, combining the flower form of the old roses with a decidedly modern colour – rich orange-yellow – and a long season that lasts from summer to autumn. The rose is named in honour of the great rosarian, Graham Stuart Thomas. H and S 1.2m (4ft). Hardy/Z 4–9.

Rosa 'Frühlingsgold'

Rosa gallica var. *officinalis*

Rosa 'Gruss an Aachen'

Rosa 'Ingrid Bergman'

Rosa 'Just Joey'

'Gruss an Aachen'

Bred around 1909, this rose is variously described as a floribunda or a polyantha, but it has the air of an old rose. The shapely, deeply cupped, fully double, delicately scented flowers, which are carried in clusters from early summer to autumn, are tinged with pink on opening then fade to creamy white. A long flowering season and low habit of growth make 'Gruss an Aachen' an outstanding bedding rose. H and S 1m (3ft). Hardy/Z 4–9.

'Handel'

A vigorous climber, branching stiffly from the base, this bears double, urn-shaped, only lightly scented flowers from midsummer to autumn. These have cream petals, which are edged with pink, creating an unusual effect. With hard pruning it can be grown as a shrub; in any case its stiff canes make it a reluctant climber. Fan the stems against a wall or spiral them up a pillar. Blackspot may be a problem. H 3m (10ft), S 2.2m (7ft). Hardy/Z 4–9.

'Iceberg'
(syn. 'Fée des Neiges', 'Korbin', 'Schneewittchen')

One of the most successful roses ever produced, this deservedly popular floribunda has retained its place in the catalogues ever since its introduction in 1958. The double, ivory-white, lightly scented flowers open from tapering, pink-flushed buds and are produced in two very distinct flushes, with, unusually, the later, autumn display surpassing the summer one. An outstanding rose of its type, it can be used for bedding, hedging or cutting, but is best, with minimum pruning, as a specimen. H to 1.5m (5ft), S 1m (3ft). Hardy/Z 4–9. The climbing form, **'Climbing Iceberg'**, is equally valuable in the garden, suited to fences or trees.

'Ingrid Bergman'
(syn. 'Poulman')

This upright, branching hybrid tea bears fully double, only lightly scented, deep red flowers from summer to autumn. Good for cutting, bedding and in containers, this is one of the best roses in its colour range. H 75cm (2ft 6in), spread 60cm (2ft). Hardy/Z 4–9.

'Ispahan'

A compact damask rose, this was first recorded in 1832 but is quite probably much older and is possibly Persian in origin. Large clusters of cupped, loosely double, reflexing, richly scented, pink flowers appear throughout summer. The grey-green foliage is attractive. 'Ispahan' has a longer flowering season than most other damasks and is in bloom for up to six weeks. H 1.2–1.5m (4–5ft), S 1–1.2m (3–4ft). Hardy/Z 4–9.

'Just Joey'

The charm of the individual flowers makes this upright hybrid tea rose worth growing. Opening from long, shapely buds, throughout summer, the flowers are a warm coppery orange-pink with slightly ruffled petals, developing creamy buff tints as they age. Disease-resistance is another virtue. H 75cm (2ft 6in), S 60cm (2ft). Hardy/Z 4–9.

'Königin von Dänemark'
(syn. 'Queen of Denmark', 'Belle Courtisane')

This tall, elegant alba is thought by many to be one of the loveliest of all old roses. The luminous pink, fully double, quartered-rosette and richly scented flowers are borne in summer, and fade to rose-pink as they mature,. It also has one of the longest flowering seasons, up to six weeks, and the flowers have good resistance to wet weather. H to 1.5m (5ft), S 1.2m (4ft). Hardy/Z 4–9.

'Korresia'
(syn. 'Friesia', 'Sunsprite')

A neat, upright floribunda, this bears clusters of shapely buds, opening to fragrant, bright golden-yellow flowers, from summer to autumn. It can be used for bedding and for cut flowers; it is similar to 'Allgold' but has bigger flowers. H 75cm (30in), S 60cm (2ft). Hardy/Z 4–9.

'Laura Ford'

This miniature climber is unusual in that its dainty yellow double flowers are also scented. Borne from summer to autumn, they appear in clusters among small, shiny, dark green leaves. A good choice for a small garden, this rose is also suitable for growing in a container. H to 2.2m (7ft), S 1.2m (4ft). Hardy/Z 4–9.

'Madame Alfred Carrière'

This reliable, free-flowering, climbing rose was introduced

Rosa 'Iceberg'

Rosa 'Ispahan'

Rosa 'Königin von Dänemark'

Rosa 'Korresia'

Rosa 'Madame Hardy'

Rosa 'Madame Isaac Pereire'

in 1879. It bears creamy white, double, cupped, fragrant flowers from summer to autumn on almost thornless stems. Although the flowers are not of individual beauty, its many virtues – length of season, health, tolerance of shade – make this one of the best choices for growing against a house wall. H 5m (16ft), S 3m (10ft). Hardy/Z 5–9.

'Madame Grégoire Staechelin' (syn. 'Spanish Beauty')

The sight of this vigorous climbing rose in full flower in early summer is unforgettable. The fully double, sweetly scented, warm pink flowers hang in clusters on arching stems. There is no repeat flowering. The large, showy hips redden in autumn, but not reliably. H 6m (20ft), S 4m (13ft). Hardy/Z 4–9.

'Madame Hardy'

An undoubted queen among roses, this damask dates from 1867. The fully double, quartered-rosette, strongly scented, white flowers are borne in profusion in summer, the petals reflexing to reveal a green button eye. It is generally considered to be one of the most sumptuous of old roses, though the flowers may be spoilt by rain. H and S 1.5m (5ft). Hardy/Z 4–9.

'Madame Isaac Pereire'

A bourbon rose, introduced in 1881, this retains its place in the catalogues on account of its strong scent, which is all but unsurpassed in a genus noted for exactly that attribute. The flower colour is also of note: a luminous, deep cerise pink. Produced throughout summer and into autumn, the flowers open as quartered-rosettes but become muddled as they mature, especially those of the first flush. A tendency towards mildew is its only drawback. H 2.5m (8ft), S 2m (6ft), possibly more if grown as a climber. Hardy/Z 4–9.

'Margaret Merril' (syn. 'Harkuly')

An upright floribunda, this bears clusters of large, shapely, double, sweetly scented, pure white flowers from summer to autumn. In addition to its versatility in the garden, it can also be grown in

containers and is useful as a cut flower. Blackspot can be a problem, but the rose is worth persevering with for its delicious scent. H 1m (3ft), S 60cm (2ft). Hardy/Z 4–9.

'Marguerite Hilling' (syn. 'Pink Nevada')

A sport of the popular 'Nevada', this shrub rose is similar in all respects apart from the colour of its semi-double flowers, which are pale pink and smother the arching canes in early summer. Healthy and vigorous, it makes an excellent specimen. H and S to 2.2m (7ft). Hardy/Z 4–9.

'Mermaid'

This beautiful climber is vigorous once established, but it can take some years to do this. The flowers are produced spasmodically from midsummer until autumn, with a handful later. The elegant, pointed buds open to reveal single, pale yellow, fragrant saucers with prominent golden stamens that

persist after the petals have dropped. The leaves are glossy and can be evergreen; the stems are viciously thorny. Tolerant of some shade, 'Mermaid' may be cut back by hard frost, so appreciates some shelter. H and S 6m (20ft). Hardy/Z 4–9.

'Mountbatten' (syn. 'Harmantelle')

The clusters of mimosa yellow flowers are beautifully set off by the glossy dark green leaves on this shrub rose. With minimum pruning this makes an excellent specimen. H to 1.5m (5ft), S to 1m (3ft). Hardy/Z 4–9.

'Mrs Oakley Fisher'

This rather spindly hybrid tea has claims to attention on account of its unusual flowers. Not only are they subtle in colour – soft apricot-yellow flowers fading to pale buff yellow – but they are deliciously fragrant and, unusually for a rose in this group, single. H and S 1m (3ft). Hardy/Z 6–9.

Rosa 'Laura Ford'

Rosa 'Margaret Merril'

Rosa 'Mountbatten'

Rosa 'Orange Sunblaze'

'Nevada'

This vigorous shrub rose, which tolerates some shade, puts on a great show in early summer, when its arching, blackish canes are smothered in semi-double, creamy white flowers; their elusive fragrance seems to hang on the air. A few flowers are occasionally produced later in the season. It is best with light pruning. H and S to 3m (10ft). Hardy/Z 4–9.

'New Dawn'

This vigorous, healthy rambler is valued for its late flowering. From midsummer there is a great profusion of deliciously fragrant, silvery pink, semi-double flowers, which continue until well into autumn. Its thorny stems and occasional stiffness of habit need to be taken into consideration when planting. H and S to 5m (16ft). Hardy/Z 4–9.

'Nozomi'

This was one of the first ground-cover roses to be bred and is still one of the best, producing clusters

Rosa 'Pascali'

of single, only lightly scented, very pale pink to white flowers in midsummer. The trailing stems, which are covered in glossy dark green leaves, will root where they touch the ground. To maintain the creeping habit, cut back upward-growing shoots in winter. It can also be treated as a miniature climber. H 45cm (18in), S to 1.5m (5ft). Hardy/Z 4–9.

R. × *odorata* 'Mutabilis' (syn. *R. chinensis* 'Mutabilis')

A China rose, of uncertain age and parentage, this was evidently grown in China for many years before its introduction to Europe in 1894. The single flowers, produced over a long period from mid-spring to autumn, are unusual: flame orange in bud, they open to coppery yellow then fade to pink, the pink deepening to purple as they age. None too hardy, this rose is best grown in the shelter of a warm wall, where it can reach a height of 3m (10ft) with a spread of 2m (6ft). In the border it can also be trained on a tripod. H 1.2m (4ft), S 1m (3ft). Borderline hardy/Z 7–9.

R. × *odorata* 'Pallida'

Introduced to Europe around 1752 but undoubtedly much older, this China rose has one of the longest flowering seasons of all roses. From summer until the first winter frosts it produces double, cupped, sweetly fragrant, clear pink flowers amid elegant, pointed leaves. None too hardy, in some areas it will need growing against a warm wall to give of its best. It can also be trained as a climber. It is sometimes known as the old blush China rose or Parsons' pink China rose. H 1–3m (3–10ft), S 2m (6ft). Borderline hardy/Z 7–9.

'Orange Sunblaze' (syn. 'Meijikatar', 'Orange Meillandina', 'Sunblaze')

A neat and dainty miniature rose, this bears fully double, only lightly scented, bright vermilion-orange flowers from summer to autumn. It is an excellent choice where space is limited or for a container. H and S 30cm (12in). Hardy/Z 4–9. There is also a

Rosa 'Queen Mother'

climbing form, 'Climbing Orange Sunblaze' (syn. 'Meiji Katarsar'), which produces a dazzling display when grown on a sunny wall.

'Pascali'

This is one of the few pure white hybrid teas (albeit lightly touched with creamy buff). Shapely double, only lightly scented flowers are displayed from early summer into autumn. The rain-resistance of the flowers is unsurpassed in this colour range; they are also exceptionally long-lasting when cut. H 1m (3ft), S 75cm (2ft

6in). Hardy/Z 4–9. **'Climbing Pascali'**, a climbing form, shares the same qualities.

'Peace' (syn. 'Gioia', 'Gloria Dei', 'Madame A. Meilland')

One of the most popular hybrid teas ever produced, this rose is surely worthy of revival. The large, fully double, only lightly scented flowers are pale yellow with pink flushes, and they appear from midsummer to autumn. Its present lack of popularity is due to its supposed coarseness – that

Rosa 'Peace'

Rosa 'Président de Sèze'

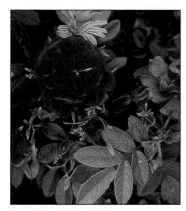

Rosa 'Roseraie de l'Haÿ'

is, it is a vigorous, spreading, bushy rose that makes a fine specimen with light pruning. H 1.5m (5ft), S 1m (3ft). Hardy/Z 4–9.

'Président de Sèze'

Richly scented, large, quartered flowers appear on this sturdy gallica rose in summer. The centre petals are rich magenta-purple, the colour fading across the flower to soft lilac-pink, almost white, at the edges. The leaves are larger than is usual for a gallica rose. A well-grown specimen is a stunning sight when in full bloom. H 1.2m (4ft), S 1m (3ft). Hardy/Z 4–9.

'Queen Mother'
(syn. 'Korquemu')

This spreading patio rose deserves its popularity. The dainty buds open to semi-double, clear pink flowers from summer to autumn. It does well in a container and is sometimes available as a weeping standard. H 45cm (18in), S 60cm (2ft). Hardy/Z 4–9.

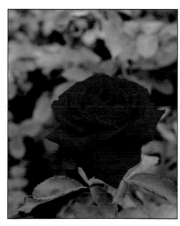

Rosa 'Royal William'

'Rambling Rector'

A vigorous rambling rose, this is covered with clusters of small, semi-double, fragrant, white flowers in summer. Small red hips follow in autumn. It is suitable for growing into a large tree, and a mature rose in full flower is an impressive sight, but it is not a rose suited to every garden. H and S 6m (20ft). Hardy/Z 5–9.

'Roseraie de l'Haÿ'

Despite its reluctance to produce the characteristic autumn hips, this is one of the best of the rugosa roses. Its value rests on its strongly scented, velvety, wine-red flowers, which open to reveal creamy stamens. The blooms are produced in abundance from summer to autumn. The wrinkled leaves redden in autumn. Dense and spreading, 'Roseraie de l'Haÿ' makes an excellent hedge and can also be planted in light woodland. H 2m (6ft), S 1.2m (4ft). Hardy/Z 4–9.

'Royal William'
(syn. 'Duftzauber '84', 'Fragrant Charm '84', 'Korzaun')

An upright hybrid tea, this rose is valued for its succession of large, fully double, fragrant, deep crimson flowers. The graceful blooms are carried on long stems from summer to autumn. This rose is excellent planted en masse for a stunning effect, or it can be grown to provide flowers for cutting. H 1m (3ft), S 75cm (2ft 6in). Hardy/Z 4–9.

'Savoy Hotel'
(syn. 'Harvintage', 'Integrity')

This bushy hybrid tea has strong stems that carry large, shapely, fully double, fragrant, light clear pink flowers from summer to autumn and with good repeat-flowering. It is a versatile rose, which provides excellent material for cutting, as long as you keep it well fed. H 1m (3ft), S 60cm (2ft). Hardy/Z 4–8.

'Schneezwerg'
(syn. 'Snow Dwarf')

A rugosa rose introduced in 1912, this has a dense, spreading habit. The anemone-like, semi-double, white flowers open flat to

Rosa 'Savoy Hotel'

reveal golden stamens. They are followed by small, orange-red, tomato-shaped hips. Although its flowers are unremarkable, this rose is perhaps at its best in autumn; the foliage does not change colour, but the flowers continue to appear alongside the reddening hips. In order to get the best of both worlds, therefore, deadhead selectively in summer. H 1.2m (4ft), S 1.5m (5ft). Hardy/Z 3–9.

'Sexy Rexy'
(syn. 'Heckenzauber', 'Macrexy')

This is an outstanding floribunda, of upright habit. It produces clusters of shapely, fully double, palest coral-pink flowers throughout summer and autumn. These are shown off by plentiful

Rosa 'Schneezwerg'

dark, glossy leaves. It is a versatile rose good for general garden use, growing in containers and for providing cut flowers. H and S 60cm (2ft). Hardy/Z 4–9.

'Sombreuil'

A distinctive and unusual rose, this is generally classified as a climbing tea, although it is not particularly vigorous, nor are its flowers tea-like, lacking a high centre. Borne from summer to autumn, the sweetly scented blooms are flat, quartered rosettes, creamy white in colour and acquiring pink tinges as they age. Wet weather will ruin them. H and S to 2.4m (8ft) when grown as a climber with support, but smaller if allowed to grow as a lax shrub. Hardy/Z 5–9.

Rosa 'Sexy Rexy'

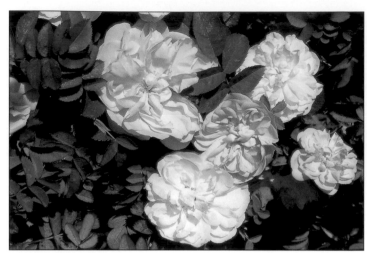
Rosa 'Stanwell Perpetual'

'Southampton'
(syn. 'Susan Ann')
This is an excellent floribunda, with an upright, branching habit and shiny, dark green leaves. Clusters of large, double, soft apricot-orange flowers, which are flushed with scarlet, are carried from early summer into autumn; the petals are wavy-edged. The scent is not especially strong. H 1m (3ft), S 60cm (2ft). Hardy/Z 4–9.

'Souvenir de la Malmaison'
This beautiful, dense, spreading bourbon rose, produced in 1843, commemorates the famous garden created by Empress Josephine at Malmaison, although it is not clear whether it was actually grown there. Repeat-flowering throughout the summer, it bears very fragrant, fully double, soft pink flowers, which open to a quartered-rosette shape as they fade to blush-white. One major drawback is that the silk-textured

flowers may be spoilt by wet weather. H and S 1.5m (5ft). Hardy/Z 4–9.

'Stanwell Perpetual'
This Scotch rose, raised in 1838, forms a dense, prickly shrub. The double, sweetly scented, attractive blush pink to white flowers open flat and are produced almost continuously throughout summer among the grey-green leaves. Tolerant of poor soil and some shade, this rose is ideal for growing in light woodland; it also makes a good hedge. H and S 1.5m (5ft). Hardy/Z 5–9.

'Sweet Dream'
(syn. 'Fryminicot')
One of the best of the patio roses, this produces an abundance of fully double, lightly scented, soft apricot-orange flowers from midsummer to autumn. It is usually well covered with glossy, healthy foliage. A good edging plant, 'Sweet Dream' is also

suitable for growing in a container. H 40cm (16in), S 35cm (14in). Hardy/Z 4–9.

'Tango'
(syn. 'Macfirwal', 'Rock 'n' Roll', 'Stretch Johnson')
This upright floribunda is chiefly of interest to flower arrangers. From summer to autumn it produces clusters of semi-double flowers of some distinction: the petals, frilled at the edges, are orange-red with white rims, yellow at the base and on the reverse. H 75cm (2ft 6in), spread 60cm (2ft). Hardy/Z 4–8.

'The Fairy'
A dainty floribunda or polyantha, this has a dense, mounding habit and is well worth considering if you are planning an autumn border. It flowers later than almost any other rose, the clusters of small, double, light pink flowers appearing only from midsummer, but then continuing in profusion until the onset of winter. H and S 60cm (2ft). Hardy/Z 4–9.

'The Queen Elizabeth'
(syn. 'Queen Elizabeth', 'The Queen Elizabeth Rose')
This is one of the best of all the floribundas, but not especially characteristic of the group. Its vigour and strongly vertical habit really make it unsuitable for most of the purposes for which the floribundas were developed. It is best used at the back of a border or as a tall, informal hedge. Its fully double, china pink flowers, which are freely carried from summer to autumn, last well when cut. H 2.2m (7ft), S 1m (3ft);

Rosa 'The Queen Elizabeth'

with minimal pruning it will easily top 3m (10ft). Hardy/Z 4–9. The climbing form, 'Climbing the Queen Elizabeth', is also well worth growing.

'Troika'
(syn. 'Royal Dane')
An outstanding hybrid tea, this has an upright, branching habit. The display of large, shapely, double, lightly scented, copper-orange flowers, sometimes veined scarlet, continues throughout summer and into autumn. Disease- and weather-resistant, this is a good choice for a massed planting and also provides good cut flowers. H 1m (3ft), S 75cm (2ft 6in). Hardy/Z 4–9.

'Tuscany Superb'
(syn. 'Double Velvet')
This erect gallica rose was raised before 1837. The large, semi-double, lightly scented, deep crimson flowers are produced in midsummer. They open flat, showing golden stamens, then fade to purple. Tolerant of poor

Rosa 'Souvenir de la Malmaison'

Rosa 'Sweet Dream'

Rosa 'The Fairy'

Rosa 'Tuscany Superb'

Rosa 'Veilchenblau'

soil, this is one of the few old roses that is suitable for hedging. It is not too thorny. H 1.5m (5ft), S 1m (3ft). Hardy/Z 4–9.

'Veilchenblau'
(syn. 'Blue Rambler', 'Violet Blue')
A vigorous rambling rose, this was introduced in 1909. In midsummer it bears clusters of sweetly scented, semi-double, violet-pink flowers with yellow stamens; the flowers fade to an unusual purplish grey as they mature. The leaves are glossy and light green. More modest than most ramblers, this rose is suitable for a small garden and is best grown with some shelter from the midday sun. H and S 4m (13ft). Hardy/Z 4–9.

'Whisky Mac'
(syn. 'Tanky', 'Whisky')
This famous hybrid tea has retained its popularity despite its propensity to die-back and fungal diseases. Its appeal lies in the unusual colouring of its sumptuous double flowers, which are a rich golden-orange of unrivalled intensity, and with a fragrance to match. Since it needs almost constant attention, this is really a plant for dedicated rose-growers only. H 75cm (2ft 6in), S 60cm (2ft). Hardy/Z 4–9.

'White Bells'
A dense, spreading groundcover rose, this bears a single, but abundant, crop of small, fully double, white flowers in summer. It is shade-tolerant, and thus useful for difficult areas of the

garden, but overall perhaps not as good as some other groundcover roses. H 60cm (2ft), S 1.2m (4ft). Hardy/Z 5–9.

'White Cockade'
This is one of the few white climbing roses. The perfectly shaped, fully double flowers appear almost continuously from summer to autumn, and the absence of a strong scent in no way detracts from its overall merit. Slow-growing, it is a good choice for growing in a container or on a short pillar. H 2.2m (7ft), S 1.5m (5ft). Hardy/Z 4–9.

'White Grootendorst'
A vigorous rugosa rose, with a dense, spreading habit, this produces clusters of small, double, scentless, white flowers, particularly notable for the frilly edges of the petals, which look like carnations. Like most of the rugosas, it tolerates some shade and poor soil, making it ideal for a wild garden. H 1.2m (4ft), S 1m (3ft). Hardy/Z 3–8.

'William Lobb'
(syn. 'Duchesse d'Istrie')
This rather sprawling moss rose is worth growing for its sumptuous rosette flowers. Richly scented, they open magenta-purple in midsummer from heavily mossed buds, then pass through a remarkable range of tones before fading to a subtle violet-grey. The ungainly habit makes it unsuitable as a specimen. Instead, try it wrapped around a tripod or as a short climber on a pillar or against a wall. H and S 2m (6ft). Hardy/Z 4–9.

R. xanthina 'Canary Bird'
This wild rose is usually one of the first to flower in the garden, offering a burst of welcome colour in late spring. The single, cupped, scented, canary yellow flowers have prominent stamens. In a good year there will be a second, though lesser, flush of flowers in autumn. It makes an attractive arching shrub, although it is sometimes available as a grafted standard, when it makes a fine specimen. H and S 2.2m (7ft). Hardy/Z 5–9.

Rosa 'Whisky Mac'

'Yellow Doll'
This spreading miniature rose has double, slightly scented, bright yellow flowers, which are produced singly or in clusters from summer to autumn. Rather unusually for a miniature, it is good for cutting; it can also be forced under glass for early flowers. It will tolerate harsh weather conditions. H and S to 30cm (12in). Hardy/Z 3–8.

'Yesterday'
(syn. 'Tapis d'Orient')
A floribunda or polyantha rose, this has an elegant, open, spreading habit and a long flowering season, from summer to autumn. The clusters of semi-

Rosa 'William Lobb'

double, fragrant, deep lilac-pink flowers open flat to reveal paler centres and golden stamens. It is good for cutting and, given lighter pruning than usual, makes an attractive specimen. H and S 1m (3ft). Hardy/Z 4–9.

'Zéphirine Drouhin'
This climbing rose is notable for its thornless stems, making it a good choice for an archway or pergola or for framing a doorway. In summer and autumn it produces clusters of double, cupped to flat, fragrant, magenta flowers. It can be prone to mildew. H 3m (10ft), S 2m (6ft). Hardy/Z 4–9. **'Kathleen Harrop'** is a pale pink sport.

Rosa 'Yesterday'

Climbers

Climbers are among the most dramatic and rewarding garden plants, lifting your eyes skywards as they reach towards the sun. They are ideal for beautifying walls, fences and ugly outbuildings and can also be draped over pergolas to provide welcome shade in summer or used to carpet banks. Some have spectacular flowers that can be deliciously scented. Others are grown for their leaves, while the evergreens provide year-round interest, a good foil to other flowering plants in summer and supplying welcome greenery in winter.

Allowed to ramble through roses and perennials, this clematis lifts its flowers to the sun.

What is a climber?

Climbers are a fascinating group of plants. Typically, a climber is a woodland dweller, with its feet in the cool, leafy soil on the forest floor. Its long, flexible stems scamper up tree trunks and into their branches, usually with considerable vigour. On reaching the canopy, it spreads sideways and produces flowers that turn to face the sun. This natural habit is one that most gardeners spend considerable efforts on circumventing.

Most climbers have woody stems, and thus are essentially shrubs, but others are soft-stemmed perennials, and some are herbaceous, dying back completely in winter. There are also some annual climbers, sweet peas (*Lathyrus odoratus*) being the best-known.

Climbers have evolved various methods of attaching themselves to their host plant in the wild. Some have special suckering pads that adhere to the host, ivies (*Hedera*), Virginia creeper (*Vitis*) and the climbing hydrangea being notable

examples. Other climbers, such as honeysuckles (*Lonicera*), have twining stems that twist themselves around the host plant. A third group have specialized tendrils – for instance, passion flowers (*Passiflora*) – or twining leaf stalks (clematis being the best example), which cling to narrow stems. A fourth group, which includes most of the roses (dealt with in their own section of this book) and bougainvillea, have thorns that allow the plant to hook itself into tree bark as it ramps upwards.

A further group should not be overlooked. This comprises so-called scandent climbers, woody plants with long, flexible stems that have no means of supporting themselves. Some clematis come into this category, as well as the popular winter jasmine (*Jasminum nudiflorum*) and the beautiful potato vines (*Solanum*). Such plants can be treated like other climbers but have to be tied to their supports as they grow.

Climbers in the garden

While most plants present their flowers at eye level or below, climbers raise your gaze skywards, and thus bring a dynamism to the garden that is unmatched by any other group. They are high-value plants in that they can fill a large amount of space above ground, while actually only occupying a small area of soil.

In the artificial environment of a garden, climbers do not need to be grown into a host plant, but can be used to clothe a wall or fence, or to cover a pergola or trellis screen. In all these cases, you have to be careful to match the vigour of the plant to the structure that will support it. Many a climber has pulled down a fence, but it is an old wives' tale that suckering climbers will damage the

mortar on house walls: only if the mortar is unsound to begin with are you likely to experience problems. Perennial climbers and some of the less vigorous clematis are effective grown on trellis obelisks or pyramids in borders. A related, but highly effective, method is to train such plants on trellis panels set horizontally in the border on posts, to create a table of flowers that you can look down on.

You can imitate the way climbing plants behave in the wild by siting them near a suitable host plant and treating this as the support. You can plan for the two plants to flower simultaneously, in complementary, toning or even clashing colours, or for the one to follow the other, thus providing for a long season of interest. The summer-flowering perennial pea (*Lathyrus*) makes a good companion for a shrub rose such as 'Nevada' or 'Canary Bird', whose moment of glory comes earlier in season. The flame creeper (*Tropaeolum speciosum*) looks

Bougainvillea and *Trachelospermum jasminoides* make an entrancing combination in this Californian garden.

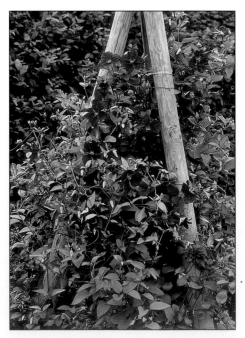

A tripod supports the vigorous hybrid clematis 'Jackmanii'. Once fully grown it will cover the support completely so it cannot be seen.

spectacular when its luminous crimson flowers light up a sombre yew hedge, and many clematis are suitable for growing into flowering shrubs. Such combinations are a matter of taste: an extreme example would be to grow *Clematis montana* into a mature conifer, a striking if bizarre sight, but honeysuckles and wisterias always strike a romantic note when allowed to ramble through mature deciduous trees.

Another use is as ground cover, a method of cultivation that is particularly effective on a bank or in a wild garden. Many climbers will actually root where the stems touch the ground (especially self-clingers such as ivy), thus creating a weed-suppressing carpet.

Many of the less rampant climbers can be grown in containers, provided these are deep enough to accommodate the root system. They can be trained on trellis panels in the same way as climbers in the open garden, or can simply be allowed to trail over the sides of the container. Ivies are very effective when grown in this way, as are some of the weaker-growing clematis.

Pruning and training climbers

Most climbers are vigorous plants that benefit from pruning occasionally to keep them under control. That said, it is generally impractical to prune climbers grown informally into trees and shrubs, and these can be given their head – hence the importance of choosing climbers that will not swamp the host.

On planting, cut out any dead, diseased or damaged stems and lightly trim back the remainder. Fan them out and tie them loosely to the support. If they are not long enough to reach the support, attach them to canes tied to the support. As the plant grows, train in the

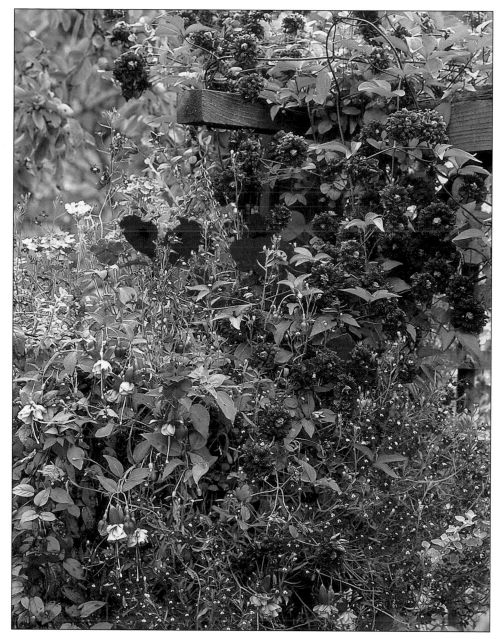

The dainty *Clematis viticella* 'Purpurea Plena Elegans' supported by the pergola dangles its flowers in among the hanging basket's traditional mix of fuchsias and trailing annuals.

stems as near to the horizontal as possible to encourage even flowering. Thorny and scandent climbers will need to be tied in. If you are training the climber up a post (for instance, the upright of a pergola), wrap the stems around the support rather than tying them in vertically.

As a general rule, prune early-flowering climbers immediately after flowering, and late-flowering ones at the start of the growing season. Once the climber has filled

its allotted space, shorten overlong shoots and remove any crossing stems. Cut back thick, old stems to ground level. You can then shorten side shoots, if necessary. A plant that has really got out of hand can be given a new lease of life by renovative pruning. In late winter, cut back all the stems to near ground level. Feed the plant well, and new growth should be vigorous.

For pruning clematis and wisteria, see their own entries in this chapter.

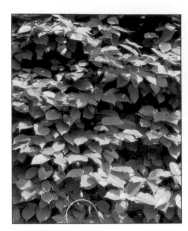

Actinidia kolomikta

The plants listed are all deciduous unless otherwise indicated.

ACTINIDIA

In addition to the ornamental species described here, this genus of twining climbers also includes *A. deliciosa* (kiwi fruit, Chinese gooseberry).
Cultivation Grow actinidias in any reasonably fertile soil in sun or light shade.

A. kolomikta

This climber from eastern Asia is grown for its leaves, which look as if they have been splashed with cream and pink paint. The leaves show different colours each year (although they are always plain green on emergence, and will remain so in a very shaded site). The plant is not to everyone's taste, but it is attractive grown into the branches of a tree. H and S 3m (10ft). Hardy/Z 4–9.

AKEBIA
Chocolate vine

An interesting genus of five species of twining climbers, with several members that deserve wider recognition than they currently receive. Few are showy, but the plants have a subtle appeal.
Cultivation Grow in any fertile, well-drained soil in sun or light shade.

A. quinata

The dark purple-brown flowers that appear in mid-spring are not particularly conspicuous and can be lost among the compound, evergreen leaves, only the vanilla scent indicating their presence.

Akebia quinata

Where two plants are grown in proximity, sausage-shaped, purple fruits can develop in autumn. H and S 4m (13ft). Hardy/Z 4–9.

BOUGAINVILLEA

These half-hardy evergreen climbers are grown not for their flowers, which are inconspicuous, but for the brightly coloured bracts that surround them. The spiny stems have to be tied to a trellis. In a conservatory, plant with caution, because if the conditions are favourable they will be rampant. In warm climates they are impressive over large pergolas or allowed to cascade down banks. Combining them with *Trachelospermum jasminoides* will provide the scent they lack.
Cultivation In a conservatory use a loam-based compost and water freely when in active growth. A potash-based fertilizer, applied from spring to early summer, will boost flowering. Keep in full light and allow the temperature to drop no lower than 10°C (50°F).

Bougainvillea 'Miss Manila'

B. × *buttiana*

This large hybrid group contains a number of desirable plants, including 'Killie Campbell', which has large, coppery-orange bracts with ruffled edges. H and S to 10m (33ft) or more. Half-hardy/Z 10.

B. 'Miss Manila'
(syn. *B.* 'Tango')

The bracts, to 5cm (2in) long, are reddish-pink. H and S to 10m (33ft) or more. Half-hardy/Z 10.

B. 'San Diego Red'
(syn. *B.* 'Hawaiian Scarlet', 'Scarlett O'Hara')

The bracts are bright red shading to orange. H and S to 10m (33ft) or more. Half-hardy/Z 9–10.

CAMPSIS
Trumpet vine, trumpet creeper

These climbers with aerial roots are not as widely planted as you might expect, given the attraction of the trumpet-shaped flowers, which are produced from late summer to early autumn. Their lack of popularity is, perhaps, because the blooms are rarely produced in quantity.
Cultivation These climbers need any reasonably fertile, well-drained soil and a position in sun.

C. radicans
(syn. *Bignonia radicans*, *Tecoma radicans*)
Common trumpet creeper

This species from the south-eastern United States has trumpet-shaped, orange-red flowers, which are borne in clusters in late summer. H and S to 10m (33ft). Borderline hardy/Z 5–9.

Campsis radicans

C. × *tagliabuana* 'Madame Galen'

A hybrid of considerable vigour, with deep apricot flowers, veined with salmon pink, and lightly hairy leaves. H and S to 10m (33ft). Borderline hardy/Z 4–10.

CELASTRUS
Bittersweet, staff vine

Unusually, this twining climber is grown for its autumn berries rather than for the flowers.
Cultivation Grow these climbers in fertile, well-drained soil in sun or light shade.

C. orbiculatus
(syn. *C. articulatus*)
Oriental bittersweet

The starry, greenish summer flowers of this species from eastern Asia are succeeded by yellow berries, which split to reveal vivid red seeds. Both male and female plants are required to ensure good fruiting. 'Diana' is female, 'Hercules' is male, but if you have room for only one plant, look for one from the **Hermaphrodite Group**. H and S to 10m (33ft) or more. Hardy/Z 5–8.

CLEMATIS

This huge genus of leaf-stalk climbers includes a few herbaceous perennials, and there are also a few non-climbing, sprawling types. There is a clematis for virtually every season of the year. Both species and hybrids are usually divided into three groups, depending on the flowering season. Group 1 clematis flower from the start of the year to late spring on growth made during the previous season. Group 2 clematis flower twice: first in late spring on the previous season's growth and later, in mid- to late summer, on the current season's growth. This group includes some double-flowered hybrids, although only the flowers borne in the first flush are double. Group 3 clematis flower from midsummer to early autumn on the current season's growth.

Best known are the large-flowered hybrids, which are excellent for growing against walls and fences. Some have plate-like flowers, but the viticella hybrids have smaller flowers, and the texensis types are like miniature tulips. There are a number of hybrids that make an even daintier effect. The species are all effective over pergolas and when allowed to romp through trees. The non-climbing clematis described below do not twine but have long, flexible, sprawling stems. They can be used to flop into other plants, or they can be fan-trained against walls and fences. When planting clematis, always bury the stems to a depth of up to 15cm (6in) to encourage stem rooting, which will enhance the plant's overall vigour.

Cultivation Grow clematis in any well-drained soil (although they seem to do best in alkaline conditions) in sun or light shade, with shade at the roots.

Prune as follows. Group 1 clematis require no regular pruning, but congested plants can, if necessary, be thinned after flowering. Harder pruning is tolerated, but the next year's flowering will be impaired. On Group 2 clematis thin congested growth in late winter, cutting back old stems to the base and shortening others as necessary, bearing in mind that these will carry the current season's flowers. Deadhead after the first flush of flowers. For a single flush of late flowers, treat as for Group 3 (although double cultivars will produce single flowers only). Prune Group 3 clematis in late winter (early spring for texensis and viticella types), cutting back all stems to near ground level. Species and very vigorous hybrids can be also be left unpruned, depending on the effect required.

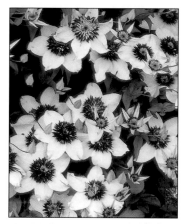
Clematis florida 'Sieboldii'

C. alpina (Group 1)
Alpine clematis
This dainty species has nodding, bell-shaped, blue flowers from spring to early summer. Selections include 'Frances Rivis', which has white-centred, mid-blue flowers with slightly twisted petals; and 'Helsinborg', which has deep purple-blue flowers. H 3m (10ft), S 1.5m (5ft). Hardy/Z 7–9.

C. armandii (Group 1)
This species, one of the few evergreen clematis, has long, leathery, dark green leaves and clusters of scented, white flowers in spring. A vigorous plant, it is best trained against a warm wall in cold areas. Selections include 'Apple Blossom', which has flowers that are initially pale pink; and 'Snowdrift', with pure white flowers that are larger than the type. H and S to 9m (30ft). Borderline hardy/Z 7–9.

C. cirrhosa (Group 1)
Fern-leaved clematis
This is usually the first of the

Clematis montana 'Continuity'

Clematis armandii 'Snowdrift'

clematis to flower: according to most books it begins to bloom in midwinter, but occasional flowers can be produced as early as autumn. These are bell-shaped, with a papery texture, and are creamy-white in colour, sometimes speckled with brownish-red inside. H 3m (10ft), S 1.5m (5ft). Hardy/Z 7–9, but best in a warm, sheltered position.

C. flammula (Group 3)
Masses of fragrant, star-like, white flowers cover the plant in late summer and early autumn. This is tolerant of poor soil and is excellent for growing through a tree. H 6m (20ft), S 3m (10ft). Borderline hardy/Z 7–9.

C. florida (Group 2)
This elegant species has two outstanding selections, both producing two flushes of passionflower-like flowers. 'Flore Pleno' has double, greenish-white flowers; 'Sieboldii' has creamy-white flowers with a central boss

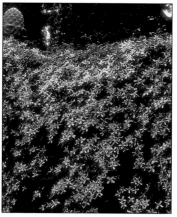
Clematis montana 'Elizabeth'

of rich purple stamens. Both are weak-growing and need a warm, sheltered spot and fertile soil. H 2m (6ft), S 1m (3ft). Borderline hardy/Z 6–9.

C. macropetala (Group 1)
The bell-shaped flowers of this species, which appear in mid- to late spring, have only four petals, but appear to be double because some of the stamens are petal-like. They are blue or violet-blue. H 3m (10ft), S 1.5m (5ft). 'Blue Bird' has semi-double, clear blue flowers. The charming 'White Moth' (syn. *C. alpina* 'White Moth') has pure white flowers. Hardy/Z 6–9.

C. montana (Group 1)
The most vigorous of the early clematis, this is the last to flower, with white flowers appearing in late spring. H 5–8m (15–25ft), S 3m (10ft). Hardy/Z 6–9. Selections include the long flowering 'Continuity' – hence the name – with creamy-white, pink-tinged flowers; 'Elizabeth', which has pale pink, richly scented flowers; and the vigorous *C. montana* f. *grandiflora*, which bears many white flowers.

C. rehderiana (Group 3)
This vigorous species produces a mass of bell-shaped, creamy yellow, cowslip-scented flowers in late summer. This is an excellent choice for growing into a sturdy tree. H 6m (20ft), S 3m (10ft). Hardy/Z 6–9.

C. tangutica (Group 3)
This species produces bright yellow, lantern-like flowers with pointed sepals and a prominent central boss of stamens, which are borne from midsummer to autumn and are followed by silky, silvery grey seedheads. There is much confusion between this species and the roughly similar *C. tibetana*, which will hybridize with it freely. H 6m (20ft), S 3m (10ft). Hardy/Z 6–9.

Hybrids
The following are large-flowered clematis, H and S around 2.4m (8ft) unless otherwise indicated. All are hardy/Z 4–9.

Clematis 'Allanah'

Group 2 clematis

'Barbara Dibley' has bright cerise-pink flowers with darker barring; 'Bees' Jubilee' is deep mauve-pink, aging lighter, and is best in shade; 'Duchess of Edinburgh' is weak-growing with double, dahlia-like, white flowers; the spectacular 'Fireworks' has luminous violet flowers with mauve-carmine bars; 'Gillian Blades' has large white flowers; 'Lasurstern' has mauve-blue flowers, fading to silvery mauve; 'John Warren' has pale greyish-pink flowers, which are veined and edged with deeper pink; 'Marie Boisselot' (syn. 'Mme le Coultre') is a free-flowering plant with pure white flowers with overlapping sepals; 'Mrs Cholmondeley' produces pale lavender-blue flowers over a long period; 'Mrs George Jackman' has creamy-white flowers, the first flush of which are semi-double; the well-known 'Nelly Moser' has pinkish-mauve flowers with carmine bars; 'Silver Moon' has

Clematis 'Gravetye Beauty'

gleaming lavender-white flowers; 'Royalty' has purplish-mauve flowers, the first flush of which are semi-double; 'Vyvyan Pennell' has rich lilac-blue flowers, the first flush of which are double.

Group 3 clematis

The sepals of the bright ruby red 'Allanah' do not overlap; the non-climbing *C. × aromatica* has small, fragrant, deep-violet flowers; 'Bill Mackenzie' has bright yellow, thick-textured, lantern-like flowers, which are followed by fluffy seedheads, H 7m (23ft), S 3m (10ft); 'Duchess of Albany' (texensis) has warm pink flowers banded with red; 'Gravetye Beauty' (texensis) produces red flowers with pink reverses to the sepals; the dainty 'Huldine' (viticella) has pearly white flowers with recurving sepals; 'Jackmanii', one of the most popular of all the hybrids, has purple flowers; the rich purple flowers of 'Jackmanii Superba' are darker than those of 'Jackmanii'; the non-climbing *C. × jouiana* 'Praecox' has small, pale purplish-blue flowers overlaid with silver; 'Kermesina' (viticella) has deep crimson flowers; 'Pagoda' (texensis) has warm pinkish-red flowers; the fully double, very distinctive flowers of 'Purpurea Plena Elegans' (viticella) are deep purplish-pink; 'Rouge Cardinal' has dusky red flowers; the flowers of 'Royal Velours' (viticella) are a deep velvety purplish-red; the young shoots of *C. × triternata* 'Rubromarginata', which has small, fragrant, pink flowers, are often decimated by slugs and snails; 'Victoria' has rose-purple flowers, fading to mauve; the flowers of 'Ville de Lyon' (viticella) are deep pinkish red.

CLIANTHUS

Hardy in only the most favoured spots, clianthus have intriguing, claw-like flowers. Though not strictly climbers, these plants have arching stems that are easily and effectively, if the flowers are to be enjoyed to the full, trained in a fan shape. They can also be grown in cool conservatories (porches).
Cultivation Grow in well-drained soil in sun, siting against a warm wall in cold areas.

Eccremocarpus scaber

C. puniceus
Lobster claw, parrot's bill, glory pea

This species, the commonest in cultivation, produces its flowers in late spring to early summer, usually in shades of gleaming red. Selections include 'Albus', which has exquisite ivory white flowers touched with green; and 'Roseus' (syn. 'Flamingo'), which has deep rose red flowers. H 4m (13ft), S 3m (10ft). Borderline hardy/Z 8.

ECCREMOCARPUS
Chilean glory vine

The species described is often grown as an annual, but it is a truly perennial plant, albeit not evergreen in cold winters, when it dies back to ground level. It looks effective when allowed to wander through a hedge.
Cultivation Grow in well-drained soil in sun. This species can also be grown in a container in an unheated conservatory.

E. scaber

The tubular orange flowers appear over a long period from summer right until the first frosts of autumn. H 3m (10ft), S 1m (3ft). Borderline hardy/Z 7–9.

FALLOPIA

The species described is one of the most rampant of all garden plants. Known as the mile-a-minute plant, it is recommended with caution. Nevertheless, it is unmatched for covering an unsightly outbuilding in record time, but any attempt to restrain its vigour is futile – it is a bottom-of-the-garden plant.

Hedera canariensis 'Gloire de Marengo'

Cultivation This will grow in any reasonable garden soil, in sun or light shade.

F. baldschuanicum
(syn. *Bilderdykia aubertii*, *Fallopia aubertii*, *Polygonum baldschuanicum*)
Russian vine, mile-a-minute plant

This species' chief claim to ornamental value lies in its generous sprays of tiny white flowers, borne in late summer. H and S 15m (50ft). Hardy/Z 5–9.

HEDERA
Ivy

These self-clinging climbers are among the most useful of garden plants, but their positive virtues are easily overlooked. *H. helix* is virtually a weed in some gardens, which should not blind you to the beauties of some of its cultivars. All ivies provide excellent evergreen cover for walls and fences, and can also do well as groundcover in the dry soil under trees where little else will grow. Another attractive use is trailing over banks with other plants, such as groundcover roses.
Cultivation Most ivies do well in any reasonable (preferably alkaline) soil in shade. Variegated ivies tend to produce plain green shoots in acid soil; large-leaved forms do best in sun.

H. canariensis
Canary Island ivy, North African ivy

Some confusion surrounds the naming of this species, which is variously listed as *H. algeriensis*, *H. canariensis* var. *algeriensis* or *H. canariensis* of gardens. No matter what it is called, the plain green species is hardly a true garden plant, and it is usually represented by one of the following selections. **'Gloire de Marengo'** has green leaves irregularly margined with cream. H and S to 4m (13ft). **'Marginomaculata'** is a dramatic plant, if none too hardy, with leaves marbled and spotted with cream and green. It is sometimes grown as a houseplant. H and S to 4m (13ft). **'Ravensholst'** has very large, shiny, green leaves on red stems. H and S to 5m (16ft). Borderline hardy/Z 8.

H. colchica
Persian ivy

The species from northern Iran and the Caucasus is usually encountered in the form of one of the following. **'Dentata'** has enormous, dull green leaves, occasionally notched at the edges. H and S 5m (16ft) or more. The leaves of **'Sulphur Heart'** (syn. 'Paddy's Pride') are irregularly marked with yellowish-green at the centre. H and S 5m (16ft). Hardy/Z 6–9.

H. helix
Common ivy, English ivy

The species is common in hedgerows and on waste ground but is seldom cultivated as a garden plant. It has a huge number of cultivars. These ivies are easily controlled by pruning. All are hardy/Z 5–9 unless otherwise stated. **'Ambrosia'** has small, slightly curled and twisted leaves, lightly variegated with cream. H and S 1.2m (4ft). Hardy/Z 5. The young leaves of **'Angularis**

Hedera helix 'Buttercup'

Aurea'** are bright golden yellow, becoming mottled with green as they age. H and S 4m (13ft). The leaves of **'Boskoop'**, a good houseplant, are claw-like. H and S 1m (3ft). Borderline hardy/Z 6. **'Bruder Ingobert'**, also good as a houseplant or in a hanging basket, has variably shaped leaves that are deep grey-green edged with creamy white. H and S 1m (3ft). Borderline hardy/Z 6. **'Buttercup'** produces its best leaf colour, a rich golden yellow, where it is in sun for at least half the day. H and S 2m (6ft). The mid-green leaves of **'Chicago Variegated'** are variegated with pale yellow. H and S 3m (10ft). The aptly named **'Curvaceous'** is a variegated sport of 'Manda's Crested', with wavy-edged, mid-green-grey leaves with cream margins. H and S 2m (6ft). **'Duckfoot'** has a bushy habit and is good for edging a border. H and S 1m (3ft). Among the variegated forms, **'Eva'** is outstanding, with leaves margined

with creamy yellow. It is good for hanging baskets and as a houseplant. H and S 1.2m (4ft). Borderline hardy/Z 8–9. The young leaves of **'Fantasia'** are cream, heavily speckled with green, turning plain green as they age. H and S 1.2m (4ft). Borderline hardy/Z 8. **'Glacier'** has grey-green leaves edged creamy white. H and S 2m (6ft). **'Green Ripple'** is a vigorous form suitable for groundcover. H and S 2m (6ft). The leaves of **'Jersey Doris'** emerge creamy white, developing green speckling before turning solid green. It is best grown in full light. H and S 1.2m (4ft). Hardy/Z 6. **'Little Luzii'** is excellent in flower arrangements and at the edge of a windowbox. The creamy gold leaves are mottled with green and hold their colour well. H and S 1m (3ft). Borderline hardy/Z 6. **'Manda's Crested'** was the first of the curly ivies. It has forked plain green leaves that turn bronze in winter. H and S 2m (6ft). The slow-growing **'Midas Touch'** has heart-shaped leaves that are basically dark green with patches of lighter green and irregularly blotched with yellow. It can scorch in an exposed site. H and S 1m (3ft). **'Oro di Bogliasco'** (syn. 'Goldheart') is very hardy, and the leaves retain their generous central golden-yellow blotch even in shade. H and S 2.2m (7ft) or more. **'Parsley Crested'** is an attractive ivy with rounded leaves that are crested at the edges and turn bronze in cold weather. It is good in a hanging basket. H and S 2m (6ft). **'Pedata'** (syn. 'Caenwoodiana') has distinctive, narrowly lobed, dark green leaves veined with greyish white. It is best against a wall. H and S 4m (13ft). **'Perkeo'** has unusual puckered leaves that are light green and turn red in cold weather. H and S 45cm (18in). Borderline hardy/Z 6–9. The leaves of **'Sagittifolia Variegata'** are variegated with golden yellow. This is a good ivy for the front of a windowbox, and it needs good light. H and S 1m (3ft). **'Spetchley'** is the smallest ivy available, with densely packed leaves that turn wine red in cold

Hedera colchica

weather. It is good as groundcover. H and S 30cm (1ft). Borderline hardy/Z 5. **'Triton'** (syn. 'Green Feather'), an eye-catching ivy, is a sprawling plant with deeply cut leaves. The three central lobes are elongated and twisted. H and S 45cm (18in).

HUMULUS
Hop

This is a commercially important genus, because hops are used to make beer, but providing one plant of interest to gardeners for its glowing foliage.
Cultivation Grow in any reasonably fertile, well-drained soil. The form described needs full sun for the best leaf colour.

H. lupulus

The straight species, a herbaceous twining climber, is not worth growing, but the selection **'Aureus'** is an outstanding plant wherever a curtain of foliage is needed. H and S to 6m (20ft). Hardy/Z 6–9.

Hedera helix 'Bruder Ingobert'

Hedera helix 'Pedata'

Humulus lupulus 'Aureus'

Jasminum officinale 'Aureum'

Lapageria rosea

Lonicera periclymenum 'Graham Thomas'

HYDRANGEA

This genus of shrubs also includes the outstanding climber described below, its single drawback being its reluctance to put on growth when young. Mature specimens are spectacular, grown either against walls or into trees.
Cultivation Hydrangeas tolerate a range of soil types, but the climbing species described does best in humus-rich, reliably moist soil in light shade.

H. anomala subsp. *petiolaris*
This self-clinging climber has creamy white 'lacecap' flowers in early summer. H and S 4m (13ft). Hardy/Z 4–9.

JASMINUM
Jasmine
For many gardeners, the heady scent of jasmine epitomizes summer; indeed, it can become almost overpowering. The winter jasmine has no scent, although the brilliant yellow flowers are undoubtedly welcome in the depths of winter.

Cultivation Grow in any well-drained soil in sun or light shade.

J. nudiflorum
Winter jasmine
Not strictly climbing, the stems of this Chinese species are lax and trailing. It can be trained against a wall or allowed to cascade down a bank. The cheery bright yellow flowers open during warm spells on the bare branches from late autumn to early spring. H and S 2m (6ft) or more. Hardy/Z 6–9.

J. officinale
Common white jasmine
This, the best-known species, is a twining climber with deliciously scented white flowers from midsummer to early autumn. 'Aureum' has leaves splashed with golden yellow. H and S to 5m (16ft). Borderline hardy/Z 9–10.

LAPAGERIA
A beautiful plant for a cool conservatory (porch) named after Empress Josephine, whose original name was Josephine de la Pagerie. There is only one species.
Cultivation Lapagerias need lime-free soil or potting compost (soil mix) in a lightly shaded position.

L. rosea
Chilean bellflower
This evergreen, twining climber has elongated bell-like, rich pinkish-red flowers that hang from the stems in late summer and autumn. H and S 3m (10ft), often less in a container. Half-hardy/Z 9–11. *L. rosea* var. *albiflora*, with white flowers, is possibly lovelier. H and S 3m (10ft). Borderline hardy/Z 10.

LATHYRUS
A large genus that includes many deliciously scented annuals and shrubs, as well as the delightful and easy-to-grow herbaceous tendril climbers described here. They are charming if allowed to wander through a hedge, but they can also be used more formally on tripods to give height to mixed borders. The flowers resemble those of the annual sweet peas.
Cultivation Grow in any well-drained soil in sun or light shade.

L. grandiflorus
Everlasting pea
This suckering species has glowing pinkish-purple flowers in summer and is good in a wild garden. H and S 2m (6ft). Hardy/Z 6–9.

L. latifolius
Everlasting pea
The species has vivid magenta flowers. Selections include the vigorous 'Rosa Pearl', which has pink flowers, and 'White Pearl', which has pure white flowers. H and S 3m (10ft). Hardy/Z 8–9.

LONICERA
Honeysuckle, woodbine
The scent of the honeysuckle is unmistakable, and fortunately can be enjoyed twice a year, since there are both early- and late-flowering varieties. These twining plants can make mounds and become congested with time. Although they can be used to cover walls and fences, they are at their best when grown more informally in a woodland or wild garden.
Cultivation Honeysuckles will do well in any soil that is not too dry, in a position where the roots are in shade.

L. periclymenum
Woodbine
This is a common woodlander throughout Europe and has deliciously scented, creamy-white flowers in summer. H and S 3m (10ft) or more. Hardy/Z 5–9. 'Belgica' (early Dutch honeysuckle) has pink and red flowers in midsummer, followed by red berries. 'Graham Thomas' bears

Hydrangea anomala subsp. *petiolaris*

Lathyrus latifolius 'White Pearl'

Lathyrus grandiflorus

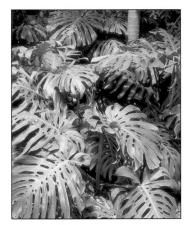

Monstera deliciosa

copper-tinted, creamy flowers all summer long. **'Serotina'** (late Dutch honeysuckle) has purple and red flowers from midsummer to autumn. Hardy/Z 5–9.

L. × tellmanniana
This hybrid would no doubt be more widely appreciated were it not for the lack of the characteristic honeysuckle scent – a drawback in the eyes of some. This is more than compensated for by the large, rich amber-orange flowers that appear in early summer, lighting up shady areas of the garden. H and S 3m (10ft). Hardy/Z 7–9.

MONSTERA
Swiss cheese plant
Popular as a houseplant, the species described here is rarely given sufficient headroom to show what it is really made of. Although tolerant enough to withstand the central heating of most living rooms, it is at its superb best in a large conservatory or greenhouse and can be used to shade orchids.
Cultivation Grow in large pots of preferably loam-based compost in light shade and mist daily to simulate rainforest conditions.

M. deliciosa
Swiss cheese plant
The common name refers to the holes that develop in the large glossy leaves as they mature. This is a scrambling plant that needs tying to its support. As it climbs higher it develops aerial roots, which can trail down to the ground. It seldom flowers in

cultivation. H 3m (10ft), S 2m (6ft), but can be considerably more. **'Variegata'** is a desirable selection, the leaves of which are splashed with creamy white. Tender/Z 10.

MUTISIA
These tendril climbers are not reliably hardy in cold areas, but they can be grown in an unheated conservatory.
Cultivation Grow in almost any well-drained soil in a sunny, sheltered site. In cold areas, train against a warm wall or grow under glass.

M. decurrens
A real connoisseur's plant, this has brilliant orange, daisy flowers in summer. H 3m (10ft), S 2m (6ft). Borderline hardy/Z 9–10.

PARTHENOCISSUS
These foliage plants are grown mainly for their spectacular autumn colour. All the species described here cling by means of suckering pads and are excellent on walls.
Cultivation Grow in fertile, well-drained soil in sun or light shade.

P. henryana
(syn. *Vitis henryana*)
Chinese Virginia creeper
This species has dark green leaves that are distinctively marked with central silvery white veins; they turn red in autumn. H and S to 10m (30ft). Borderline hardy/Z 7–9.

P. quinquefolia
(syn. *Vitis quinquefolia*)
Virginia creeper
This species is well known by its common name, its claim to garden merit lying in its vivid red autumn leaf colour. Eye-catching as cover for a large wall, it can also be dramatic weaving through the branches of a large tree, such as a silver birch. H and S 15m (50ft). Hardy/Z 4–9.

P. tricuspidata
Boston ivy
This vigorous species has maple-like green leaves that turn rich orange-red in autumn. H and S 15m (50ft). **'Beverley Brook'** is less vigorous and has smaller

Parthenocissus quinquefolia

leaves. The leaves of **'Lowii'** are tinged with purple when they emerge. The leaves of **'Veitchii'** open purple, mature to green, then turn red-purple in autumn. Hardy/Z 5–9.

PASSIFLORA
Passionflower
The range of these tendril climbers has increased considerably over the past few years, and a number of new forms, mostly conservatory plants, have been introduced. The flowers are highly distinctive: ten outer petals surround a crown of central filaments, inside which are the prominent stamens and styles.
Cultivation The hardy *P. caerulea* can be grown in any well-drained soil in sun in a sheltered position. Conservatory plants need to be in large pots of fertile compost with some protection from hot sun.

P. caerulea
This species can be evergreen, but if cut down by frosts will usually

Passiflora caerulea 'Constance Elliot'

Passiflora caerulea

regenerate from ground level. The summer flowers are white, with filaments banded blue, white and purple. H and S to 10m (30ft), but generally much less in cool climates. **'Constance Elliot'** has fragrant, creamy white flowers with red stigmas. Borderline hardy/Z 7–9.

P. quadrangularis
Giant granadilla
This South American species produces large, fragrant flowers in summer, with striking, twisted, violet and white filaments. H and S 10m (30ft), less in a container. Tender/Z 10.

PHILODENDRON
Well known as houseplants, the two root-climbing, evergreen species described here are fine foliage plants, which look good trained up moss poles.
Cultivation Use standard potting compost and keep sheltered from direct bright sunlight. Winter temperatures should not fall below 15°C (59°F).

P. melanochrysum
(syn. *P. andreasum*)
Black-gold philodendron, velour philodendron
This Colombian species has velvety textured, heart-shaped leaves, with a pronounced coppery tint when young. They can be up to 1m (3ft) long and 30cm (1ft) across. H 3m (10ft), generally much less as a container plant. Tender/Z 10.

P. scandens
Sweetheart vine, heart leaf
This well-known houseplant has shiny, mid-green, heart-shaped leaves with pointed tips. H and S 3m (10ft), but easily restrained. Tender/Z 10.

Pileostegia viburnoides

Schisandra rubrifolia

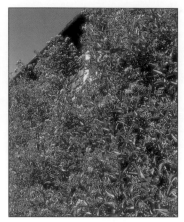

Solanum crispum 'Glasnevin'

PILEOSTEGIA

The evergreen species described is a dramatic root climber related to *Hydrangea*. The fact that it is not reliably hardy has probably kept it out of most gardens, but it is well worth trying in a sheltered situation, either growing up a tree trunk or across a wall.
Cultivation Grow in any reasonably fertile soil in sun or light shade with some shelter from severe cold.

P. viburnoides

This self-clinging climber from China and India has glossy, leathery leaves and clusters of small creamy-white flowers in late summer and autumn. H and S to 6m (20ft). Borderline hardy/Z 7–10.

PLUMBAGO
Leadwort

These South African climbers are grown for their flowers, which are mostly an appealing clear blue, although there are also white forms. The plants do not climb unaided but need to be tied to some form of support.
Cultivation Grow in pots of high-fertility compost such as John Innes No. 3 (loam-based soil mix) and keep in a sunny or lightly shaded spot.

P. auriculata
(syn. *P. capensis*)
Cape leadwort

The clusters of pale sky-blue flowers are produced from summer to early winter. H and S 1.5m (5ft) or more in a favourable site. Tender/Z 9–10.

SCHISANDRA

These twining climbers are hardy but seem to do best in sheltered gardens. They are delightful when grown so that they can climb into trees in light woodland or against walls, but the species described has one drawback for owners of small gardens: for reliable fruiting, plants of both sexes must be grown in proximity.
Cultivation Grow in sun or light shade in fertile soil that does not dry out excessively.

S. rubrifolia

This twining species produces scarlet to dark red flowers in early summer, followed, on female plants, by red berries. H and S 10m (30ft). Hardy/Z 8–10.

SOLANUM

These delightful climbers deserve to be better known. They produce an abundance of potato flowers over a long period and are generally easy in cultivation. Both the species described are lax

Plumbago auriculata

climbers, which need to be tied to their supports.
Cultivation Grow solanums in any well-drained soil in full sun.

S. crispum
Chilean potato tree

This species, which can be evergreen, is usually represented in cultivation by the form 'Glasnevin', which is reputedly hardier. The deep blue flowers, with prominent central yellow 'beaks', are carried in clusters over many weeks in summer. H and S to 5m (16ft). Borderline hardy/Z 8–9.

S. jasminoides
Potato vine

The straight species has grubby, grey flowers, but the selection 'Album' is a real beauty, with yellow-centred, white flowers. In cold areas, this is best trained against a warm wall. A harsh winter may kill the topgrowth, but it should recover if the base of the plant is protected with a dry mulch. H and S 3m (10ft). Half-hardy/Z 8–10.

STEPHANOTIS

A lovely plant for a conservatory (porch) or as a houseplant, the species described has richly scented, waxy white flowers.
Cultivation Use standard potting compost and keep in good light, but not direct sunlight. In winter, the temperature should not drop below 13°C (55°F).

S. floribunda
Bridal wreath, floradora

This twining evergreen has thick,

glossy, pointed leaves and can flower at any time when in growth. H and S to 3m (10ft), but usually much less when container-grown. Tender/Z 10.

THUNBERGIA
Clock vine

These climbers are too tender to grow outdoors in any but frost-free gardens, but the twining species described can be treated as an annual. In addition to providing temporary cover against a small trellis, it is also effective on tripods in borders or containers or allowed to trail without support from a hanging basket or large trough.
Cultivation Thunbergias will grow in any reasonable garden soil – or standard potting compost (soil mix) for container-grown plants – in a warm, sunny spot.

T. alata
Black-eyed Susan

The simple yellow or orange flowers, produced over a long period during summer and into autumn, have pronounced dark purple-brown throats – hence the common name. H to 2m (6ft), S 25cm (10in) or more if grown as a perennial. Tender/Z 10.

TRACHELOSPERMUM

The genus contains about 20 species, and the one described is among the most worthwhile of all climbers, with attractive, evergreen leaves and a long succession of small but incomparably scented flowers from summer until autumn. It deserves a prime spot in any garden and makes an excellent companion to *Bougainvillea* in a frost-free climate.
Cultivation Grow in sun or light shade in any well-drained soil. In a cold climate, train against a warm wall.

T. jasminoides
Star jasmine, confederate jasmine

This species from China and Japan has leathery, pointed, glossy green leaves on twining stems, although these need tying to their support initially. The white flowers are curiously twisted. H to 9m (30ft), but usually much less in cold climates. Borderline hardy/Z 8–10.

Trachelospermum Jasminoides

Tropaeolum speciosum

Vitis vinifera 'Purpurea'

TROPAEOLUM

As well as the highly desirable climber described here, the genus includes the popular annual nasturtiums. A yew hedge festooned with this plant is an eye-catching sight in late summer, but it does not always prove easy to establish in gardens, a cool, damp climate appearing to suit it best.
Cultivation Grow in reliably moist, lime-free soil in sun or light shade. It does not like hot, dry conditions.

T. speciosum
Scottish flame flower, flame creeper

The common names of this herbaceous perennial make appropriate reference to the colour of the brilliant red flowers, which appear throughout the summer. H and S to 3m (10ft). Borderline hardy/Z 7–9.

VITIS

This genus of tendril climbers is important commercially for the production of grapes, both for the

table and for wine-making. The plants described here are principally of ornamental value and are good for covering walls or clothing pergolas.
Cultivation Grow in poor soil in sun.

V. 'Brant'

This vigorous and attractive hybrid is a value-added plant in that its bloomy purple-black grapes are edible; these ripen in autumn as the leaves, which are veined yellow-green, turn dark purple-red. H and S to 12m (40ft) or more. Hardy/Z 5–9.

V. coignetiae
Crimson glory vine

This species from Japan and Korea is really valued for its spectacular autumn leaf colour – yellow, orange and deep scarlet – although it also produces crops of inedible, bloom-covered black grapes. H and S 15m (50ft). Hardy/Z 5–9.

V. vinifera
Tenturier grape

The species is the parent of the many varieties grown for edible crops and also of a number of purely ornamental selections. 'Purpurea' is one of the most widely grown. The leaves mature to purple, then develop even richer hues in autumn as the blackish, unpalatable fruits ripen. H and S 9m (30ft). Hardy/Z 6–9.

WISTERIA

Possibly the most desirable of all flowering climbers, wisterias bear dramatic racemes of scented pea flowers in late spring to early

summer. Old specimens trained against house walls are breathtaking, as are those trained to embrace arching bridges over water. They are also spectacular trained over arches, pergolas or – in a less formal garden – allowed to ramp into sturdy host trees. When shopping for wisterias, look for named varieties grafted on to vigorous rootstocks, expensive though these are. Seed-raised wisterias often have poor flowers, and plants raised from cuttings can lack vigour.
Cultivation Grow in any deep, fertile, well-drained soil in sun or light shade. Although fully hardy, they flower best when trained hard against a warm wall to ripen the stems. Prune young plants each year in late summer, cutting back any of the current year's growth that exceeds the allotted space and tying in suitably placed new stems to fill in the framework. Once the framework is established, in late summer cut back all stems that exceed the

framework. Shorten laterals to five or six leaves. In midwinter, cut these back further to two or three buds from the base of the stem. These are the spurs that will carry the flowers.

W. floribunda
Japanese wisteria

The species has hanging racemes, up to 30cm (12in) long, of fragrant, violet-blue flowers in early summer. Selections include **'Alba'** (syn. 'Snow Showers', *W. multijuga* 'Alba'), a desirable white-flowered form; **'Kuchi-beni'** (syn. 'Lipstick', 'Peaches and Cream'), which has lilac-pink and white flowers; and **'Multijuga'** (syn. 'Longissima', 'Macrobotrys'), which bears purple flowers in racemes to 60cm (2ft) long. H and S to 9m (30ft). Hardy/Z 4–10.

W. × *formosa*

This hybrid group includes one of the most dramatic of all wisterias, **'Yae-kokuryû'** (syn. 'Black Dragon', 'Kokuryû'), which produces long, hanging racemes of rich purple, double flowers. H and S to 9m (30ft). Hardy/Z 6–9.

W. sinensis
Chinese wisteria

This wisteria is somewhat more vigorous than the Japanese species. In its typical form, it has faintly-scented violet-blue flowers in late spring; **'Alba'** has white flowers; and **'Caroline'** has fragrant, deep blue-purple flowers. H 15m (50ft) or more, S 9m (30ft). Hardy/Z 5–9.

Vitis 'Brant'

Wisteria floribunda 'Kuchi-beni'

Wisteria sinensis

Gardening techniques

To maintain a healthy and attractive garden display successfully all year round, you will need to master a few important skills. In order to avoid mistakes and get the most from your garden you must give it the right care at the right time. From choosing the right plant for the right place and planting and sowing techniques to routine care, regular pruning and renovating overgrown plants; this chapter is a step-by-step guide to mastering and implementing essential skills, so that your garden can reach its fullest, most verdant potential.

As well as being the ideal place to store your tools, equipment and other gardening materials, a shed can be an attractive retreat in its own dusty way.

Buying trees and shrubs

Trees and shrubs are permanent additions to the garden and so need to be chosen with care. Many grow into large specimens, taking up a lot of garden space, so make sure you choose varieties that offer more than one season of interest to ensure they offer real value for money.

Buying plants

Trees and shrubs can be bought as container grown, containerized (grown in the field; potted for sale), rootballed or root wrapped (grown in the field; lifted with soil around the roots) or bare root (grown in the field; lifted without soil around the roots) depending on the type of plant and the supplier. Generally, container-grown plants will establish more quickly but are more expensive. Rootballed and bare-root plants are usually available in the autumn or early spring, while container-grown plants are available all year round.

Choosing trees

Most gardens can accommodate just one or two fully grown trees, which will take up a large proportion of the available planting space. It is vital, therefore, to make the correct choice. There is quite a wide range of trees available from garden centres and an even wider choice from specialist nurseries and by mail-order or on the Internet.

To make choosing easier, the first thing you should do is disregard those types of trees that are simply not suitable. Unless you have a very large garden, most can be rejected on the basis of their ultimate size. But other criteria, such as the preferred position (sun or shade) and the soil type in your garden, can also be used to narrow down the choice available. Plant labels, plant catalogues and websites will give this information, or you can check your selections in a reliable plant encyclopedia.

With a much-reduced list of possible candidates, the next step is to consider what features you want the tree to have. Should it be evergreen? When should it bear flowers or fruits? Is scent important? Would your garden benefit from autumn colour or winter interest such as attractive stems or bark? Again, use the information at the point of sale to help you decide.

Once you have made a choice, the next decision is the size of tree you buy (see right). Large trees make an instant impact and might be the best option if your garden is newly laid out and would benefit from the added height and structure a large tree would offer. However, younger specimens – three to five years old, say – generally establish more quickly than older trees. After a few years young trees will often catch up with and even overtake larger ones. Smaller trees are also much cheaper.

MAIL-ORDER PLANTS

Many trees and shrubs are available from mail-order companies. The young plants are mailed in special packages that minimize damage during transit.

ROOTBALLED PLANTS

A rootballed *Taxus* (yew). The ball of soil around the roots of the plant is held together by a net and strong elastic bands. It protects the roots and prevents desiccation.

BARE-ROOT PLANTS

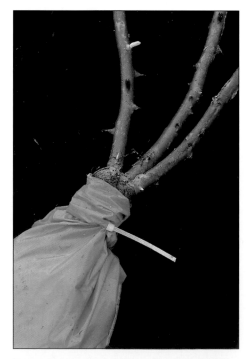

During the dormant season, bare-root plants are often sold with a wrap to protect their roots. If it is too frosty or wet to plant them, leave in the wrappings until conditions improve.

Specialist nurseries carry a wide range of trees and shrubs. Many have a mail-order service, which can be invaluable if the nursery is not easy for you to reach.

What size tree?

Trees are generally sold as two sizes: standards and half-standards, although you may find variations from some suppliers. Standards have a clear trunk to 1.8m (6ft) or so and are ideal for large trees that will form a specimen in a lawn or at the back of a border. Half-standards have a clear single stem, to at least 1.2m (4ft), and are useful planted in a mixed border or to provide a focal point nearer the edge. You can also buy trees as single-stemmed young plants (known as whips) or with new side branches (known as feathered maidens), which you can train yourself into a half-standard or standard by removing the lower branches as the tree grows.

Choosing shrubs

A garden or area of a garden can accommodate more shrubs than trees, so you can choose plants that offer spectacular displays for a relatively short period. However, it is important to create collections of shrubs that flower at different times to extend the period of interest. If you are planting a large area, plant shrubs in groups of threes or fives to achieve a more natural-looking overall display. Also include a proportion of evergreens to provide structure and colour to the borders in winter – as a rule, aim for about two-thirds evergreen to one-third deciduous plants.

What to look for

When buying trees and shrubs, whether container grown, rootballed or bare root, the signs to look out for are the same. Choose a plant with a well-balanced shape and healthy looking foliage with no signs of pest or disease damage. Grafted plants should have a strong, well-healed union. Look for plants that are well established in their pots but avoid those that have roots coming through the bottom of the pot or where roots are circling inside the pot because these have been left too long in their container. Also avoid plants with unnaturally yellowing leaves or weeds in the container because they have been neglected. Faded labels are also a sign the plant has been hanging around too long.

Look for healthy plants of bushy habit (centre) without any signs of leaf yellowing (right), stunted, straggly growth (left), or premature leaf fall, which may be caused by irregular watering.

Planting trees and shrubs

Trees and shrubs need to get off to the best possible start if they are to establish quickly. The secrets of success are preparing the ground well, preventing competition from other plants and keeping the new specimen well watered.

When to plant

Generally, the larger the specimen, the more work it will be to plant successfully. Container-grown deciduous plants can be planted at any time of the year, but they will establish more quickly and be easier to look after if they are planted in spring or autumn when the soil is moist and warm, which encourages rapid root growth and so establishment. Bare-root specimens, however, have to be planted during the dormant season, which is between autumn and spring. Evergreens, particularly conifers, are best planted in late spring so that they have time to establish before the onset of winter.

How to plant

If planting in a lawn, remove a 1m (3ft) wide circle of turf. Dig a hole large enough to accommodate the full spread of the roots (for bare-root plants) or twice as wide as the rootball for all other types. The hole should be the same depth as the rootball. Fork over the soil in the bottom of the hole. Place all excavated soil on a sheet near to the planting hole. Traditionally, the soil would be augmented with well-rotted manure and a handful of bonemeal, but recent research has shown that it is more beneficial to mulch after planting to prevent competition from weeds and to help retain soil moisture around the roots.

Water the rootball thoroughly before planting and allow it to drain. If staking, drive in a stake at this

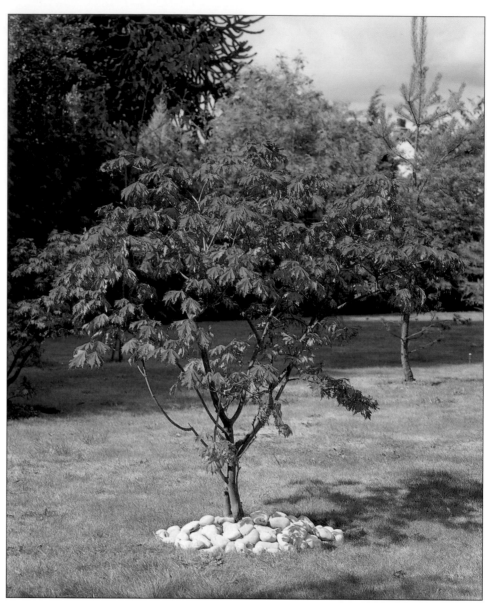

Trees often look best planted in isolation on the lawn. Here, the pale pebbles at the tree's base draw the eye to the feature, and enhance the decorative red leaves.

HOW TO PLANT A CONTAINER-GROWN SHRUB

1 Before you start, check that the plant has been watered. If not, give it a thorough soaking, preferably at least an hour before planting. This ensures that the rootball is moist and has the ability to absorb water after it has been planted.

2 If the soil in the bed has not been recently prepared, fork it over, removing any stones, weeds and other debris. Add a slow-release fertilizer and fork it into the soil well. If you use bonemeal, apply the fertilizer wearing rubber or vinyl gloves.

point. Position the tree or shrub at the same depth as it was in the pot or the nursery bed – there is usually a tell-tale dark soil mark on the stem about 5cm (2in) above the highest root. With container-grown specimens, tease out the roots from around the rootball before planting to encourage them to spread into the surrounding soil. Check the planting depth by laying a cane across the planting hole, then add or remove soil as necessary.

Backfill the first few centimetres (inch) of the hole with the excavated soil, and give bare-root trees or shrubs a gentle shake to settle the soil. Firm the first layer around the roots with your heel before adding a second layer and repeating the process until the hole is filled. This will prevent any air pockets. Also check that the specimen is upright from time to time as you work. With trees that you are staking, fit the tie. Water well, then cover the soil around the new tree or shrub with an 8cm (3in) deep layer of well-rotted, loose organic mulch. In exposed gardens, protect the tree or shrub after planting by erecting a windbreak and add rabbit guards if these are a pest in your garden.

How to stake a tree

If you are planting a tree over 1.5m (5ft) tall, hammer in a stake on the windward side of the tree to leave just 60cm (2ft) above ground level. Normally this can be done before positioning the tree.

If planting a large specimen you may need to put in the stake after planting, angling it to avoid the rootball. When planting bareroot specimens, spread the roots around the stake.

1 Place a strong stake of rot-resistant wood or one treated with preservative in the hole, knocking it in so that it cannot move.

2 Place the tree in the hole, pushing the rootball up against the stake, so that the stem and stake are 8–10cm (3–4in) apart.

3 Firm down the soil around the plant with the heel of your boot.

4 Although it is possible to use string, proper rose or tree ties provide the best support. Fix the lower one 15cm (6in) above the soil.

5 Fix the second tie near the top of the stake, slightly below the head of the plant.

6 Water the ground around the plant thoroughly and mulch with chipped bark or a similar material.

3 Dig a hole twice as wide as the rootball. Place the plant, still in its pot, in the hole and check that the hole is deep enough by placing a stick or cane across the hole: the top of the pot should align with the top of the soil. Adjust the depth of the hole accordingly.

4 Remove the plant from its pot, being careful not to disturb the rootball. If it is in a plastic bag, cut the bag away rather than trying to pull it off. Place the shrub in the hole and pull the earth back around it. Firm the soil down around the plant and water well.

5 Finally, mulch round the shrub, covering the soil with 5–8cm (2–3in) of chipped bark or similar material. This will not only help to preserve the moisture in the soil but will also help to prevent weed seeds from germinating.

Moving trees and shrubs

It is of course best to plant a tree or shrub in its final position, but even in the best planned garden this isn't always practical. Moving established plants, even small ones, is hard work and needs careful forethought. However, with a few helpers and good preparation, many plants can be moved successfully.

When to move trees and shrubs

The best time for transplanting most established trees or shrubs is during the dormant season (late autumn to early spring). However, the soil should not be waterlogged or frozen as this will damage the soil structure and make it more difficult for the plant to re-establish itself. Spring planting gives a full season's growth before the winter; an autumn move allows the plant to develop a good root system before spring. Evergreens, including conifers, are best moved in mid-spring when the soil is moist and warm enough to encourage rapid root growth.

What size rootball?

The rootball diameter and depth should depend on the size of the plant you are trying to move. The diameter should be about the same as the spread of the branches of shrubs and about one-third the height of a tree. The depth of the rootball depends on the type of soil in your garden. The lighter the soil the more penetrating the roots and so the deeper the rootball will have to be. For example, a 30cm (12in) deep rootball on clay soil may need to be twice that depth on a light, sandy soil. Bear in mind that rootballs with soil attached can literally weigh a ton if you are moving a small tree or large shrub. Make sure you have sufficient help before you start.

HOW TO MOVE A SMALL SHRUB

1 Before moving a shrub, make sure that the planting site has been prepared and the hole excavated. Water the plant well the day before moving it.

2 Dig a trench around the plant, leaving a large rootball (the size depends on the size of the plant). Carefully sever any roots that you encounter to release the rootball.

3 Dig under the shrub, cutting through any vertical taproots that hold it in place.

4 Rock the plant to one side and insert sacking or strong plastic sheeting as far under the plant as you can. Push several folds of material under the rootball.

5 Rock the shrub in the opposite direction and pull the sacking or plastic sheeting through, so that it is completely under the plant.

6 Pull the sacking round the rootball and tie it firmly at the neck of the plant. The shrub is now ready to move. If it is a fairly small plant, one person may be able to lift it out of the hole and transfer it to its new site.

7 If the plant plus the soil is heavy, it is best moved by two people. Tie a length of wood or metal to the sacking. With one person on each end, lift the shrub out of the hole.

8 Lower the transplanted shrub into the prepared planting hole. Unwrap and remove the sheeting from the rootball. Make sure that the plant is in the right position, refill the hole, and water well.

Root pruning

The chances of successfully moving very large shrubs and trees can be improved by pruning the roots in advance of the move, a technique known as root pruning. It should be done up to a year before the move.

To root prune, simply dig the vertical trench at the correct distance from the tree or shrub and sever any roots you find, then refill the trench with soil. The plant will produce more fibrous roots in the soil nearer to the trunk, and these will form part of the rootball, increasing the plant's chances of survival after the move.

Making moves

Before you start, decide on the new position of the plant and prepare the planting hole, which should be about twice as wide and as deep as the rootball. Fork over the bottom of the hole, incorporating a bucketful of grit on heavy soils to improve drainage.

Use a spade to cut a slit-trench around the tree or shrub being moved to mark out the size of the rootball and to sever any roots near to the surface. Then cut a second slit-trench about 30cm (12in) further out and dig out the soil in between to form a trench around the specimen. Make this trench as deep as the rootball.

Undercut the rootball from the trench by inserting the spade at an angle of about 45 degrees all the way round. Small rootballs should then be completely undercut and can be wrapped. Larger rootballs may need further excavation to expose any vertical roots under the middle of the rootball.

After the rootball has been freed, carefully rock it back and slip a sheet of folded heavy-duty polythene or hessian (burlap) under one side then

A shrub may need to be moved because it is too vigorous and is crowding out other plants, or because the re-design of its bed makes a move desirable. Prune the shrub after planting if required to create a balanced shape. Water the shrub well throughout the first growing season.

rock it over the other way and then pull the folded polythene through. Tie the corners of the sheeting over the top of the rootball around the main stem to form a neat package, so that the soil is held firmly. Use rope or strong string to reinforce the rootball on all sides.

Move the tree or shrub by pulling on the polythene sheeting, not the trunk. Use a short plank (board) or pair of planks as a ramp out of the hole and then drag it to its new position or get a gang of helpers to lift it. It may be easiest to fix a pole to help carry the tree or shrub.

Replant immediately and water and mulch well. Stake if necessary. Spray the foliage of evergreens after planting and every few days for the first month to help prevent scorching. It is also worth putting up a windbreak around conifers. Keep all transplants well watered throughout the first growing season.

Even very small conifers such as this *Chamaecyparis lawsoniana* 'Bleu Nantais' are hard work to move. Always check the final height and spread of a plant before choosing where to plant it.

Aftercare of trees and shrubs

Once they are established, most trees and shrubs will look after themselves. However, it can take more than a growing season to reach this point of independence. There are also some ornamental types that produce much better displays if they are given a little extra pampering.

Watering techniques

The main reason new trees and shrubs fail in their first season is because they cannot take up sufficient water. Since they have not had time to root into the soil, new specimens should be treated like container-grown plants elsewhere in the garden. Water them thoroughly once a week in dry weather or if your soil is well drained, rather than giving them a light sprinkling every day. Aim to give new shrubs at least a full watering can of water and new trees twice this amount each time you water.

It is essential that the water soaks the soil around the plant and doesn't run off elsewhere. There are a number of techniques you can employ to make sure this happens. Insert a plastic pipe at an angle into the soil

This evergreen *Pieris japonica* had sufficient water in its first year after planting, and now produces an everchanging display of foliage with very little maintenance required.

so that the bottom is at the root zone and the top just proud of the soil surface. Fill the pipe with gravel so that other rubbish cannot accumulate in it and pour water into the pipe each time you water. Alternatively, ridge up the soil about 30cm (12in) away from the main stem to create a

moat each time the plant is watered. The water will then have time to soak into the soil exactly where it is needed. A more sophisticated method is to use circles of seep hose or leaky pipe with a snap-lock connector around individual plants and clip these to a hosepipe (garden hose) each time you water. The water will be released slowly without running off. If you are planting a whole garden, consider installing an automatic watering system.

Mulching

There are many benefits to mulching the newly planted tree or shrub with organic matter. It smothers the ground, preventing weed seeds from germinating and getting established. It also prevents water evaporation from the soil, helping to conserve soil moisture. As it is incorporated into the ground by soil-living creatures, such as earthworms, it helps improve the soil structure and

HOW TO LOOK AFTER TREES AND SHRUBS AFTER PLANTING

A newly planted tree or shrub needs to be watered well in order to become established.

Mulch with straw or garden compost to conserve the moisture in the soil.

releases valuable plant nutrients as it decomposes. A mulch also helps to insulate the soil from excessive heat in summer and cold in winter.

A wide range of materials can be used for mulching. Apply a 5–8cm (2–3in) deep layer around new plants and top up to this layer each spring thereafter. Around established shrubs and trees you can use grass clippings as a free organic mulch. Although some nitrogen is removed from the soil by micro-organisms as the clippings are broken down, only the very surface layer is affected.

Weed control

Limiting weed growth is important in the first few years but is less so as the canopy fills out. Keep all weeds under control during the early years. Use a hoe shallowly around each plant to avoid damaging the roots and hand weed near shallow-rooted plants, such as azaleas, as well as trees and shrubs, such as lilac, that are prone to suckering (throwing up shoots from below ground level) if they suffer root damage. If a weed gets established, use a chemical spot weedkiller to deal with it.

WEEDING AROUND TREES AND SHRUBS

Using a hoe to remove weeds from around young trees or shrubs is the surest way of catching them all. It is best carried out in hot weather so that any weeds hoed up die quickly.

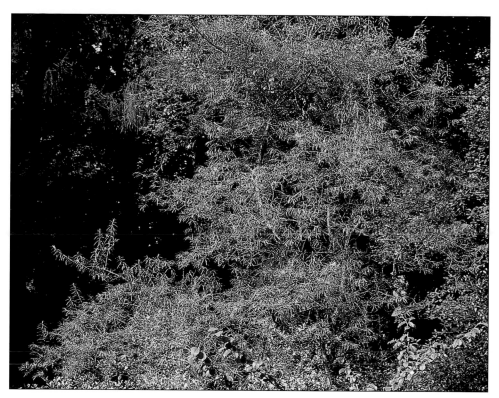

As its name suggests, *Hippophaë rhamnoides* (sea buckthorn) is tolerant of strong, salt-laden winds and can be planted as a windbreak to protect frailer plants. Its long, silvery green leaves, yellow flowers and orange berries are all decorative in their own right.

Windbreaks

A severe winter storm can cause considerable damage to trees and shrubs, sometimes breaking whole branches. If your garden is exposed you should consider erecting some sort of windbreak. In the short term this can be a special plastic windbreaker, but in the longer term it is probably better to create a more permanent solution by planting a living windbreak. A number of trees and shrubs can be used for this, and it should be fairly easy to find one that fits seamlessly into your garden design.

Leyland cypress grow very fast, and, for this reason, they are often used as windbreaks, but are best avoided for more suitable alternatives. They are thirsty, hungry plants that take a lot of nutrients from the soil for some distance around the roots. They also continue to grow rapidly past their required height.

It is best to get the windbreaks established before the shrubs or ornamental trees are planted, but if time is of the essence, plant them at the same time, perhaps temporarily shielding both from the winds with windbreak netting.

Good windbreak plants

Acer pseudoplatanus (sycamore)
Berberis darwinii
Buxus sempervirens (box)
Cotoneaster simonsii
Fraxinus excelsior (ash)
Griselinia littoralis
Hippophaë rhamnoides
  (sea buckthorn)
Ilex (holly)
Ligustrum ovalifolium (privet)
Lonicera nitida (box-leaf honeysuckle)
Pyracantha (firethorn)
Rosmarinus officinalis (rosemary)
Sorbus aucuparia (rowan)
Taxus baccata (yew)

Routine care

Some trees and shrubs need regular maintenance to produce their best displays. Pruning is the main task, but there are a few other important techniques worth carrying out.

Feeding

Trees and shrubs are often fed with bonemeal at planting time but, once established, feeding should not be necessary except in a few special circumstances. If your soil is very poor or free-draining give an annual application of a general fertilizer around each plant in spring. Some free-flowering shrubs, such as roses and lilacs, will produce a better display if given a high-potash fertilizer such as tomato fertilizer or rose feed, in spring and early summer.

Foliar feed can also be applied as an emergency measure when soil nutrients are in short supply or unavailable because of drought, for example. The feed is very dilute and can be easily applied, even to quite large plants and large areas, using a hose-end feeder fitted to the end of a garden hose. The nutrients are readily absorbed through the leaves.

Get better, long-lasting displays from flowering shrubs by applying a high-potash feed in spring.

Deadheading

The removal of fading, dying or dead flowerheads after flowering (known as deadheading) not only improves displays directly by tidying up the plant, but also prolongs and improves flowering over time by encouraging the plant to put its energy into growth and flower production rather than producing seeds. With nearly all trees and most shrubs deadheading is not practicable, but it is particularly worth the effort for repeat-flowering shrubs, such as large-flowered (hybrid tea) and cluster-flowered (floribunda) roses, as well as free-flowering plants such as lilacs. Pinch off the old blooms between finger and thumb or

HOW TO DEADHEAD RHODODENDRONS

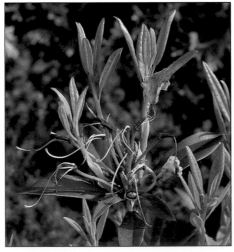

1 Deadheading stops the plant putting energy into seed production that could be used for new flowers or foliage. New growth emerges below the flower truss.

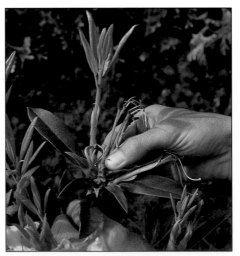

2 Pinch out the dead flowerheads, using your finger and thumb to minimize potential damage to the emerging new leaves.

3 After the flowerhead is removed, the point at which soft and tender new leaves will emerge can clearly be seen.

HOW TO DEADHEAD HEATHERS

Trim heathers with shears after flowering. Cut just below faded flowers but avoid cutting into the old wood because it will not resprout.

use a pair of garden snips or secateurs (pruners) for tougher stems. Shrubs that produce a lot of small flowers, such as heathers, are usually easier to deadhead using a pair of shears.

A few shrubs, such as magnolias and rhododendrons, produce next year's blooms just behind those produced this year, so you need to be careful not to break these off too. Hydrangeas are the exception to the deadheading rule because the old blooms should be left on the plant to protect next year's buds in winter. Only in early spring should the faded flowerheads be removed.

Winter protection

If you have any shrubs that are of borderline hardiness for your area, it is worth protecting them over the winter. Even normally hardy shrubs may need protection during a severe

Shrubs worth deadheading

Azalea	Paeonia
Camellia	Pieris
Choisya	Rhododendron
Erica	Rosa
Hypericum	Syringa
Kalmia	

or unseasonably cold spell. Cold and wind or a combination of the two are the main problems. Evergreens in particular can be scorched by cold winds in winter, especially if the soil is frozen, because the plant is unable to replace the water it loses through its leaves. The easiest way to protect individual plants is to erect a windbreak supported on wooden stakes. Groups of small shrubs can be protected by covering them with netting firmly anchored on all sides and held off the plants on canes topped with upturned pots. A more long-term solution is to choose hardy trees or shrubs as windbreaks.

Some shrubs, such as hardy fuchsias and eucalyptus, will die down to ground level in cold winters and sprout again in the spring. In severe spells of cold weather, however, the roots can be killed, so they are worth protecting with an insulating layer of leaves or straw. Make an enclosure over the root area using plastic mesh and fill it with dry leaves in autumn, or cover the roots with a 15cm (6in) layer of bark chippings. This can be removed in spring and used as a border mulch.

HOW TO PROVIDE WINTER PROTECTION

1 To protect a tender shrub using a shield, insert three stout stakes firmly into the ground around the plant, then wrap a plastic sheet or several layers of horticultural fleece around the outside of the stakes. Tie securely and peg down the bottom to secure.

HEAVY SNOW FALLS

Some evergreens, particularly conifers, are susceptible to damage caused by the weight of accumulated snow. The plant can be either pulled out of shape or have limbs broken. Prevent damage by tying up susceptible plants before winter or routinely knock heavy falls of snow from exposed plants before damage is caused.

A few shrubs, such as bay, cordylines and myrtle, are worth wrapping up in winter. Make an insulating duvet out of two layers of fine-mesh netting stuffed with insulating material. Wrap the plants in late autumn or early winter and uncover them in early spring.

2 If you don't want to erect a shield, perhaps on aesthetic grounds, cover the plant with a large plastic bag or horticultural fleece sleeve, pegged to the ground, when very severe weather is forecast. Remove it afterwards.

Basic pruning for trees and shrubs

Most trees and shrubs will need an occasional prune to maintain health, control their size and improve the display of flowers or foliage. It is a straightforward process provided you use the correct pruning technique and get the timing right.

Pruning tools

Despite having acquired a reputation for being difficult, all pruning follows a few basic rules, which are easy to understand and to put into practice. The first rule is to have good quality tools with sharp, clean blades. Sharp well-maintained blades will make clean cuts without damaging the surrounding tissues left on the plant. By keeping the blades clean you will also minimize the chance of spreading disease when you prune. If you are removing diseased material it is a good idea to use a garden disinfectant to wipe the blades between cuts.

It is also important to use the right pruning tools for the thickness of the stem. For cutting stems up to 1cm (½in) thick use a pair of secateurs (pruners), for stems 1–3cm (½-1¼in) thick a pair of long-handled loppers would be best. For stems more than 3cm (1¼in) thick you will need a pruning saw.

Pruning cuts should also be made in the right way. As a rule, cut just above an outward-facing, healthy looking bud (or pair of buds) so that new growth does not increase the congestion in the centre of the plant. Make the cut angled away from the bud so that it sheds water. With shrubs such as potentilla and spiraea, which have a lot of thin, wiry stems, pruning in this way is not practicable. You will get just as good a result if you use shears to cut back the plant. Indeed, recent research has shown that even thick-stemmed bush roses can be "rough pruned" without a noticeable decline in their health or flowering potential.

Simple pruning

Most shrubs and trees do not require regular pruning, but some will produce bigger and better displays of flowers

GOOD AND BAD PRUNING CUTS

1 A good pruning cut is made about 3mm (⅛in) above a strong bud. It should be a slanting cut, with the higher end above the bud. The bud should generally be facing outward from the plant rather than inward; the latter will throw its shoot into the plant, crossing and rubbing against others, which should be avoided. This is an easy technique and you can practise it on any stem.

2 If the stem has buds or leaves opposite each other, make the cut horizontal, about 3mm (⅛in) above the buds.

3 Always use a sharp pair of secateurs (pruners). Blunt ones will produce a ragged or bruised cut, which is likely to provide easy access to disease spores.

4 Do not cut too far above a bud. The piece of stem above the bud is likely to die back and the stem may well die back even further, causing the loss of the whole stem.

5 Do not cut too close to the bud, otherwise the bud might be damaged by the secateurs (pruners) or disease might enter. Too close a cut is likely to cause the stem to die back to the next bud.

6 It is bad practice to slope the pruning cut towards the bud because this makes the stem above the bud too long, which is likely to cause die-back. It also funnels rain on to the bud, and moisture can collect in the join which may cause rot or other problems.

HOW TO PRUNE

1 Cut any diseased or damaged wood back to sound wood, just above a strong bud. It may be necessary to cut right back to the main stem. The wood is quite easy to spot. It may not be dead, but still in the process of turning brown or black. Damaged wood will not grow and may harbour diseases.

2 Crossing stems should be removed while they are still young, otherwise friction may damage them and let in disease spores. They also make the bush look congested if not removed, and make it harder to prune. Use secateurs (pruners) to cut the stem at its base where it joins the main branch.

3 Tips of stems often die back, especially those that have carried clusters of flowers. Another cause of die-back is when the young growth at the tip of shoots is killed by frost. If the die-back is not cut out, it can eventually kill off the whole shoot. Cut the shoot back into good wood, just above a strong bud.

if they are pruned in the right way and at the right time. If left to their own devices, however, even those types that don't normally need pruning will become congested with unproductive wood. For this reason the most basic form of pruning can be applied to all woody plants and is often known as the three Ds: the removal of dead, diseased and damaged stems. This can be done at any time of the year.

If you want to go a step further the pruning method you use and the time you prune will depend on what you are trying to achieve. For example, if you are pruning to

improve flowering you will need to know whether the shrub you are about to prune blooms on wood produced during the previous season or on new wood produced during the current season. However, if you do not know anything about the shrub

you could use the fail-safe one-in-three method. Prune one-third of the shrub back to the ground every year, choosing the oldest stems, so no stem is more than three years old. The one-in-three technique is also a good way of rejuvenating old shrubs.

No-prune shrubs

Aucuba japonica
Berberis thunbergii
Choisya ternata
Cordyline australis
Cotoneaster microphyllus
Euonymus fortunei
Fatsia japonica
Genista lydia
Magnolia stellata
Prunus laurocerasus
Skimmia japonica

This *Olearia* x *haastii* puts forward a glorious display of white flowers in summer. After flowering, prune back the oldest one-third of the shoots following the one-in-three method.

Established tree pruning

With proper initial training most trees are set up for life and apart from a regular check-up rarely need much attention. It is possible to ignore their pruning totally and the tree will still thrive, much as they all do in the wild. However, a healthy tree is a far safer one as well as a prettier one, and so it is worth spending a short while each year checking any trees over.

The three Ds

The one gardening task that must be carried out at least once a year is a survey of all the trees in the garden in order to check that there is no dead, diseased or damaged wood. Any that is found should be cut out and the wounds cleaned up. It is probably a good idea to check at the end of the growing season, in autumn, and again after the winter during which strong winds and frost may have caused damage to your trees.

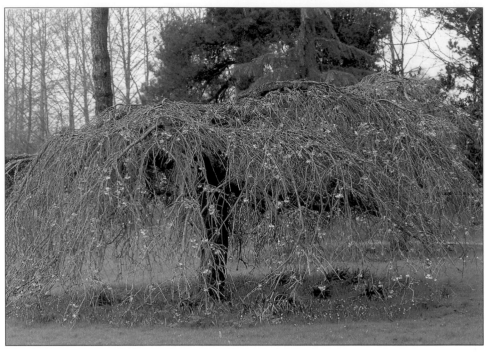

ABOVE Unusual trees, such as this weeping cherry, need special attention or they will lose the quality that makes them such an attractive feature in the garden.

Fallen branches should have the snags cut off and any tears should be cleaned with a sharp knife to remove all fragments of loose wood. Any heavy branches that are to be removed should be cut off in sections to prevent splitting and tearing. There is no need to dress wounds even from cuts left by the removal of large branches.

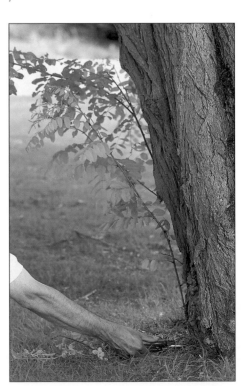

ABOVE Many trees produce suckers from the base of the trunk. These should be cut out as tightly to the trunk as possible.

ABOVE It is essential that any dead, damaged or dying wood should be removed from your trees. Autumn and winter storms can be a cause of damage that will need dealing with in the spring. Here, a pair of long-handled pruners is being used to remove a dead branch.

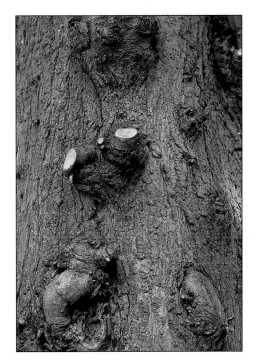

ABOVE Clean any larger cuts with a sharp knife to remove any ragged or torn bark.

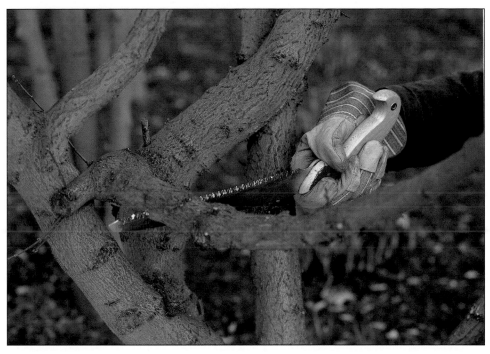

ABOVE Usually little pruning is required for trees, but it is likely to help if any crossing or over crowding branches are removed.

Unwanted growths

Most trees at some point produce branches that cross others, creating congestion and often wounds where the bark of one rubs against that of another in the wind. Any such crossing wood should be removed. If you are creating a branch-headed standard then it is also a good idea to thin the timber in the centre of the tree so that air and light can circulate.

Many trees from time to time throw out wayward growths – an odd stem will suddenly shoot off into space – spoiling the shape of the plant. These should be removed at some point within the shape of the tree. Similarly, if the tree is a variety with variegation or non-standard foliage, it may occasionally throw out reverted stems, with leaves that are plain green, like those of the parent species. These should be removed back at their point of origin.

Some trees produce water (or epicormic) shoots. These are shoots that appear around wounds where, for example, a branch has been removed or where a lawn mower has

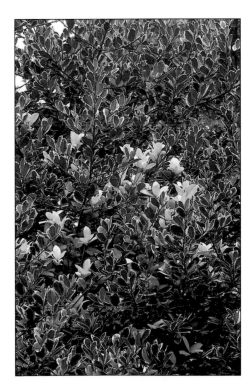

ABOVE Variegated trees can throw out shoots on which the leaves revert to their original green. Remove these when you see them.

DEALING WITH EPICORMIC SHOOTS

1 Some trees – lime (*Tilia*) in particular – produce what are known as water or epicormic shoots on their trunks.

2 The best way of dealing with them is to rub them out with your fingers as soon as you see them.

REMOVING A LARGE TREE BRANCH

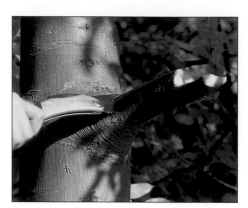

1 Make a cut about 20–25cm (8–10in) out from where the final cut will be on the underside of the branch. Cut about a third of the way into the branch.

2 Make a cut about 10cm (4in) nearer the position of the final cut, cutting until the branch snaps. The initial undercut prevents the wood splitting or bark from stripping.

3 Position the saw for the last cut to avoid damaging the swollen area at the base of the branch. The cut will heal in a couple of seasons. No wound painting is necessary.

damaged the bark at the base of the trunk. Cut these out at their base. If the tree has been grafted, then any shoots that appear from below the graft union should be removed, even if they look as though they might be in the ideal place, as these will be different from the rest of the tree. Similarly, suckers often appear from below ground. These may come from a grafted rootstock or just as a natural suckering habit. Unless you want to develop a multi-stemmed tree, these should all be removed back at their point of origin. Dig below soil level, if necessary.

Controlling size

In an ideal world it would be nice to allow trees to grow to their full potential, but there are often factors, such as a lack of space, which dictate that the tree should be kept to a certain size. In some cases this may simply be a question of removing a few side branches, perhaps even spoiling the shape. In other cases, it may mean reducing the size of the whole tree. One technique is known as dropcrotching: all the branches are reduced in length, so that the original outline of the tree is kept the same but much reduced in size. This should be done before the tree reaches its ultimate size, while the branches are still quite young, so that the shaping will not be too unsightly. Repeat every two or three years. Do not cut too deeply back into the tree or it may never recover its shape.

Letting in light

It has already been mentioned that it can sometimes be beneficial to open up the canopy to let in more light and air, particularly with fruiting trees. In addition, you may wish to grow other plants below trees, and too dense a shade will often prevent this. In order to let in more light (and, indeed, water in the form of rain), rather than remove the whole tree it

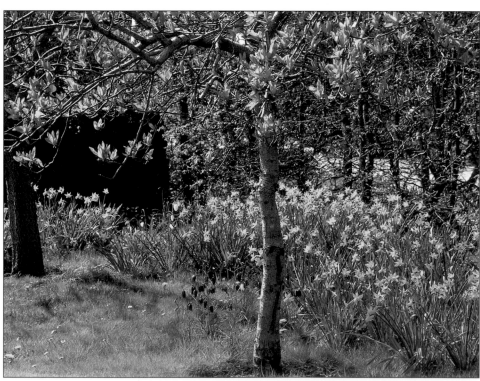

ABOVE In gardens where space is limited or where there is close planting, established pruning is required to control the size of a tree and so prevent it from smothering other plants.

ABOVE Working with ladders can be dangerous for those not used to them. This stepladder with a wide base is a much safer option.

is often possible to remove some of the lower branches. This is often done with oak trees, the shape of which is not unduly spoilt by such pruning. It allows grass and other plants to be grown beneath them.

Feeling their age

As with humans, trees age. In oaks, this may well be only after several hundred years, but it might be only after 30 in the case of birches. There are several problems associated with this. One is the development of stags' heads. This is most noticeable in oaks but can also occur in other trees. Some of the branches die, leaving them bare and stripped of bark (often looking like a stag's horns, hence the name). In some cases this makes the tree look venerable, but others will simply look diseased and unsightly. The tree is usually perfectly healthy, and the removal of the branches will return the tree to its normal appearance.

The other problem is that branches may start to sag and fall away. A similar and more frequent occurrence is when the trunks of multi-stemmed trees start to fall apart. These can be braced if the tree is an important one. This is best done by experienced professionals, as an inadequately braced tree may fall on somebody with dire consequences all round.

Safety

Ladder work may be necessary when pruning tall trees. If you do not feel confident or have not had the necessary experience of cutting large branches from a tree, especially those that are some way from the ground, call in a tree expert. It may cost money but not lives. If you do the work yourself, wear adequate safety gear, especially a hard hat.

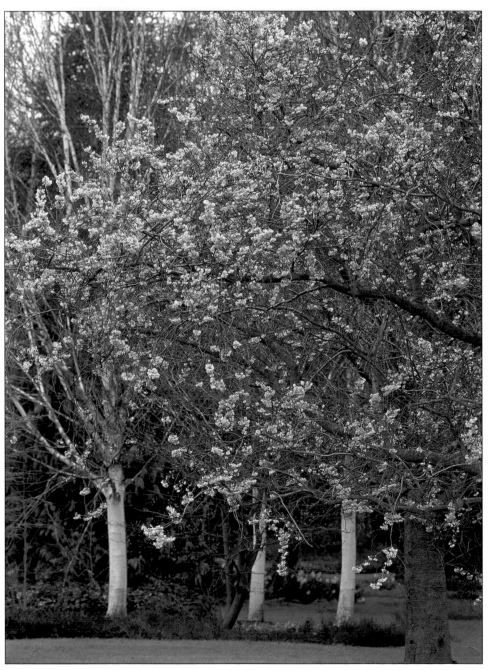

ABOVE Most fully grown trees, such as these ornamental cherries (*Prunus*) or the birches (*Betula*) in the background, need little in the way of pruning.

Renovating trees

When you take over an old garden, or acquire a new one which was part of a field or wood, there may be old trees in it that have been neglected or never been pruned. You may well be forced to decide whether to take the trees out and start from scratch, or try to renovate them. Trees take a long time to grow to maturity and leave a large gap when felled, so if possible it is best to try to bring them back to their former glory. There may also be preservation orders on the trees, so it would be illegal to remove them without permission. It may even be illegal to carry out major renovation without permission, so it is always best to check before you start.

Prune it step by step

Your aim with a neglected and overgrown tree is to turn back the clock and do all the things that should have been carried out in previous years. The best time to rejuvenate an old tree is in the late autumn or early winter. Start, as always, by removing any dead, diseased or damaged wood. This should remove quite a bit of material and allow you to begin to see the structure of the tree. Next remove any water or epicormic shoots along with any weak growths, especially those that have developed in the centre of the tree. Where branches cross over or rub against other branches, cut them out. The tree should now begin to look the way it should.

Examine the tree closely to assess whether there is still any overcrowding and whether anything else needs to be removed. Perhaps the tree has been regularly "pruned" by somebody who has simply gone over the outside of the tree

RENOVATING AN OVERGROWN TREE

1 (*left*) Some trees, such as this contorted hazel, can become overgrown and need to be renovated in order to bring back their shape and interest.

2 (*above*) Start the renovation by removing all the dead and damaged wood. This will allow you to see what remains much more clearly.

3 (*left*) Next thin some of the branches to reduce the congestion, especially towards the middle of the tree. Remove old and weak growths first.

4 (*above*) The dead stub shows how poor pruning can cause die-back, as the previous cut was made too high. Cut tightly back as shown here.

PRUNING KNOBBLY SPURS If a tree has been severely cut back over a number of years, the ends of the branches become a mass of spurs. Cut these back drastically to one or two in order to return the tree to its original shape.

Tree renovation times

**Mid- to late winter
(before growth starts)**
Maple (*Acer*)
Horse chestnut (*Aesculus*)
Birch (*Betula*)
Conifers
Juglans (walnut)
Salix (willow)

Any season apart from spring
Carpinus (hornbeam)
Fagus (beech)
Quercus (oak)
Tilia (lime)

**Summer (before end of
mid-summer)**
Ornamental plums and cherries

TREE RENOVATION TECHNIQUES

In general, most ornamental trees can be left to their own devices, but sometimes it is essential to remove the lower branches or thin the crown in order to allow more light and rain to reach any plants that are growing under the tree.

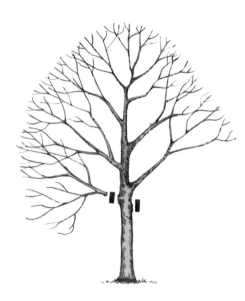

CROWN RAISING More light can be obtained below a tree by removing some of the lower branches so that the light comes in under the canopy.

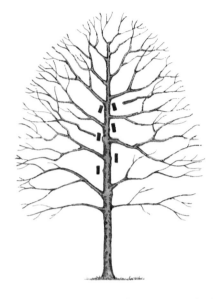

CROWN THINNING An alternative method is to thin out some of the branches from the crown so that dappled light filters its way through the canopy.

removing the new extension growth on the tips of the branches, so that it has thickened up around the perimeter, a bit like a hedge. You will have to reduce and thin this growth drastically to bring the tree back to something resembling a normal appearance.

Not all trees like to be pruned hard all in one go, as it can often kill them. It is usually better to prune them over a number of years, taking out just a bit each time. This means that the tree will look untidy over this period, but this is better than a dead tree.

Aftercare
Renovation is a drastic treatment for any tree, so make certain that it is fed and kept watered during any dry spells the following summer. Mulching will help to preserve soil moisture.

Safety
A lot of the pruning work on an overgrown tree inevitably takes place well above the head of the gardener, usually on ladders. If you do not feel confident to carry out this work yourself, then employ a specialist firm who will have had a lot of experience in dealing with this kind of renovation work. This is particularly important if you need, for example, to take out a dead crown from a large tree.

ABOVE Overgrown trees will inevitably contain a lot of dead and damaged wood. This should be one of the first things to be removed.

ABOVE If a tree has been neglected, there are likely to be branches that cross over or rub against others. These should be removed.

Conifers

After years in the wilderness, slow-growing dwarf conifers are now coming back into fashion. They are easy to grow, require practically no maintenance and offer year-round interest.

Grouping conifers

Conifers can be grown as single specimens or in groups, in a mixed border with other shrubs, perennials and bulbs or in a special conifer area, where a variety of forms can be combined to good effect. Although an evergreen conifer display is very low maintenance and looks good all year, it can seem static, because it remains exactly the same from one season to the next.

Choosing a position

Most conifers prefer a position in full sun, but many will tolerate partial shade or being in deeper shade for just part of the day. They will not grow well in dense shade or waterlogged soil, however. If your soil is heavy, you could try draining it, improving the structure, by adding plenty of well-rotted organic matter and grit before planting, or creating a special conifer raised bed. Many slow-growing dwarf conifers also do well in containers.

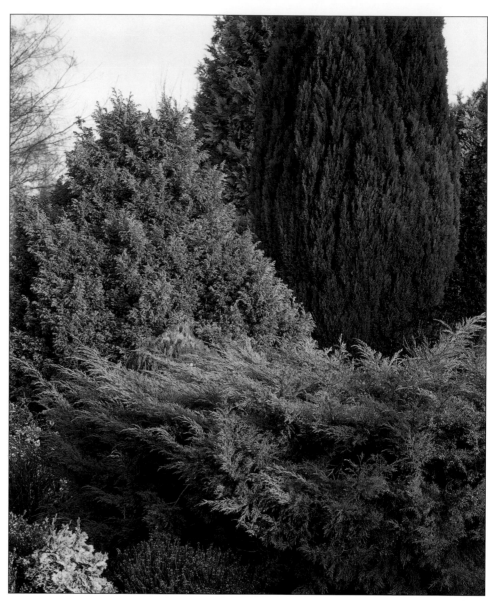

Conifers develop a range of habits, including upright, conical and spreading. Planted together in the garden they can make a striking group.

HOW TO PLANT A CONIFER

1 Place the conifer in the prepared hole and check the planting depth. The soil mark should be at the same level as the surrounding soil.

2 When the plant is in position, untie the wrapper and slide it out of the hole. Avoid disturbing the ball of soil around the roots.

3 Replace the soil around the plant and firm down to eliminate large pockets of air. Apply fertilizer, if necessary, and water well.

Planting

The best time to plant conifers is mid-spring, when the soil is moist and starting to warm up. This allows the plants to establish before the onset of winter. However, container-grown conifers can also be planted at other times of year (particularly early autumn), provided they are kept well watered in summer and protected from cold winds in winter. If the weather or soil conditions are not suitable for planting when the conifers arrive, plant them roughly in a trench in a sheltered spot (known as heeling in) until conditions improve. Do not take container-grown plants out of their pots until you are ready to plant them properly.

Plant conifers in the same way as other trees and shrubs but after planting protect the plants from cold and drying winds by erecting plastic windbreak netting held up on well-anchored posts as a windbreak. Once the conifer is well established this protection can be removed. Tall trees may also need staking to prevent damage from storms.

Do not feed conifers unless they are showing signs of starvation (unnatural yellowing foliage). If they are given too much food, conifers

4 It is worth mulching the ground after planting. It will conserve moisture, and some mulches, such as chipped bark, look attractive.

HOW TO REMOVE A COMPETING LEADER

1 Where two or more leaders have formed a fork in the conifer tree, leave the strongest unpruned. Cut away the other stem or stems at the point of origin.

will grow more quickly, producing lush, often uncharacteristic, growth that does not look attractive and is prone to damage caused by drying and cold winds.

Pruning

Conifers do not need extensive pruning and most are best left to assume their natural shape, with the occasional pruning of an overly long shoot. Occasionally, however, you may need to undertake more substantial pruning if the conifer starts to get too big for its position.

Plants can be clipped annually with shears to keep them small and neat. Do not prune back to leafless brown stems because these will not re-sprout. Cut back whole stems to restrict the size of ground-hugging conifers, making the cut under a newer, shorter shoot that will hide it. Conifers that have become too overgrown should be removed.

Another problem that should be pruned out as soon as it occurs is reversion: all-green growth on variegated forms. Use secateurs (pruners) to remove these vigorous shoots, otherwise they may dominate the more decorative foliage.

2 If the remaining leader is not growing strongly upright, tie a cane to the conifer's main stem. Tie the new leader to the cane to encourage vertical growth.

Most conifers produce resinous sap that bleeds freely from the stems if they are cut while the tree is in active growth. Pruning is therefore best carried out from autumn to mid-winter while the tree is dormant. Use sharp, clean pruning tools as blunt blades will snag the wood and may provide an entry point for disease. Wear gloves and goggles and, if you are using power machinery, the protective clothing recommended.

Aftercare

Once established, conifers will largely look after themselves. Mites and aphids can be problems on pines and spruces respectively, causing the needles to drop and producing unsightly bare stems. Aphids are easy to control with insecticidal sprays, but mites are more persistent (you may wish to get in a professional to treat an affected specimen). Mites are particularly active during warm, dry years when conifers are under stress. You can help prevent outbreaks by watering conifers during a drought and spraying the foliage occasionally to increase air humidity. Do this in the evening to avoid scorching the foliage on a sunny day.

Hedges

A living screen makes an excellent marker for a garden boundary and an attractive garden divider. Hedges will be around for a long time, so careful preparation before planting and regular maintenance are essential to keep them looking good.

Choosing a hedge

Many shrubs and some trees make excellent hedging plants, and the species will be largely a matter of personal preference. However, there are a few key points to bear in mind when you are making your selection.

First, decide whether you want a deciduous or evergreen hedge. An evergreen hedge will provide cover throughout the year but a deciduous one is often hardier and so is better in cold or very exposed positions. A few deciduous plants, such as hornbeam and beech, offer the best of both worlds because they keep their dead leaves on the plant until spring. You will also have to decide whether you want to grow it informally (unclipped) or formally (clipped).

Perhaps the most important consideration is the desired height of the hedge, and you must match the vigour and ultimate height of the hedging plant to this. If you choose a fast-growing variety for a small hedge, for example, the results will be quick, but you will need to trim it many times each growing season and the overall appearance of the hedge may deteriorate with time. Remember that the taller the desired height of the hedge, the more work it will be to maintain – anything over 1.5m (5ft) will be difficult to clip from ground level.

How much time and effort you are prepared to devote to your hedge is also something to consider. Although the thought of having a hedge that needs clipping just once a season can be appealing, the growth that it puts on means the trimming task is a lot of work. You may prefer to spread the work by choosing a hedge that responds to pruning several times each growing season. Alternatively, if you want a low-maintenance option choose a compact, slow-growing variety or consider having a no-prune informal hedge instead.

Planting a hedge

Hedges are planted in the same way as other trees and shrubs. Instead of making a planting hole for each plant, however, you simply prepare the planting trench for the whole hedge in one go. Bear in mind that this will be hard work, especially on heavy soils.

In the autumn, when weather and soil conditions allow, dig over a strip 60–90cm (2–3ft) wide, double digging down its entire

HOW TO PLANT A HEDGE

1 Prepare the ground thoroughly. Excavate a trench at least 60cm (2ft) wide and fork in plenty of manure or garden compost.

2 Add fertilizer at the rate recommended by the manufacturer. Use a controlled-release fertilizer if planting in the autumn.

3 Use a garden line, stretched along the centre of the trench, as a positioning guide. If the area is windy or you need a particularly dense hedge, plant a double row.

4 Use a piece of wood cut to the appropriate length as a guide for even spacing. Make sure the roots of bare-root plants are well spread out. If planting container-grown plants, tease out some of the roots before planting.

5 Firm the plants in and water well. Water the hedge regularly in dry weather for the first season. Mulch to keep down weeds until the hedge is filling out, after which it should suppress weeds naturally.

length. For shorter, less vigorous hedges you can get away with single digging. Remove any weeds and other debris as you proceed and incorporate plenty of well-rotted manure or garden compost into the soil and a handful of bonemeal for every 1m (3ft) of hedge. Allow the soil to settle for a fortnight before planting or delay planting until spring.

Aftercare

The general care after planting a hedge is exactly the same as for any other tree or shrub. However, as a general rule, vigorous deciduous hedging plants, such as privet, should be cut back to 15cm (6in)

and evergreens and flowering shrubs cut back by about one-third after planting to encourage thick growth from the base of each plant. Pruning is not required after planting for slower growing deciduous plants, such as beech, and all types of conifers until they have reached the desired height of the hedge.

Annual pruning of an established hedge will vary according to the variety. As a general rule, prune flowering hedges, such as quince or firethorn, after the flowering is over and use secateurs (pruners) rather than shears or hedge trimmers for hedges of large-leaved plants such as cherry laurel.

SHAPING A CONIFER HEDGE

Conifer hedges are best shaped with an inward slope, called a batter, to prevent damage by heavy snowfalls and allow light to reach lower parts of the hedge.

HOW TO PRUNE A HEDGE

1 Take the hard work out of clearing up trimmings by laying down a cloth or plastic sheet under the area you are clipping and move it along as you go.

2 When you use shears, try to keep the blades flat against the plane of the hedge as this will give an even cut. If you jab the shears forward with a stabbing motion, the result is likely to be uneven.

3 When trimming the top of a formal hedge, use canes and string as a guide to help you get it completely flat.

4 Keep the blades flat when you cut the top of a hedge. If it is a tall hedge, you will need to use steps rather than trying to reach up at an angle. Stand back from the hedge periodically to check that the trim is even.

5 Power trimmers are much faster than hand shears and, in consequence, things can go wrong more quickly. Concentrate on what you are doing and have a rest if your arms feel tired. Wear adequate protective gear and take the appropriate precautions if you are using an electrically operated tool.

6 Some conifers are relatively slow growing and produce only a few stray stems, which can be cut off with secateurs (pruners) to neaten them. Secateurs should also be used for large-leaved shrubs, such as *Prunus laurocerasus*. This avoids the leaves being cut in half by mechanical or hand shears, which always looks a bit of a mess and can encourage die-back.

Once a shrub is fully established and growing away happily, it will need regular attention to keep it healthy and in shape. Many shrubs only need minimal treatment (a few can even be left to their own devices), but most need at least some attention.

Types of shrub

For pruning purposes, shrubs are usually divided into several categories: those that need no or minimal pruning (*Daphne, Ceanothus, Magnolia*), those that flower on the current year's growth (*Buddleja, Lavatera*), those that flower on the previous year's growth (*Forsythia, Philadelphus*) and those which are evergreen (*Elaeagnus, Osmanthus*). The main difference between the needs of the different categories is the timing of pruning and the amount required.

When to prune

Pruning is an ongoing activity, spread throughout the year, although the majority can be done in winter and spring. There is an old garden adage that says you should do things when you think of them, but although unlikely to kill the plant, pruning at the wrong time of year could at least curtail its flowering for the following season. For example, if you prune in the winter a shrub that flowers on the previous year's wood, you are likely to remove all the shoots that have flowering potential. These need time in the previous year to develop that wood and so should be pruned as soon after flowering as possible. Many of them, such as forsythia, are early flowering, leaving plenty of time for growth. The shrubs that flower on new wood are ones such as buddleja, which flower around mid- or late summer, once they have had a chance to produce new growth. These are usually best

ABOVE Not all shrubs need to be cut hard back. This *Ceanothus thyrsiflorus* only needs the longer new growth to be cut back by about a third after flowering.

pruned in the early spring. Evergreens usually only need minimal pruning, in spring.

Minimal pruning

In most cases, all that is needed is to look for and cut out any dead, dying or diseased wood. Some of these shrubs also benefit from being lightly trimmed over to reduce the length of the new growth, but only to prevent the shrub getting too large or outgrowing its position. If the shrub does get too large for its position, you can try cutting it back heavily. But often these shrubs will

Shrubs that need little or no pruning

Amelanchier	Daphne mezereum
Aronia arbutifolia	Enkianthus
Berberis	campanulatus
Callicarpa	Magnolia
bodinieri	Nandua (sacred
Calycanthus	bamboo)
Clerodendron	Phlomis
trichotomum	Rhododendron
Clethra alnifolia	(azalea)
Corylopsis	Salix helvetica
Crataegus	Salvia (sage)
(hawthorn)	Stephandra
Cytisus (broom)	Thymus (thyme)

Reversion

Sometimes shrubs with variegated leaves, most frequently evergreens, throw up a shoot which has reverted to the original green leaves of the parent species. If this shoot is ignored, it will gradually take over the whole bush and the variegation will be lost. So it is essential to cut out this green shoot at the base.

The reverse sometimes happens, where a green bush throws up a variegated shoot. If this is an interesting colour or pattern, it may be worthwhile taking a cutting and rooting it to see if you can produce a whole shrub with this variegation. This is how a lot of variegated plants are originally produced. Plain cream shoots that occasionally appear on variegated hollies are usually the result of cold weather. These cannot be used for propagation, as they lack chlorophyll.

Shrubs flowering on old wood

Corylus (hazel)	(beauty bush)
Cotinus (smoke bush)	*Philadelphus* (mock orange)
Forsythia	*Ribes*
Hydrangea	*sanguineum*
Kerria (Jew's mantle)	(flowering currant)
Kolkwitzia	*Rubus* (bramble)

Shrubs flowering on old and new wood

These two categories of shrub are basically treated in the same way, the only major difference being the timing. Firstly, remove any dead, damaged or diseased wood. Take out any branches that cross over others. These may be rubbing against each other or just producing congestion, preventing the circulation of air and light. Any thin weak growths that are not going to produce healthy shoots should also be taken out. You can

not make new growth from old wood, so you may have to remove it altogether and start again. Occasionally you may need to cut out an individual shoot that has suddenly decided to grow faster than the others and spoils the shape of the shrub.

PRUNING SHRUBS THAT FLOWER ON THE PREVIOUS SEASON'S GROWTH

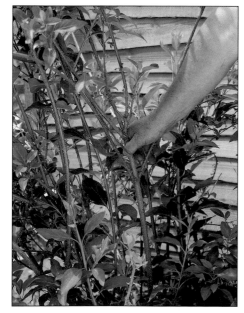

1 The best time to prune is soon after flowering. Count the number of stems and decide which third look the oldest (these will usually be the thickest and darkest).

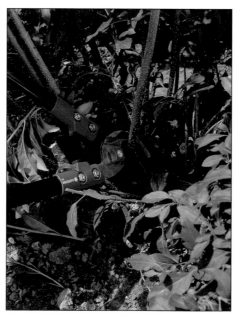

2 Cut back the oldest third just above ground if the branches rise from ground level or to a stump near the base if there is thick old wood. Cut just above a new shoot near the plant base.

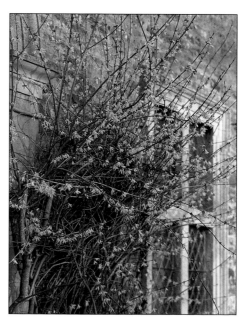

ABOVE If this forsythia is pruned after it has flowered in the spring, then plenty of replacement shoots will grow during the summer to flower the following year.

PRUNING SHRUBS THAT FLOWER ON THE CURRENT SEASON'S GROWTH

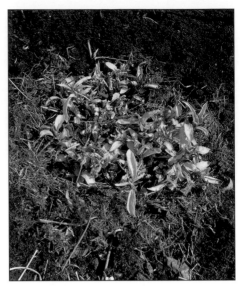

1 Many shrubs, such as this hardy fuchsia, flower on the current season's growth. In spring, all the older material that flowered the previous year will have to be cut out.

2 During the spring this old growth is cut back – as far as the ground in the case of the fuchsia. In other shrubs it may just be back to the first sound bud or shoot.

3 Once growth starts again, new shoots appear and quickly grow to flowering size. These require no further pruning until the following spring.

promote new healthy growth by removing some of the older wood. Old shoots, which are usually easy to identify, should be removed to the base, but if they are already producing vigorous new growth from just above the base, cut just above these new shoots. Take out a few of these older stems so that the bush retains its shape and appearance. If necessary, you can remove up to a third of the bush annually, so that over a three-year period a new shrub is formed. Normally it is only necessary to do this every few years, when the shrub has become congested or tired. Finally, look at the shrub to

assess its shape and see if any of the remaining shoots need trimming to improve its overall appearance. It may be that some of the longer stems need cutting back to contain its size.

Evergreens

Most evergreens need very little pruning other than the routine

removal of any dead, dying and diseased wood. They may need to be lightly trimmed over each year in order to maintain the size if that is important in the context of your garden. If the foliage is variegated, as in the case of some hollies, it is also important to remove any shoots that revert to the original green.

Shrubs flowering on new wood

Buddleja	Hypericum
Caryopteris	calycinum
Cassia	Indigofera
Ceanothus 'Gloire	Lavatera
de Versailles'	Leycesteria
Ceratostigma	Potentilla
Fuchsia	Sambucus (elder)

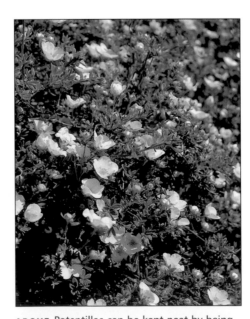

ABOVE Potentillas can be kept neat by being trimmed over after flowering. Apart from taking out the odd old stem to keep the plant vigorous, little other pruning is required.

Evergreen shrubs

Abelia	Garrya
Azara	Hebe
Berberis	Laurus nobilis
Buxus (box)	(bay)
Camellia	Mahonia
Ceanothus	Osmanthus
Choisya ternata	Photinia
(Mexican	Pieris
orange	Pittosporum
blossom)	Prunus
Convolvulus	lusitanicus
cneorum	(Portuguese
Cotoneaster	laurel)
Daphne	Rhododendron
Elaeagnus	Sarcococca
Escallonia	Skimmia
Euonymus	(Christmas box)
fortunei	Viburnum tinus

PRUNING EVERGREEN SHRUBS

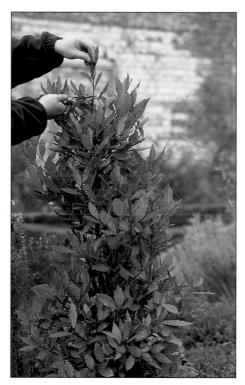

1 Evergreen shrubs usually need little pruning, but sometimes, as in the case of this bay (*Laurus nobilis*), they may need to have their shape checked or improved.

2 After you have removed any dead or damaged wood, look at the top of the shrub and cut back any straggly stems in order to improve its shape.

Deadheading

Most flowering shrubs benefit from deadheading. A plant requires a lot of energy in order to produce seed for reproduction. By removing the faded flowers, seeding is prevented and this energy is diverted into the new growth, sometimes producing a second flowering, which is always welcome. Another reason for deadheading your shrubs is that many of them look decidedly unsightly when they are covered with dead flowers, particularly those that have white flowers. As well as looking ugly themselves, dead flowers also tend to detract from the impact of those that are still at their best: remove the dead ones and then the look of the remainder will be greatly improved. Simply cut the flowering stem back to the first leaves as the flowers begin to fade.

3 Remove any long stems well back into the bush, as these could grow away and completely distort the shape of the plant.

4 Then, complete the pruning by trimming back any wayward shoots near the base of the plant. The ⋯ ⋯ ed bush looks much tidier.

ABOVE Dead flowers not only look ugly but also detract from the remaining flowers. They will sap the plant's energy, so remove them.

Renovating shrubs

It is not uncommon to be faced with a shrub that has not been pruned for many years, and is now in desperate need of renovation. Although the task may look daunting, it should not be a problem provided you take a systematic approach.

Clearing the way

The first stage, as with all pruning jobs, is to remove the dead wood. Next, take out any damaged, diseased or otherwise dying wood. In an overgrown shrub this often amounts to a great deal of material. Once it has been removed, the shrub already looks better and you can now see the framework you have to work on. Also remove any suckers around the plant. A neglected sumach (*Rhus*), for example, is likely to produce quite a number of suckers and these should be removed below ground level where the shoot joins the root.

If the shrub is badly diseased, it is best to remove it completely and start again, as it is highly unlikely that you will be able to resurrect it successfully.

RENOVATING AN OVERGROWN SHRUB Most shrubs can be renovated by removing dead wood and some of the oldest stems, as well as reducing the length of the remainder.

Reinvigoration

Remove any weak growth and any branches or stems that rub against or cross over other branches. The next thing to do is to try to reinvigorate the shrub. Remove some of the old wood to stimulate fresh new growth. Generally, several of the oldest main stems should be cut out completely or cut back to any new

REMOVING SUCKERS

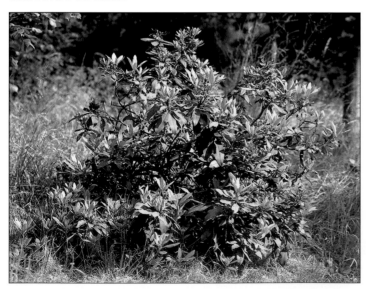

1 Some shrubs form a thicket as suckers grow around the base of the plant, often from the roots, but also from the base of the trunk.

2 Suckers should be removed by cutting them close to the trunk, or underground, close to the roots.

growth starting from near the base. Up to one-third of the oldest wood can be taken out. Repeat this process over the next three years until the shrub has completely regenerated itself. Some shrubs, such as *Ceanothus*, are reluctant to produce new growth from old wood. In this case, either omit this stage or remove the plant entirely and put a new one in its place.

Shaping up

A shrub that has been heavily pruned in this way is likely to be rather straggly and it may be necessary to reduce the remaining branches so that a better shape is achieved. The amount that can be removed will vary from shrub to shrub, but it can be up to about a half. However, some, such as *Ceanothus*, should only be trimmed over to remove the previous year's growth, as they will not reshoot from old wood.

Cutting down to the ground

There are some shrubs that can be simply cut to the ground and they will start again. Lilac (*Syringa*), elder

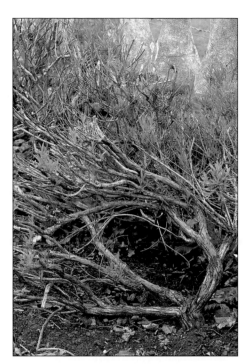

ABOVE Many shrubs that have grown straggly, such as this lavender, will not reshoot easily from old wood and should be replaced with new plants.

(*Sambucus*) and hazel (*Corylus*) are examples. Remove some of the top growth initially, so that the weight is removed from the main stems, then cut these off at about 15–30cm (6–12in) from the ground. If it is a grafted shrub, be certain to cut above the graft.

ABOVE With shrubs such as spiraea, you can remove one or two of the oldest shoots each year to promote the growth of new shoots.

Replacing

There are some shrubs that are virtually impossible to regenerate. If you cut back into the older wood, no new growth will appear and the plant will die. The best way to cope with this is to ensure that the shrubs are properly pruned in the first place and therefore do not become in need of renovation. However, if you inherit such overgrown plants when you move to a new garden, the only way to cope with them is to dig them out and replace them.

HOW TO RENOVATE A SHRUB

1 The first job when renovating any shrub is to cut out any dead branches or shoots right back to sound wood.

2 You need to remove any damaged wood, through which diseases can enter, as well as any dead wood.

Planting roses

Choosing new roses for the garden is one of the most enjoyable of all gardening activities, for it carries with it the anticipation of many years of pleasure from these generally long-lived shrubs. It is most important to consider the space that you have available and to select a rose variety of a suitable size so that it will not rapidly outgrow the allotted space.

Buying roses

Roses are sold as either container-grown or bare-root plants – that is, those that have been lifted from the open ground while dormant and the roots shaken free of soil. Both types eventually make equally good plants, although container-grown roses usually establish more quickly.

Whichever type of rose you buy, good soil preparation before planting is essential if the rose is to perform well, and will considerably minimize maintenance of the plant later on.

Where to plant?

Most roses grow best in full sun but with some protection from wind. Very exposed sites are suitable only for the tough rugosas, which will also tolerate some degree of shade,

ABOVE If possible slide a container-grown rose from its container before buying so that you can check that the root system is healthy. The roots should fill the pot but should not be crowded.

although flowering is less profuse. A few roses tolerate dappled shade, although growth and flowering will be less vigorous. No rose will perform well in deep shade.

Good air circulation around the plants is important and lessens the likelihood of mildew and other fungal diseases. Take time to consider the spread of the full-grown rose before you plant. Even roses intended to make a hedge should be placed at least 1m/3ft apart. Planting a rose too close to

other shrubs in your garden will also limit the moisture and nutrients available to both plants.

Planting

Before planting, the site should be prepared thoroughly by digging and forking it over to break up and aerate the soil. Remove any large stones you come across. Organic matter greatly improves the texture of all soil, opening up heavy soil that clogs by binding it into crumbs, while aiding water retention on

PLANTING A BARE-ROOT ROSE

1 Dig a hole large enough to take the roots when they are spread out and deep enough not to bend them. Incorporate garden compost or well-rotted manure in the base if this has not already been added to the soil when the bed was prepared.

2 Work a handful of bonemeal into the planting hole (wear gloves), then spread out the roots evenly, with the plant placed centrally. If the roots grow in just one direction, do not bend them, but plant the rose to one side of the hole.

3 Trickle the soil between the roots, shaking the plant occasionally as the hole is filled to settle the soil. Tread around the base of the plant to firm the soil, and make sure the budding is completely covered to prevent suckers.

PLANTING A CONTAINER-GROWN ROSE

1 Excavate a hole twice the width of the container and a little deeper. Break up the soil in the bottom with a fork, incorporating humus-forming material, such as compost or well-rotted manure, if this has not already been done in the general preparation of the bed.

2 Remove the rose from its pot. Gently tease out some of the roots from around the edge to encourage them to grow out into the surrounding soil, then position the rootball in the hole. Lay a cane across the hole to check the depth, adding or removing soil as necessary.

3 The graft union (the point where the rose was budded on to its rootstock) should be about 2.5cm/1in below the level of the surrounding bed. Backfill with soil and firm in with your foot to ensure there are no large air pockets where the roots will dry out.

4 If you are planting in spring or early summer, apply a general garden fertilizer or one formulated for roses, and fork it in lightly. Water well, then mulch with more organic material, such as garden compost or chipped bark, to reduce water evaporation and suppress weeds.

light, sandy ground. Fork in garden compost or farmyard manure at the rate of about one bucketful per square metre/yard.

Take great care to remove all trace of weeds completely, especially perennial weeds such as couch grass and ground elder. Weeds are much easier to eradicate before the rose is planted, as the roots of the two plants quickly become entangled.

Bare-root roses should be planted as soon after purchase as possible, during a mild spell. If the ground is unworkable, because it is frozen or waterlogged, the rose can be stored unopened for up to six weeks in a cool, dark, frost-free place. When you are ready to plant, remove the packaging and cut back any damaged or twiggy growth. Lightly trim the root, then soak the rose for about an hour in a bucket of water.

Container-grown roses can be planted at any time of year, except when the ground is frozen or waterlogged, or during periods of drought. If you cannot plant

immediately, keep the rose in a sheltered place and water it regularly.

If you are intending to plant your new rose on a spot where roses have been grown for several years, you should take action to minimize the risk of soil sickness. Well-established roses are thought to drain a soil of nutrients, and new roses planted on the same site can sometimes suddenly fail to thrive and begin to die back. When you are removing the old plant, dig out a hole at least 1m/3ft across and 45cm/18in deep and replace the old soil with fresh compost that has not already had roses growing in it.

Once planted, a rose should be watered regularly until it is established. Adding a top-dressing such as chipped bark will help to keep water evaporation to a minimum, and also help in the suppression of weeds.

Roses planted in the spring should quickly put forward new shoots, and may even flower the following year.

BELOW With proper year-round care, your roses will grow vigorously and produce many beautiful blooms.

Pruning bush and standard roses

For years rose pruning has been presented as a complicated affair of well-defined rules and precise, well-timed cuts. Then, a few years ago, new research showed it might all be a waste of time. So how should you prune your roses?

Why do roses need to be pruned?

Rose pruning is important for two main reasons. The first is that, left unpruned, the plant will get big and straggly, with an ugly bare base; the second is that the stems will bear flowers for only a few years before becoming exhausted. Pruning tackles both problems in one go, keeping the plant small and the shoots young and vigorous.

Pruning roses correctly

The same basic rules apply when rose pruning as for any other shrub, so use sharp, clean blades and a pair of thornproof gloves.

Bush roses The traditional method of pruning bush roses is probably still the most reliable. Cut back all the stems of large-flowered (hybrid tea) roses by about half their length. Cut back old stems of cluster-flowered (floribunda) roses to the base. The remaining younger stems of cluster-flowered roses should be pruned back to about 45cm (18in).

All cuts should be made just above a healthy, outward-facing bud using a cut that slopes slightly away from the bud so that the lower edge of the cut is still above the top of the bud. You should also remove all dead, damaged or weak wood and thin out the centre of the plant. Pruning should be carried out annually in early spring.

It is now known that, although the results won't be quite as good, all bush roses can be pruned roughly, cutting all stems back to 15–20cm

LARGE-FLOWERED BUSH

Cut out any badly positioned, diseased or dead wood (shown here coloured orange-brown) close to the base. This will leave fewer stems about which pruning decisions have to be made, and the extra space makes the job easier. Shorten the remaining stems by about half, cutting to an outward-facing bud.

STANDARDS

Prune an ordinary standard rose (left) by shortening the summer's growth by about half. Prune a weeping standard (right) by cutting back each long shoot to a point where there is a new one to replace it. If no suitable replacement shoots can be found, do not prune the main stems; instead, shorten the sideshoots on the flowered stems to two buds.

(6–8in) once every few years without worrying about cutting to just above a bud. You can even use a hedge trimmer if you have a lot of roses and time is short.

CLUSTER-FLOWERED BUSH

First cut out any badly placed or very old shoots that are dying or diseased (shown here coloured orange-brown), then shorten the remaining main shoots to about 45cm (18in), or about one third of their length. Cut back to an outward-facing bud where possible.

SHRUB

Pruning should always be modified to suit the growth characteristics of the plant but, as a guide, shorten the main stems by between a quarter and a half, and any sideshoots that remain by about two-thirds. Cut out any badly positioned growth and remove weak, diseased or dying stems completely.

Standard roses Prune lightly as cutting back severely will encourage over-vigorous shoots that may spoil the shape. Shorten the main stems in the head and any sideshoots.

Newly planted roses

It is worth pruning new roses in early spring to encourage new shoots from the base. Reducing the amount of top growth will also give the roots a chance to get established. The stems of bush roses and new growth on standard roses should be cut back by about half their length while those of shrub roses and miniatures should be cut by about a quarter.

Prune standards in late winter or early spring, but prune weeping standards after flowering, in summer.

Shrub roses Prune lightly, either annually or once every other year. Remove between a quarter and a half of the new growth and cut out any dead, diseased or congested growth.

Miniature roses These require little or no pruning other than to keep growth thick and compact. Use shears to trim back vertical new growth in spring. Again cut out any dead, diseased or weak growth.

ABOVE This floribunda rose has been well pruned and now displays plenty of new, vigorous growth and an abundance of flowers.

HOW TO PRUNE ROSES

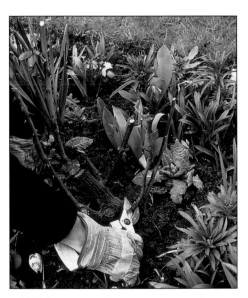

1 Moderate pruning is the most appropriate for established large-flowered roses. Cut back all the main stems by about half, or to within 20–25cm (8–10in) of the ground. Cut to an outward-facing bud to keep the centre of the bush open, with no congestion.

2 You can treat cluster-flowered roses in the same way, but if you prune some shoots severely and others lightly, flowering may be spread over a longer period. Prune the oldest shoots back close to the base, but those that grew last year by about one third only.

3 Whichever type of rose you are pruning, cut back any dead or diseased shoots to healthy wood. Also remove any very thin, spindly shoots, cutting either to their point of origin or to two or three buds from the base of the shoot.

Planting climbers

Most climbers should be planted in the same way and at the same time as trees and shrubs, although the technique varies slightly depending on the type of support they are being trained against.

Preparing the soil

The soil next to vertical surfaces, such as walls and fences, is usually drier than the soil in the rest of the garden because the ground is in the rain shadow of the wall or fence. Walls also draw water from the soil, further reducing the moisture content. It is essential, therefore, to improve the water-holding capacity of the soil before planting and to set the climber a little way away from the wall so that the roots have a chance to spread out. This is also the best method when planting next to free-standing supports. Before you plant a new climber it is a good idea to put up the support. Prepare the soil by digging it over thoroughly and removing any debris, which can include builders' rubble if the border has not been properly dug before. Incorporate plenty of organic matter as you go.

Planting

Once the soil has settled, dig a hole 30–45cm (12–18in) away from the wall or fence, large enough to accommodate the full spread of the roots (for bare-root plants) and about twice as wide as the rootball for container-grown types. The planting hole should be the same depth as the rootball.

As you dig, place all excavated soil on to a sheet next to the planting hole. Fork over the soil in the bottom of the hole. Add well-rotted manure or organic matter, such as garden compost to the soil as well as a handful of bonemeal and gently fork it in (use latex gloves for protection when handling bonemeal). Remove container-grown specimens

Match the vigour of the climber to the climbing space available. This *Rosa* x *alba* 'Alba Semiplena' grows to 2m (6ft) high.

from their pots and tease the roots out from around the rootball before planting to encourage them to spread into the surrounding soil.

With the exception of clematis, position the climber at the same depth as it was in the pot or the nursery bed – look for a soil mark on the stem – angling it back at 45 degrees towards the bottom of the support. Check the planting depth by laying a cane across the hole, then add or remove soil as necessary.

Backfill the first few centimetres (inches) of the hole with the excavated soil and give bare-root climbers a gentle shake to settle the soil. Firm the first layer around the roots with your hands before adding a second layer and repeating the process until the hole is filled. Water in well and cover the soil around the new specimen with an 8cm (3in) deep layer of well-rotted, organic mulch but take care not to pile it up against the stems.

HOW TO CHOOSE A CLIMBER

1 Many climbers are sold in containers. Look for strong-growing plants with plenty of shoots arising from the base of the plant.

2 Small plants with fewer stems are sometimes available. They are usually cheap but will probably need good aftercare if they are to establish themselves properly.

3 Check the root system by sliding the plant from its container. Reject the plant if the roots are congested or tightly coiled around the pot. The root system of this plant is in good condition.

HOW TO PLANT CLIMBERS

1 Dig over the proposed site, loosening the soil and removing any weeds. If the ground has not recently been prepared, work some well-rotted organic material into the soil to improve soil texture and fertility.

2 Add a general or specialist shrub fertilizer to the soil at the dosage recommended on the packet. Work into the soil around the planting area with a fork. A slow-release organic fertilizer is best.

3 Water the plant in the pot. Dig a hole that is much wider than the rootball. The hole should be next to a free-standing support or at least 30cm (12in) from a wall or fence, and angled back towards the support.

4 Stand the plant in its hole and place a cane across the hole to check that it is at the same level. Take the plant from the pot or cut the bag away. Holding the plant steady, fill in the soil. Firm as you go with your hands.

5 Train the stems of the climber up individual canes to their main support. Tie the stems in with string or plastic ties. Even twining plants or plants with tendrils will need this initial help. Spread them out, so that they ultimately cover the whole of their support.

6 Water the climber thoroughly. Put a layer of mulch around the plant, to help preserve the moisture and prevent weed growth. Do not pile mulch up against the stems of the climber, however.

Planting near established plants

The soil next to established trees and shrubs is often dry and full of roots and it may be difficult for a climber to become established.

The best position for a new plant is at the edge of the tree or shrub canopy, where water will run off when it rains – the "drip zone". When digging the planting hole try as far as possible to do this without disturbing the surrounding soil or any major roots. Cut off any minor roots that become exposed in the planting hole. Improve the soil with well-rotted garden compost and bonemeal, and then line the sides of the planting hole with pieces of old timber. This will give the climber a chance to establish without suffering from too much competition from surrounding plants. The timber will eventually rot away without you having to remove it.

Planting clematis

It is good practice to plant clematis about 8cm (3in) deeper than other types of climber so that the bottom of the stems are below ground level. Then, if the clematis suffers from wilt, which kills all top growth, it will be able to produce new shoots the following year from unaffected buds at the base of the stems underground.

Providing wall support

When choosing a support for a climbing plant it is important to take into consideration the method by which it climbs. Some climbers such as ivy can be grown on a bare brick wall, but most will need a trellis to support them as they grow.

Types of climbers

Climbers hold on to their supports in a number of ways. Some are self-clinging and can cover a vertical surface without the need for any support at all. Ivies and climbing hydrangeas, for example, produce modified roots on their stems that attach themselves to rough surfaces, while other climbers, such as Virginia creeper, produce tiny suckers that will stick to any surface, including glass. Many self-clinging climbers need a support or another plant to climb up but will hold on by themselves. Clematis, for example, have twining leaf stalks, and passion flowers and sweet peas produce tendrils. A few plants, such as akebia, honeysuckle and wisteria, have twining stems that coil snake-like

SELF-CLINGING CLIMBERS

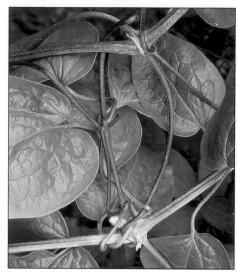

Hydrangea anomala subsp. *petiolaris* clings to wall surfaces by putting out modified roots.

around their supports. There are also climbers, including climbing and rambler roses, that are not self-clinging and need to be tied in to their supports.

Supports for vertical surfaces

There are several types of support to choose from, but it is important to provide one that matches the size and vigour of the climber it is to

TWINING CLIMBERS

Clematis have twining leaf stalks that grow round a supporting structure.

support. Against a wall or fence you have the choice of fixing trellis panels, expanding trellis or plastic mesh to the surface or attaching a series of sturdy parallel wires.

Trellis panels Wooden or plastic panels are very strong and look attractive. They are also easy and quick to erect, but they are fairly costly. Trellis panels are available only in a small range of specific

HOW TO TRAIN A CLIMBER OR WALL SHRUB ON WIRES

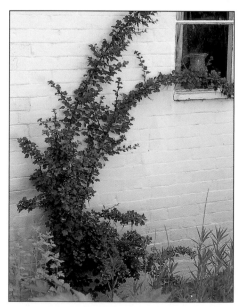

1 Without supporting wires or a trellis, a wall shrub will grow out in all directions.

2 Drill pilot holes into the wall and insert vine eyes to support the wires. If you use vine eyes with a screw fixing, insert a plastic or wooden plug in the wall first. Vine eyes are available in several lengths, the long ones being necessary for vigorous climbers, such as wisteria, that need wires further from the wall.

3 The simplest vine eyes are wedge shaped. Hammer them directly into the masonry and then feed the wire through a hole. Although wedge-shaped eyes are suitable for brick and stone walls, the screw type are better for wooden fences and posts.

HOW TO FIX A TRELLIS TO A WALL

1 The trellis should be sturdy and in good condition. Ensure it has been treated with wood preservative. Take the trellis panel to the wall and mark its position. The bottom of the trellis should be about 30cm (12in) from the ground. Drill holes for fixing the spacers and insert plastic or wooden plugs.

2 Drill the equivalent holes in the wooden batten and secure it to the wall, checking with a spirit (carpenter's) level that it is horizontal. Use a piece of wood that holds the trellis at least 2.5cm (1in) from the wall. Fix another batten at the base, and one halfway up for trellis more than 1.2m (4ft) high.

3 Drill and screw the trellis to the battens, first fixing the top and then working downwards. Check that the trellis is straight using a spirit level. The finished trellis should be secure, so that the weight of the climber and any wind that blows on it will not pull it away from its fixings.

sizes, so are suitable for only some climbers and walls.

Expanding trellis This is sold in a compact form, is easier to transport than panels, but is not as strong. It comes in specific sizes, but expansion can be adjusted to fit an area.

Plastic mesh This is cheap but less robust than trellis panels. It is also less pleasing to the eye until it is covered with growth.

Wires and netting Fixing vine eyes into a wall to support galvanized wire is time-consuming, but once up, wires are a good support for climbers. Even when not covered with plants they are barely visible, and are very versatile, covering any shape or size of surface. If you are growing annual climbers, such as morning glory and sweet peas, less robust netting or even string can make a suitable support.

Access for maintenance

To make maintenance of the wall easier in the future, consider attaching the bottom of the trellis panel to the bottom spacer batten with galvanized hinges so that when the screws fixing the panel to the other battens are removed the panel can be swung away from the wall or fence, providing easy access for repointing or painting.

4 Thread galvanized wire through the hole in the vine eye and wrap it around itself to form a firm fixing. Thread the other end through the intermediate eyes (set at no more than 2m/6ft intervals and preferably closer) and fasten the wire around the end eye, keeping it as taut as possible.

5 Spread out the main stems and attach them to the wires, using either plastic ties or string. Tie at several points, if necessary, so that the stems lie flat against the wall and do not flap about in the wind.

6 When all of the stems are tied in to the wires they should form a regular fan shape. Tying the stems in like this, rather than allowing the climber to grow up the wall naturally, covers the wall better and encourages the plant to produce flowering buds all along the top edge of the stems.

Providing free-standing support

It is not always convenient to grow a climber against a wall, and a free-standing support gives flexibility in planning which climbers to grow and where to place them. Climbers can be used to shield an unsightly part of the garden from view as well as adding variety to already attractive areas.

Growing into established plants

If you wish to grow a climber through a tree or a shrub, you must make sure that you have compatible candidates. Neither plant should compete unduly for moisture or nutrients or both will suffer. The established plant must also be strong enough to bear the weight of a full-grown climber, which can be considerable. Hedges and apple trees are good candidates for large climbers. The tree should be neither too young nor too old: a young tree may be smothered by the vigorous climber, while the additional burden may be too much for an older, weaker tree during winter storms.

Position the climber on the side of the prevailing wind so that it will blow the stems into the support as it grows. After planting the climber, hammer in a short stake next to it and attach one end of a piece of rope to the stake. Tie the other end of the rope up into the canopy of the supporting plant. Untie the climber from its supporting cane that was supplied when you bought it and unravel the stems. The climber can then be tied into the rope and the longer stems up into the canopy of the tree or shrub. Do not, as is sometimes recommended, secure the bottom of the rope by looping it under the rootball because the climber is likely to be pulled out of the ground by the first strong gust of wind that catches the branch holding the other end of the rope.

Arches and pergolas

Garden structures, such as arches and pergolas, are available in a wide range of styles. The style you choose should fit in with the rest of the garden design and be strong and large enough to support the chosen climbers. There are many ready-made kits on sale in a variety of materials.

PLANTING A CLIMBER NEXT TO AN ESTABLISHED SHRUB

1 Choose a healthy shrub, such as this *Salix helvetica*, and preferably one that flowers at a different time from the climber.

2 Dig a hole at the edge of the supporting shrub so that the climber will receive rain. Improve the soil if necessary.

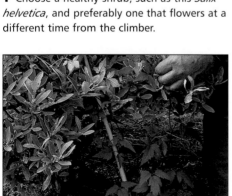

3 Using a cane, train the climber, such as this *Clematis alpina*, into the shrub. Spread out the shoots so it grows evenly through the shrub.

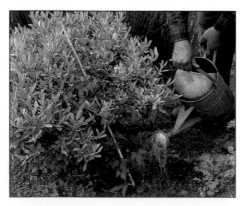

4 Water the new plant thoroughly and mulch if necessary. Continue to water, especially in dry weather, until the climber is established.

The white flowers of the scented rambling rose 'Seagull' look spectacular against the dark green of the conifer it is climbing through.

Single posts, tripods and hoops

Many climbers are suitable for training up single posts, often called pillars, although it is probably best to avoid very vigorous climbers. If space permits, a series of pillars can be erected along a path, linked garland-fashion by chunky rope along which climbers can grow. Climbers also look effective trained up tripods or, alternatively, you can make your own supports from canes.

Training a climber over a hoop allows you to direct the growth so that it covers the available space with an abundance of flowers. Bending the new growth into curving arches encourages flowering buds to be formed along the whole stem rather than just at the tip. A hoop will also keep the climber in proportion to the border in which it is growing, and is a useful method of growing vigorous plants in a limited space.

Whichever free-standing support you choose, it is essential that it is anchored securely into the ground.

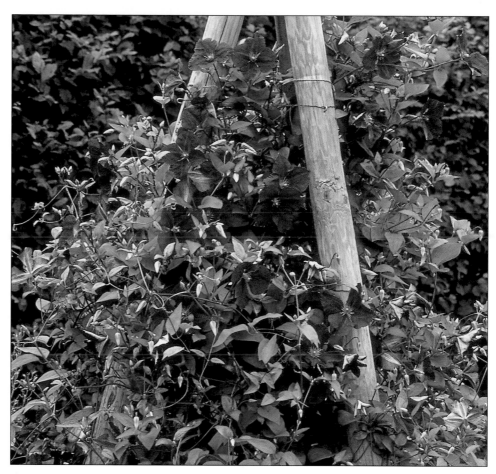

The rich purple flowers of *Clematis* 'Jackmanii' can be seen clearly as it climbs up a tripod, bringing interest to an otherwise neglected corner of the garden. Once it is fully grown, the clematis will cover the support completely, so that the tripod cannot be seen.

HOW TO ERECT A PILLAR FOR A CLIMBER

1 Dig a hole at least 60cm (2ft) deep. Put in the post and check that it is upright. Backfill with earth, ramming it firmly down as you work. In exposed gardens a more solid pillar can be created by filling the hole with concrete.

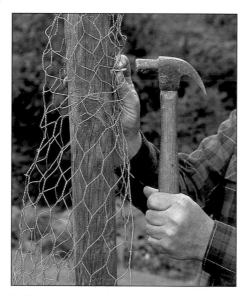

2 Plants can be tied directly to the post but a more natural support can be created by securing wire netting to the post. Self-clinging climbers such as clematis will then be able to climb by themselves with little attention from you other than tying in wayward stems.

3 Plant the climber a little way from the pole. Lead the stems to the wire netting and tie them in. Self-clingers will take over, but plants such as roses will need to be tied in as they grow. Twining plants, such as hops, can be grown up the pole without wire.

Aftercare of climbers

Most climbers are easy to look after and, apart from pruning, require the minimum of care. Do keep an eye out for potential problems, however, as early action is most effective. A little general maintenance will keep your plants in tip-top condition.

Watering and mulching

Most climbers are planted in dry soil at the base of walls and fences, which is why they are more likely to suffer from drought during prolonged dry spells. Always keep climbers well watered until they are established. Thereafter, soak the soil thoroughly once a fortnight during a period of drought or if the climber is showing signs of stress.

Each spring top up the loose organic mulch so that it is about 8cm (3in) thick but is not piled against the stems of the climber. The mulch will not only help to retain moisture in the soil but will also prevent any competition from weeds.

Feeding

With new plants, apply a general-purpose fertilizer on the surface of the soil in spring. Thereafter, if your soil is very poor or free-draining apply an annual dressing of a general fertilizer around each plant in spring. Some free-flowering climbers, such as roses, will produce even better displays if given a high-potash fertilizer, such as rose feed, in spring and early summer. Foliar feed can also be applied using a hose-end feeder fitted to the end of a garden hose. The nutrients are readily absorbed through the leaves.

Keeping plants tidy

Tie in new growth while it is still flexible enough to be bent into position against the support. Prune out any dead, diseased or dying growth as well as any unwanted, crossing stems. Also remove any all-green shoots produced on variegated climbers (known as reversion) to

Using grass clippings

For a free organic mulch use grass clippings (not treated with weedkiller) in an unobtrusive area, such as at the back of a border or the bottom of the garden, to mulch established climbers each spring. Top it up throughout the mowing season. This is not only a cheap and effective mulch but is also a convenient way of getting rid of lawn clippings.

prevent these more vigorous green shoots from overwhelming the rest of the climber. Check old ties to make sure they are secure and are not constricting the stems.

The removal of fading flowers (known as deadheading) on climbers is desirable although not always practicable if the climber is large or not very accessible. Deadheading not only makes the climber look neater, but also encourages better and longer-lasting flowering displays by stopping the climber wasting energy in producing unwanted fruits and seeds. Where the fruits or seedheads are of ornamental value, simply deadhead parts of the climber that are hidden from view so that you get the best of both worlds.

Winter protection

Although walls and fences give some protection in winter, climbers that are of only borderline hardiness may need extra protection during cold years or in colder areas. Draping a sheet of hessian (burlap) over the climber is the traditional method, but a double layer of horticultural fleece will also do the trick. For real protection, create an insulating duvet by stuffing straw or other insulating material under the sheeting. Remove all winter protection when milder weather returns in spring.

HOW TO TIE IN NEW SHOOTS

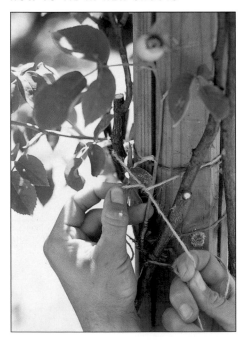

Once you have pruned out the old stems of ramblers and climbers, tie in vigorous new shoots to replace them.

HOW TO DEADHEAD CLIMBERS

As the flowers die, remove the flowerheads. This not only makes the climber tidier but also promotes further flowering. With tall climbers, however, this may not always be practicable.

CLEMATIS WILT

Some forms of clematis, mainly large flowered hybrids and *montana*, are susceptible to wilt. This disease is caused by the fungus *Ascochyta clematidina*. The top-growth dies back and, left unchecked, the disease may affect the whole plant. If your clematis shows signs of wilt prune it hard. If it has been planted deeply enough it will usually recover. Drenching with fungicide at monthly intervals in the growing season may help, but if wilt is a persistent problem, replace your clematis with one less susceptible to the disease.

HOW TO PROTECT AGAINST FROST

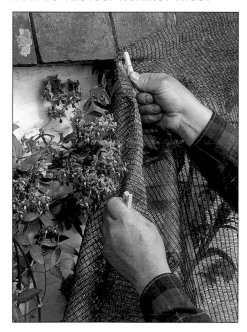

For light protection against unseasonal frosts a temporary cover such as shade netting or hessian (burlap) can be used to protect new shoots and early flowers. If the climber is grown against a wall, hang the cover from the gutter or from some similar support. Fasten the netting securely so that it remains attached, even in windy weather.

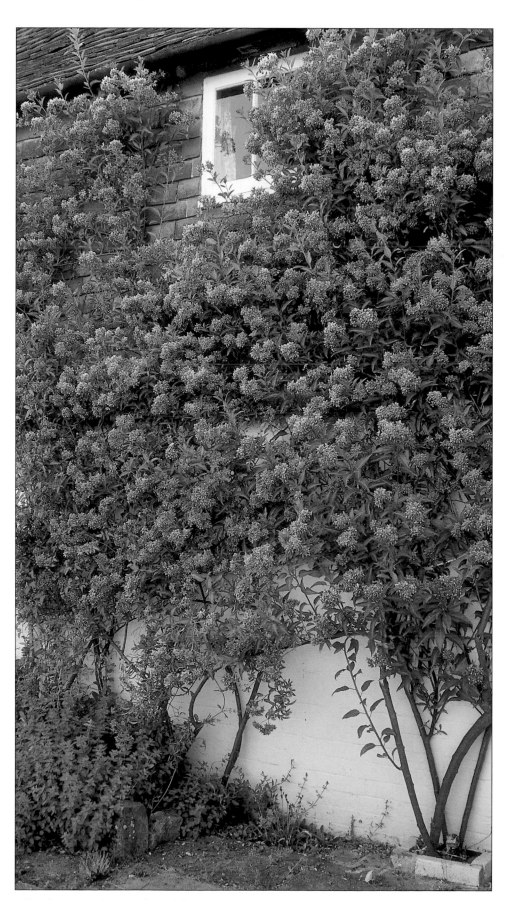

This *Solanum* has been well cared for and is in good condition. The plant has been securely tied to its support, and trained so that it is not growing over the windows or into the guttering. Regular mulching and feeding with a high-potash fertilizer will help improve flowering.

Pruning clematis and wisteria

Most climbers can be kept in good shape and flowering well by simply removing unwanted growth and pruning out any dead, dying or diseased stems. A few popular types, however, including clematis, wisteria and roses, require special pruning for best results.

Pruning clematis

Clematis has gained a reputation for being difficult to prune, mainly because not all clematis are pruned in the same way. However, as long as you know when your clematis flowers and can tell whether it produces blooms on old stems or new growth produced during the current year, you won't go far wrong.

Clematis can be divided into three groups: those that produce all their flowers on old wood (known as pruning group 1); those that produce blooms on both old wood and new growth produced during the current season (known as pruning group 2); and those clematis that flower only on new growth (known as pruning group 3).

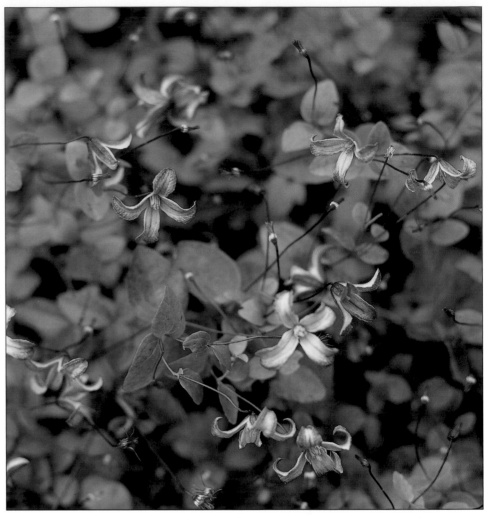

Clematis 'Pagoda' is a group 3 clematis, so the flowers are borne on new stems. Hard pruning in winter will lead to a good display of flowers the following summer.

CLEMATIS PRUNING GROUPS

Group 1 These clematis need pruning only when they outgrow their space. Cut out sufficient branches to reduce congestion and take those that encroach beyond their space back to their point of origin.

Group 2 After cutting out all the dead, damaged or weak growth, remove any wood that is making the clematis congested, cutting back to a pair of buds.

HOW TO PRUNE WISTERIA

1 In late summer shorten the long shoots produced this year. Unless required for further spread, cut back to about four or six leaves.

2 In midwinter shorten the summer's growth further, cutting back to just two or three buds, so the shoots are 8–10cm (3–4in) long.

WISTERIA TWO-STAGE PRUNING

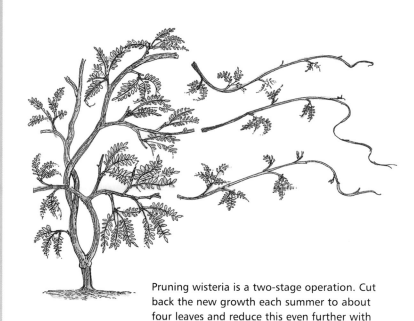

Pruning wisteria is a two-stage operation. Cut back the new growth each summer to about four leaves and reduce this even further with a winter pruning.

Group 1 The spring-flowering clematis belong to this group. Some are vigorous, such as *C. montana*, while others are more restrained. Cut back vigorous species as necessary to keep them in check, but others in this group need little pruning other than the removal of dead, damaged or diseased stems. Prune back unwanted stems to their point of origin or to a pair of plump buds.

Group 2 This group includes late spring and early summer varieties that flower mainly on old wood early in the season and later produce a smaller flush on this year's growth. They need little pruning other than the removal of dead, damaged or diseased stems. Congested growth can be thinned out by pruning back stems to their point of origin or a pair of plump buds. Alternatively, cut half the stems back to a pair of buds before growth starts to increase the number of blooms produced later in the year.

Group 3 The clematis in this group flower in late summer. Cut back all stems during the winter or early spring to the lowest pair of buds.

Pruning wisteria

Wisteria has an undeserved reputation for being difficult to prune, but in this case it is because it is pruned in two stages, in late summer and then in winter. The pruning itself is straightforward: simply cut back all the whippy new growth to four or six leaves in late summer and then, when the leaves have fallen and it is easier to see what you are doing, cut the same stumps to just two or three buds from the main stem.

Group 3 These clematis should have all the growth cut back in winter or early spring to the first pair of sound buds above the ground.

Clematis pruning groups

Group 1	Group 3
C. alpina	'Abundance'
C. armandii	'Bill MacKenzie'
C. cirrhosa	'Comtesse de
C. macropetala	Bouchaud'
C. montana	'Duchess of
	Albany'
Group 2	'Etiole Violette'
'Barbara	*C. flammula*
Jackman'	'Gravetye
'Daniel Deronda'	Beauty'
'Ernest	'Hagley Hybrid'
Markham'	'Jackmanii'
'Lasurstern'	'Perle d'Azur'
'Marie Boisselot'	*C. rehderiana*
'Nelly Moser'	*C. tangutica*
'The President'	'Ville de Lyon'
'Vyvyan Pennell'	'Victoria'

Pruning climbing roses and honeysuckle

Climbers that are grown for their flowers, such as roses and honeysuckles, require only light pruning from time to time to achieve a profusely flowering plant.

Climbing roses

When trained up walls or along fences climbing roses may not need pruning annually, other than to remove dead or dying growth, but regular pruning will keep the plant vigorous and flowering well, with the blooms low down, where they can be appreciated. Roses trained over free-standing supports need annual pruning to keep them within bounds.

Climbing roses can be divided into two main groups: those that produce blooms in one flush on short sideshoots from an established framework of stems, and those that are repeat-flowering, bearing blooms in a series of flushes throughout summer. Once-flowering climbers should be pruned after flowering by removing up to one-third of the stems, starting with the oldest. Cut

back near to the base or to a new sideshoot produced low down. If there isn't much new growth, cut back older branches to about 30cm (12in) to encourage more next year. Trim sideshoots on other stems to two or three leaves.

Repeat-flowering climbers or those that produce attractive hips should be pruned in winter to remove the weakest and oldest stems. Trim any sideshoots on the remaining stems to within two or three buds.

Rambler roses

These roses have a single flush of blooms in summer, which are produced on growth that was formed the previous year. They produce long shoots from the base. For each vigorous new young shoot prune out an unproductive old one back to ground level after flowering. Do not prune out an old shoot unless there is a new one to replace it, but remove completely any very old, dead or diseased wood.

PRUNING A CLIMBING ROSE

On a well-established, once-flowering climber, cut out one or two of the oldest stems to a point just above a new shoot near the base.

PRUNING A RAMBLER ROSE

Ramblers are straightforward to prune. Cut out old canes that have flowered, taking them back to a point where there is a new replacement shoot.

HOW TO PRUNE A ONCE-FLOWERING CLIMBING ROSE

1 These climbing roses have a stable framework of woody shoots and are always pruned in summer after flowering, so they can seem intimidating to prune. Fortunately, these roses usually flower even with minimal pruning, provided you keep the plant free of any very old stems and any dead and diseased wood.

2 Cut out one or two of the oldest stems each year to encourage new growth. Cut old stems off just above young replacement shoots near the base. If there are no low-growing shoots, choose one that starts 30–60cm (1–2ft) up the stem, and cut back to just above this level.

3 If there are strong young replacement shoots, prune back a proportion of stems that have flowered to just above the newer growth. Tie them in if necessary. If possible, always prune to an outward-facing bud or shoot.

4 Go along the remaining stems and shorten the sideshoots, pruning back to leave two or three buds. Do not remove more than a third of the stems, otherwise flowering will suffer next year.

HOW TO PRUNE A RAMBLER ROSE

1 Prune the rambler rose after flowering – late summer is a good time. Older, congested plants can be more off-putting than younger ones, but all rambler roses are fairly straightforward to prune if you work on them methodically.

2 Once you have a well-established rambler, try to balance the shoots that you remove with those available to replace them. First, cut out any dead or damaged shoots or those that are very weak and spindly. Do not remove very vigorous, young shoots.

3 Cut out old stems that have flowered, but only where there are new shoots to replace them. This will vary from plant to plant and year to year. Shorten the sideshoots on old stems that have been retained (those that have flowered) to leave two or three leaves.

4 Tie in the flexible new shoots to the support. Wherever possible, tie loosely to horizontal wires or a trellis. After pruning, rambler roses will produce new stems from the base, rather than growing taller on existing stems, which gives them a lower, more spreading habit.

Honeysuckle

These climbers can be divided into two groups: those that flower on the current year's growth and those that bear blooms on stems produced last year. Those that flower on new wood do not need regular pruning unless they outgrow their allotted space. In this case, cut back all stems in winter to allow for the new growth the following season. If the climber gets overcrowded remove about one-third of the oldest stems, cutting back to near ground level. Honeysuckles that flower on the previous year's growth should have old growth that has flowered cut back to a newer shoot produced lower down on the stem.

HOW TO PRUNE HONEYSUCKLE

1 Prune honeysuckle only if it has become sparse at the base and the flowers are too high, or if the tangled mass of stems is too thick. This sometimes happens if the plant is grown on a trellis of limited height: when the stems reach the top, they cascade downwards and begin to grow upwards, using the already tangled stems for support.

2 If you prune back hard you will lose flowers for a season or two. Avoid this by shearing off only dead or badly placed shoots, especially those beneath healthy growth. You could use secateurs (pruners), but the job will be very tedious among the mass of tangled stems.

3 If it is done carefully, the plant will not look very different yet much of the redundant growth will have been removed. As you will almost certainly have severed stems that remain entangled, you may notice dead stems, which will need to be pulled out; sever the stems in several places if this helps to disentangle them.

Tackling overgrown climbers

Overgrown and unproductive climbers can be given a new lease of life by hard pruning. The method you use will depend on the type of climbers you are tackling.

Renovation pruning

If your climbers have got out of control or produce all their flowers out of sight at the top of the plants, you may need to take decisive action. The best time to carry out drastic pruning of climbers is during the dormant season, between autumn and spring. When there are no leaves it is easier to see what you are doing and make the cuts in the right place. Choose a mild day to make the task as pleasant as possible and arm yourself with a good pair of secateurs (pruners) and long-handled loppers. For stems over 3cm (1½in) thick you will also need a special pruning saw.

HOW TO PRUNE A SELF-CLINGING CLIMBER

1 Vigorous self-clinging climbers can reach great heights if planted against a tall wall. They may need pruning to keep shoots clear of windows and doors, or areas where they can cause damage such as blocking gutters or loosening roof tiles.

2 The actual pruning, best done in early spring, is very simple but you may need ladders to reach the offending stems. If necessary pull the shoots clear of the wall (this may require some force) so that you can use the secateurs (pruners) freely.

3 On this wall, a hard edge after the plant has been cut back is acceptable, but around windows you may prefer to cut the shoots by different amounts to avoid a clipped or straight-line appearance.

Evergreen plants such as this ivy 'Green Ripple' can be particularly difficult to prune as it is hard to see the stems under the leaves. When pruning is necessary, carry out the task methodically, working your way along the wall.

Overgrown clematis

Clematis are often left unpruned for years so that the climber ends up as a mass of bare, non-flowering stems at the base with the few blooms produced way up on top. All clematis respond well to pruning back hard: cut back stems to within 1m (3ft) of the ground. Those that flower on new wood can be cut back even harder, to 30cm (12in). If your clematis flowers on old wood, you will not get any blooms for a year or two, but thereafter the climber will flower with renewed vigour.

Climbing and rambler roses

If they are neglected climbing roses slowly get bigger and bigger, forming large gnarled bare stems at the base with the flowers produced on growth higher up on the plant. Tackle an overgrown monster by removing one stem in three back to a newer shoot lower down or cut right back to the base if there is not one. Repeat over a three-year period to reinvigorate the plant completely.

Rambler roses by contrast throw up new shoots from the base, and these form impenetrable thickets of thorny growth if left to their own devices. In this case, thin out the tangle of stems by removing all but the newest shoots.

Honeysuckles

These often form a top-heavy mass of spindly shoots, and when they are grown on free-standing supports and fences they tend to catch the wind and rock the support. The best way to tackle an overgrown honeysuckle is to trim back all the thin growth on the top to reveal the main stems. These can then be pruned with secateurs (pruners). Reduce their number by removing awkwardly placed stems and the oldest ones

HOW TO RENOVATE A NEGLECTED CLIMBER

1 This neglected climbing rose has lost vigour and is flowering very poorly, and so needs renovative pruning.

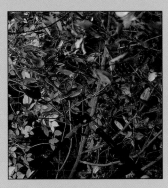

2 Use loppers to cut back old growth that is too thick for secateurs (pruners).

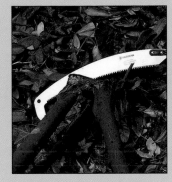

3 Thick stems may need a pruning saw. Support the branch to prevent it tearing off bark from the main stem.

4 Use a sharp knife to pare off the rough edges of any large pruning wounds.

first. If all else fails, honeysuckles respond well to hard pruning, so if yours gets out of hand try cutting it back in winter to within 30cm (12in) of the base. It should regrow, although it may be a couple of years before it is flowering well again.

RENOVATING HONEYSUCKLE

If you prune honeysuckle hard you will lose flowers for a season or two, but in the long term you will have fresh growth that you can retrain. This drastic treatment means that the support will look bare for a while, but new shoots should grow fairly rapidly in the first summer. Tie the new shoots in or train them to the support to give even and relatively untangled growth.

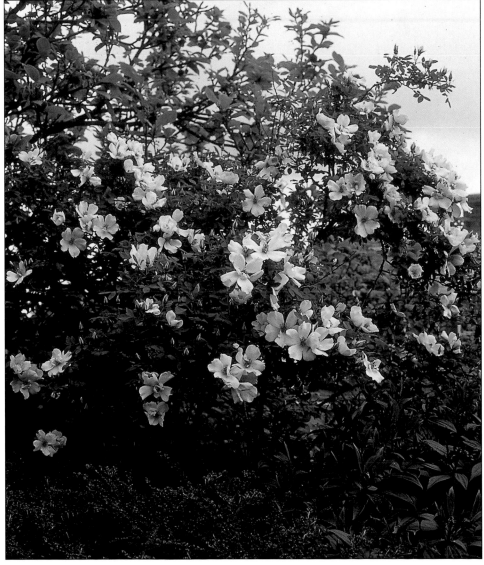

Hard pruning can sometimes restore all of the former glory of a rose, such as this 'Frühlingsgold', which is now showing a healthy crop of primrose-yellow flowers.

Recommended planting lists

The following lists offer a guide to plants adapted to certain conditions. Most of the entries relate to entire genera. For more detailed information on the preferences of individual species, refer to the relevant entry. Remember that some plants are tolerant of a range of conditions, hence their presence in more than one list.

PLANTS FOR DRY SOIL IN SUN

TREES
Cercis
Gleditsia

CONIFERS
Juniperus
Pinus
Thuja

SHRUBS
Artemisia
Ballota
Buddleja
Ceanothus
Cistus
Genista
× *Halimiocistus*
Helianthemum
Hibiscus
Lavandula
Lavatera
Olearia
Perovskia
Phlomis
Potentilla
Rosmarinus
Ruta
Salvia
Santolina

Teucrium
Thymus
Yucca

PLANTS FOR DRY SOIL IN SHADE

SHRUBS
Buxus
Elaeagnus
Hypericum
Kerria
Sarcococca
Vinca

CLIMBERS
Hedera

PLANTS FOR MOIST SOIL IN SHADE

TREES
Acer

SHRUBS
Aucuba
Hamamelis
Hydrangea
Kalmia
Mahonia
Sarcococca

PLANTS FOR EXPOSED SITES

TREES
Acer
Carpinus
Crataegus
Fagus
Fraxinus
Populus
Prunus
Salix
Sorbus

CONIFERS
Chamaecyparis
× *Cupressocyparis*
Cupressus
Juniperus
Pinus
Thuja

SHRUBS
Berberis
Buddleja
Calluna
Erica
Euonymus
(deciduous)
Ilex
Kalmia
Prunus

PLANTS FOR ACID OR LIME-FREE SOIL

TREES
Acacia
Arbutus
Eucryphia
Magnolia

Hosta 'Golden Prayers'

CONIFERS
Abies
Picea
Pinus

SHRUBS
Callistemon
Calluna
Camellia
Daboecia
Erica
Fothergilla
Hamamelis
Kalmia
Magnolia
Pieris
Rhododendron

CLIMBERS
Lapageria

PLANTS FOR CHALKY SOIL

TREES
Aesculus
Betula
Carpinus
Cercis

Crataegus
Fagus
Fraxinus
Gleditsia
Laburnum
Laurus
Malus
Paulownia
Prunus
Pyrus
Robinia
Sophora
Sorbus

CONIFERS
Juniperus
Taxus

SHRUBS
Berberis
Buxus
Ceanothus
Cistus
Cotoneaster
Daphne
Deutzia
Euonymus
Forsythia
Fuchsia
Genista
Hebe
Helianthemum
Ilex
Kerria
Lonicera
Olearia
Osmanthus
Paeonia
Phillyrea
Phlomis
Rosmarinus
Sarcococca
Syringa

Viburnum
Vinca
Weigela
Yucca

CLIMBERS
Clematis
Hedera
Lonicera
Parthenocissus

PLANTS FOR CLAY SOIL

TREES
Acer
Alnus
Arbutus
Carpinus
Fraxinus
Salix

CONIFERS
Abies
Chamaecyparis
Cryptomeria
Metasequoia

SHRUBS
Cornus
Magnolia
Weigela

CLIMBERS
Lonicera
Wisteria

PLANTS FOR COASTAL SITES

TREES
Acer
Arbutus
Ilex
Trachycarpus

CONIFERS
Chamaecyparis
Cupressocyparis
Pinus

SHRUBS
Artemisia
Ceanothus
Cistus
Cotoneaster

Stachys byzantina

Sarcococca hookeriana var. dignya

Calluna vulgaris 'My Dream'

Sempervivum arachnoideum

Wisteria × formosa 'Yae-kokuryû'

Cytisus	*Phlomis*	**AUTUMN AND**	*Malus*	*Larix*	*Daboecia*
Elaeagnus	*Pittosporum*	**WINTER COLOUR**	*Populus*	*Taxodium*	*Erica*
Erica	*Potentilla*		*Prunus*		*Euonymus*
Euonymus	*Rosmarinus*	TREES	*Pyrus*	SHRUBS	*Fothergilla*
Fuchsia	*Santolina*	*Acer*	*Quercus*	*Berberis* (deciduous)	*Hamamelis*
Genista	*Spiraea*	*Aesculus*	*Robinia*	*Ceratostigma*	*Paeonia*
Halimium	*Yucca*	*Arbutus*	*Sorbus*	*Calluna*	*Photinia*
Hebe		*Betula*		*Cornus*	*Pyracantha*
Hydrangea	CLIMBERS	*Cercidiphyllum*	CONIFERS	*Cotinus*	*Spiraea*
Ilex	*Fallopia*	*Crataegus*	*Cryptomeria*	*Cotoneaster*	*Viburnum*
Lavandula	*Wisteria*	*Eucryphia*	*Ginkgo*	(deciduous)	(deciduous)

Plant Hardiness Zones

This map was developed by the Agricultural Research Service of the U.S. Department of Agriculture. Every plant in the directory is given a zone range. The zones 1–11 are based on the average annual minimum temperature. In the zone range, the smaller number indicates the northernmost zone in which a plant can survive the winter and the higher number gives the most southerly area in which it will perform consistently. Bear in mind that factors such as altitude, wind exposure, proximity to water, soil type, snow, night temperature, shade, and the level of water received by a plant may alter a plant's hardiness by as much as two zones.

■	Zone 11	Above 4°C (40°F)
■	Zone 10	-1 to 4°C (30 to 40°F)
■	Zone 9	-7 to -1°C (20 to 30°F)
■	Zone 8	-12 to -7°C (10 to 20°F)
■	Zone 7	-18 to -12°C (0 to 10°F)
■	Zone 6	-23 to -18°C (-10 to 0°F)
■	Zone 5	-29 to -23°C (-20 to -10°F)
■	Zone 4	-34 to -29°C (-30 to -20°F)
■	Zone 3	-40 to -34°C (-40 to -30°F)
■	Zone 2	-45 to -40°C (-50 to -40°F)
■	Zone 1	Below -45°C (-50°F)

Index

Acknowledgements

The Publisher would like to thank the
following gardens and garden owners
for kindly allowing photography to take
place on their premises:

Andrew Mikolajski, Northamptonshire;
Bedgebury Pinetum, Kent; Batsford
Arboretum, Gloucestershire; Brogdale
Horticultural Trust, Faversham, Kent;
Chenies Manor, Buckinghamshire;
Chiffchaffs, Dorset; East Lambrook
Manor, Somerset; Elsing Hall, Norfolk;
Headland Garden, Cornwall; Fiona
Henley Design; Lamport Hall,
Northamptonshire; Merrist Wood,
Surrey; Pine Lodge Gardens, Cornwall;
Renishaw Hall, Sheffield; RHS Chelsea
Flower Show 2004; RHS Hyde Hall,
Essex; RHS Gardens Rosemoor, Devon;
RHS Gardens Wisley, Surrey;
Rodmarton Manor, Cirencester;
Spinners, Devon; Westonbirt
Arboretum, Gloucestershire; Wollerton
Old Hall, Shropshire; Writtle College,
Essex; Wyken Hall, Suffolk; Yalding
Organic Gardens, Kent.

A special thank you goes to STIHL Ltd.
who lent some of the equipment used in
the book. A list of worldwide suppliers
of Stihl products can be found on their
website: www.stihl.com

Picture acknowledgements
The Publisher would like to thank
the models in the photography sessions:
Jeff Clayton; Nick Robinson;
Peter Sedgewick; Robin Whitehead;
Stephen Coling.

The publisher would like to thank
the following picture libraries for
permission to use their photographs.

A–Z Botanical
15t, 17tr, 17br, 19tl, 19br, 24br, 26tr,
26br, 105bl.

Jonathan Buckley
12, 14, 15b, 30, 33t, 42, 44t, 94, 97.

Andrew Mikolajski
6, 10t, 11r, 22tr, 23tl, 70tl, 96l, 99tr.

Peter McHoy
47tl, 52tl, 52tc, 52tr, 53br, 54tl, 55br,
58b, 60bc, 61br, 63tc, 63tr, 63bl, 64t,
64bl, 65tl, 65tr, 65br, 66tr, 67tc, 67br,
68tl, 68tc, 69tl, 76tc, 76bl, 77br, 98tl,
98tc, 98tr, 98b, 100tc, 102tc, 103tl,
103tc, 104tl, 104tc, 104b, 105tl.

Additional step-by-step text: Peter
McHoy, Richard Bird, Andrew
Mikolajski, Ted Collins, Blaise Cooke,
Christopher Grey-Wilson, Lin
Hawthorne, Jessica Houdret, Hazel Key,
Peter Robinson, Susie White.